# HERE'S JOHNNY!

# HERE'S JOHNNY!

*Thirty Years of America's Favorite Late-Night Entertainer*

Revised Edition

## STEPHEN COX

Cumberland House
Nashville, Tennessee

*For my dad*
*who, in his smoking days,*
*flicked an ash with more flair*
*than Bogie or Gleason.*
*I'm glad he stopped.*

A previous edition of this book was published by Harmony Books, a division of Crown Publishers Inc.

Published by
  Cumberland House Publishing
  431 Harding Industrial Drive
  Nashville, Tennessee 37211
  www.cumberlandhouse.com

Cover design: Unlikely Suburban Design
Interior design: Mary Sanford

**Library of Congress Cataloging-in-Publication Data**
Cox, Stephen, 1966-
   Here's Johnny! : thirty years of America's favorite late-night entertainer / Stephen Cox--Rev. ed.
       p. cm.
Includes index.
   ISBN 1-58182-265-0 (pbk. : alk. paper)
  1. Carson, Johnny, 1925–  2. Tonight show (Television program)  3. Television personalities--United States--Biography.  I. Title.
   PN1992.4.C28 C68 2002
   791.45'028'092--dc21

                                            2002009593

Printed in the United States of America
1 2 3 4 5 6 7—08 07 06 05 04 03 02

Gregory Peck • Don Rickles • Bob Hope • Orson Wells • Jodie Foster • Gene Kelly • Mickey Mantle • Edgar Bergen • Ronald Reagan • Bing Crosby

d • Mel Blanc • Sam Kinison • Gore Vidal • Fred Astaire • Lucille Ball • Freddie Prinze • Danny Thomas • Buddy Rich • Truman Capote • Anthony Q

Curtis • Sid Caesar • Eva Gabor • Clint Eastwood • Red Skelton • Adriana Caselotti • Elizabeth Taylor • Burt Mustin • Robert Easton • Robin Willia

Burns • Joan Crawford • Selma Diamond • Boy George • Marlon Brando • Barry Manilow • F. Lee Bailey • William Demarest • Vincent Price • S

er • Harvey Korman • Larry Gatlin • Rita Coolidge • Joey Heatherton • Dick Van Dyke • Buddy Greco • Edward Asner • Harry Chapin • Rev. Robert Sch

Stiller & Anne Meara • Joan Rivers • Johnny Bench • Cathy Lee Crosby • Michelle Pfeiffer • Annie Potts • Ella Fitzgerald • Alfred Hitchcock • Norman M

Nabors • Howard Cosell • William Blatty • Dudley Moore • Dizzy Gillespie • Ron Ely • Steve Lawrence & Eydie Gorme • Deidre Hall • Harvey Fierste

Connery • Richard Boone • Andrew Lloyd Webber • Kirk Douglas • Keenen Ivory Wayans • James Stewart • Phil Foster • Michael J. Fox • Walter Cronk

cCartney • Styx • Trisha Yearwood • Jeane Dixon • Billy Crystal • Al Jarreau • Elaine Stritch • Michael Caine • Weird Al Yankovic • Elle MacPherson • Tor

la • Richard Simmons • Anne Baxter • Arnold Schwarzenegger • Rhonda Fleming • Corbett Monica • Broderick Crawford • Joan Collins • Peter Fon

y Garland • Kris Kristofferson • Peter O'Toole • Jo Ann Pflug • McLean Stevenson • Ricardo Montalban • Lainie Kazan • Regis Philbin • Dusty Spring

Whitman • Agnes Moorehead • Otto Preminger • Art Carney • John Ritter • Madonna • Nancy Wilson • Kay Starr • Helen Gurley Brown • Richard N

l Channing • Karen Valentine • Marty Allen • Yonely • Zsa Zsa Gabor • Count Basie • Pete Rose • Warren Beatty • Natalie Cole • Irene Ryan • D

man • Roseanne Barr • Jim Backus • Sugar Ray Leonard • Bill Cosby • Jim Carrey • Arnold Palmer • Tim Allen • Don Adams • Rex Reed • Bill Dana • S

• David Steinberg • George Peppard • Arte Johnson • Joey Bishop • Roy Rogers • Billie Jean King • Mario Andretti • Frank Capra • Mel Torme • Mic

n • Dick Van Patten • Olivia Newton-John • Art Buchwald • Florence Henderson • Neil Diamond • Petula Clark • Paul Williams • Louis Armstrong • Ge

an • Diana Ross • Martin Short • Whoopi Goldberg • Foster Brooks • Elizabeth Ashley • Julie London • Bobby Troup • The Smothers Brothers • Paul Si

Ballard • Gig Young • Allen Funt • Judy Collins • Cleo Laine • Pete Sampras • Carol Lawrence • Robert Blake • Susan Sarandon • Zero Mostel • Sar

• Herve Villechaize • Bert Convy • Ethel Merman • Alan Alda • Jack Klugman • Danny Kaye • Roger Maris • Sally Struthers • Sammy Davis Jr. • S

man • Woody Allen • Buddy Ebsen • David Brenner • Jerry Vale • Ralph Nader • Ellen Corby • Dwight Yoakam • Kenny Loggins • Kathryn Kuhlman • H

r • Little Richard • Harry Anderson • Randy Newman • The Temptations • Bonnie Hunt • Drew Carey • Randy Travis • Henny Youngman • Dody Good

Elliot • Bernadette Peters • Frank Gorshin • Nipsey Russell • Alice Faye • James Taylor • Diane Keaton • Sandy Baron • Louise Lasser • James Cobu

Gish • Jim Fowler • Kate Capshaw • Bette Davis • Roberta Flack • Dack Rambo • Hugh Downs • Liza Minnelli • The Harlem Globetrotters • Bob Cra

& Cher • Billy DeWolfe • Jack Lemmon • Roy Clark • Debbie Reynolds • Rodney Dangerfield • Cliff Robertson • Jo Anne Worley • Charles Grodin • Sa

n • Kreskin • Rodney Allen Rippy • Ernest Borgnine • Lauren Hutton • Madelyn Rhue • Orson Bean • Mary Tyler Moore • Andy Rooney • Frank Zap

Crosby • Jack Palance • Oliver Reed • Aretha Franklin • Jack Benny • David Horowitz • Susan St. James • Dick Cavett • John Denver • Ben Vereen •

• Red Buttons • Helen O'Connell • Marty Brill • James Coco • Paul Rodriguez • Michael Keaton • David Bowie • Eddy Arnold • Albert Brooks • N

au • Buck Henry • Slappy White • Charles Durning • Willie Mays • Karen Black • Ed Ames • Lola Falana • Pearl Bailey • Mac Davis • Charles Schu

her • William Devane • Dolly Parton • Ray Bolger • Paul Reiser • Paula Poundstone • Victor Borge • Dick Shawn • Ruth Gordon • Lou Rawls • Burl Iv

Rogers • Peter Ustinov • Joey Lawrence • Henry Winkler • Jerry Van Dyke • Phil Collins • Trevor Howard • Tracey Ullman • Charlie Callas • Dionne War

Boone • Jerry Lewis • Lily Tomlin • Barbara Walters • Suzanne Pleshette • Don Ho • George Segal • Peter Nero • Elliott Gould • Elke Sommer • Jose Felic

ard Crenna • The Mills Brothers • Jan Murray • Glen Campbell • Dom DeLouise • Burt Reynolds • Joan Blondell • Martin Luther King Jr. • Dean Ma

Lanchester • David Niven • Fernando Lamas • Leo Durocher • The Lennon Sisters • Michael Landon • Vikki Carr • Vic Damone • John Byner • Desi A

Fitzgerald • Cloris Leachman • David Janssen • Frank Sinatra • Anthony Newley • Godfrey Cambridge • Tennessee Ernie Ford • Edwin Newman • Luc

tti • Eli Wallach • Lou Brock • Irene Cara • Joe • Jean Arthur • Jack Nicholson • Ray • Cyndi Lauper • Dr. Joyce Brothers • Victor Buono • Marilyn H

Fountain • Marvin Hamlisch • Howie Mandel • Willie Nelson • Johnny Yune • Pete Barbutti • Arlene Golonka • Sarah Vaughan • Steve Landesberg • Wil

n • Liberace • Carl Sagan • Jim Stafford • Spiro T. Agnew • Charles Nelson Reilly • James Garner • Suzanne Somers • Barbara Eden • Joe Cocker •

• Jean Marsh • David Brenner • Christie Brinkley • Garry Shandling • Chet Atkins • The Cowsills • Sheena Easton • B.B. King • The Oak Ridge Boys • Ca

• Tim Conway • Bette Midler • Tippi Hedren • Mel Brooks • Ike & Tina Turner • Bill Maher • Jack Jones • Martin Mull • William Frawley • Ally Shee

math • Richard Benjamin • Rosemary Clooney • Donald Sutherland • Garson Kanin • Victoria Jackson • Greg Louganis • David Huddleston • Liz Torr

g • Roy Orbison • Muhammed Ali • Ryan O'Neal • ZZ Top • Jerry Seinfeld • Charo • Andre Agassi • Flip Wilson • Larry Storch • Andy Williams • Grou

• Sean Penn • Della Reese • Jackie Gleason • Buddy Hackett • Robert Morse • Al Hirt • James Caan • Rev. Billy Graham • Dinah Shore • Ross Martin •

• George Kirby • Rich Little • Robert Merrill • Jacqueline Bisset • Robert F. Kennedy • Wayne Gretzky • Rex Harrison • Kate Jackson • Julie Andrews •

Jack Cassidy • Chuck Berry • John McGiver • The Carpenters • Lawrence Welk • Gladys Knight & the Pips • Mitzi Gaynor • Ian Whitcomb • Merie Ea

Marceau • Mickey Rooney • Trini Lopez • Minnesota Fats • Lana Turner • Ethel Waters • Artie Shaw • Goldie Hawn • Eartha Kitt • Mark Spitz • Dan Ro

Martin • Evel Knievel • Johnny Mathis • Arte Johnson • Rip Taylor • Itzhak Perlman • Lynn Redgrave • Tom Wolfe • Courtney Cox • Celine Dion •

tt • Siskel & Ebert • Brooke Sheilds • Ozzie & Harriet Nelson • Bobby Vinton • Sidney Poitier • Yvonne De Carlo • Raymond Burr • Tiny Tim • Andy Gri

ard Nixon • Kermit the Frog • Telly Savalas • Candice Bergen • Yul Brynner • Maureen O'Hara • Alan Shepard • Barry Goldwater • Abbe Lane • Rock Hud

Ameche • Lee Trevino • Burt Lancaster • Gene Hackman • Charles Bronson • Redd Foxx • Soupy Sales • Hal Holbrook • Dennis Hopper • Dustin Hoff

ne Newton • Carly Simon • David Frost • Glenn Close • Celeste Holm • June Allyson • Omar Sharif • Rod Steiger • Dennis Wolfberg • Faye Dunaw

Cronyn • Lee Marvin • Bruce Dern • Angela Lansbury • Phil Silvers • The Beach Boys • Imogene Coca • Kathy Bates • Valerie Bertinelli • Leonard Nim

arles • Ted Danson • Burt Bacharach • Tony Danza • Michael Douglas • Cyd Charisse • Jay Silverheels • Doris Day • Nanette Fabray • Douglas Fairba

lfre Woodard • Jon Voight • Robert Young • Kareem Abdul-Jabbar • Dave Garroway • Christopher Plummer • Rich Hall • Ruth Buzzi • Joe Piscopo

nan • Billy Wilder • Tony Bennett • The Doobie Brothers • Anjelica Huston • Anthony Hopkins • Cicely Tyson • Larry Hagman • Richard Chamberla

Glover • Pet Shop Boys • Julio Iglesias • Shari Lewis • Dyan Cannon • Hope Lange • Bo Derek • Kevin Costner • Bruce Willis • Tom Hanks • James

• Steven Wright • Jacques Cousteau • Cathy Guisewite • David Lynch • Kevin Pollak • Magic Johnson • Jon Lovitz • Paul Sorvino • Ricky Schroder • Bel

le • Kate Mulgrew • Placido Domingo • Hugh Downs • Boris Becker • Bob Costas • Jack Webb • Mark Rydell • Gary Grimes • Ben Gazzara • Dub Tayl

Vallee • Karl Malden • Mel Tillis • James Hampton • Totie Fields • John Cassavetes • Lorne Greene • Norman Fell • Eubie Blake • Betty Buckley • E

ny • Honor Blackman • Glynis Johns • The Andrews Sisters • Wally Cox • Kelly Monteith • Dr. Lendon Smith • Sally Field • Jack Albertson • LeVar Bu

Baez • Marilu Henner • Richard Dawson • Louis Nye • Dave Barry • Jane Morgan • Clint Walker • Jerry Reed • Andy Kaufman • Bill Clinton • Tony Rar

n Hayes • Connie Stevens • Juliet Prowse • Troy Donohue • Garry Marshall • John Amos • George Maharis • Tom Jones • Patsy Kelly • Helen Reddy • Gra

Brad Garrett • Sandra Bernhard • James Franciscus • James Galway • Michelle Lee • Ellen Burstyn • Hal Linden • Hoyt Axton • Robby Benson •

line • George Segal • Marsha Mason • Park Overall • Ted Danson • Joe Williams • Pam Grier • Doug Henning • Charles Aznavour • Tim Reid •

es • Cindy Williams • Gay Talese • Jon Cryer • George Kennedy • Sherman Hemsley • Lyle Lovett • Charles Fleischer • Raquel Welch • Mark Kay Place

s • Dr. Paul Erlich • Lesley Ann Warren • Elaine Joyce • Erma Bombeck • Michael Crichton • Sharon Gless • Jeff Greenfield • Barbara McNair • Jeff Ces

vin Hagler • Willie Tyler & Lester • Larry Blyden • Tony Martin • James Mason • Art Linkletter • Gypsy Rose Lee • Peter Lawford • John Gary • Diah

l • Gilda Radner • Neil Sedaka • Teresa Ganzel • Margaret Whiting • Tom Dreesen • John Goodman • Victoria Jackson • Hubert Humphrey • Cliff

Csonka • Alex Haley • Loni Anderson • Roddy McDowall • Kim Hunter • Kevin Nealon • Byron Allen • Barbara Carrera • Maximillian Schell • Will

y • Ray Stevens • Dave Thomas • Abigail Van Buren • Cleavon Little • Paul Lynde • Pigmeat Markham • Ann-Margret • Bobby Darin • Glenn Ford •

**Johnny's Guests . . .**

# CONTENTS

Foreword: A Twenty-One-Star Salute     *viii*
Acknowledgments     *xi*
Introduction     3

**1** The Evolution of *The Tonight Show*     21

**2** The Monologue: "That's Good Stuff"     47

**3** Memorable Moments     67

**4** Celebrities on *Tonight*     97

**5** Civilians     123

**6** A Comic's Dream     141
*by Joe Rhodes*

**7** Paging Johnny Carson     157

**8** Carson's Wild Kingdom     169

**9** Television's Parade of Humanity: Grand Marshall, Johnny Carson     179
*by John Lofflin*

**10** Farewell     205

**11** A King and His Court     211

*Index*     *240*

# Foreword: A Twenty-One-Star Salute

Envision the ultimate lineup on a perfect *Tonight Show*, or a star-laden Friars Club roast. In 1991, while Johnny was preparing to make his exit into the night, a group of his friends toasted him with a few words exclusively for this tribute. Sadly, time has marched on and some of these legendary folks are no longer with us, but their sentiments are as telling as the moment they were spoken. In this book we remember, we savor Johnny Carson's years on *The Tonight Show.* So don't just raise a glass, go ahead and tip it a few times in honor of America's favorite talk show host, the man who was welcome in nearly every home in the country for three decades. Although, it should be noted that Jonathan Winters did say he wanted to rescind his comments because he hasn't gotten a Christmas card from the Carsons in ten years.

*And now . . . "Cheers Johnny!"*

I don't remember exactly how I met him, but I vividly recall spending an hour with Johnny Carson when we were both in our early twenties in the bar of the old Astor Hotel in Times Square. We were yakking about show business and our hopes and dreams, and I was tremendously impressed with this guy. At the end of our talk, I was convinced of two things: I wasn't sure if I was going to make it, but I was dead certain the young man across from me was going to impress the hell out of everybody. I think I was right.

—Jack Lemmon

I warned Johnny that nobody could replace Jack Paar. I talked to him like a Dutch uncle. I said, "Don't do it, John! Wait until the first person tried to and then when that bombs—because it surely would—then step in." And I was right, because he's about to lose the show. I don't think he lasted twenty-seven, twenty-eight years.

—Tom Poston

It's a simple fact, that throughout show business history, there has never been such a success story. Who in the world has had thirty years in one spot? It never happened before. There's nothing to compare it to. Sometimes old-timers hang on and they're not so good, but the audience likes them and forgives. You don't have to forgive him. He's as good as the day he started.

—Phyllis Diller

HERE'S JOHNNY!

Over all other hosts, I prefer Johnny Carson. I've always had a lot of fun with Johnny. I attribute many things to Johnny. He's been on for thirty years, and nobody's been able to bump him. His only threat was Rick Dees—only Rick Dees was in a car. He tried to kill Johnny.

—JONATHAN WINTERS

I loved being on *The Tonight Show with Johnny Carson.* Nobody listened as good as Johnny. He's also a great actor. He laughed at my jokes like he'd never heard them before.

—GEORGE BURNS

I sure am sorry to see him leave the show. And I join with a great number of people that are sorry. I think he's done an amazing job, and there's a tremendous number of people who have enjoyed him for quite some time.

—JIMMY STEWART

He is, he was, and will always be the best there ever was. It's been thirty years of the best television we will ever have. There is not another Johnny Carson . . . unless there'll be another Charlie Chaplin.

—JERRY LEWIS

I knew Mr. Carson since he was a young man. I knew from the start he could never hold a job. They say he is retiring, but how can you tell? In the thirty years, consider the amount of people who have watched him; he kept a lot of people off the street after 11 at night, but on second thought, those who watched his show from the bed created a lot of criminals that are running around.

—RED SKELTON

I've known Johnny Carson for many years. I didn't think it conceivable over the years, that it is possible to be Gentile and genuinely funny. Johnny's a gem, and I owe a great deal of my success to my appearances with him. He shall be missed.

—ALAN KING

I have nothing but the greatest admiration for him. I think that when he quits, it's kind of an end of an era.

—JACK PAAR

I will personally miss Johnny and thank him in the same breath, for assisting me in my career and for giving me the ultimate exposure in nighttime TV. Love you much, Johnny! And I wish you success in whatever you endeavor. Love,

—DIONNE WARWICK

I clearly recall tuning in to see the very first *Tonight Show with Johnny Carson*. It was a rerun. Sincerely,

—ANDY ROONEY

Somebody once said that volume is an important thing when judging talent. If Beethoven had only written Eroica, he would be considered one of the great composer, but he wouldn't be considered a genius. It's the amount of things that Beethoven and Mozart turned out; the longevity of creative people like Johnny Carson is a mark of talent. We're gonna miss a friend, and nobody takes the place of a friend.

—CARL REINER

As a veteran of twelve appearances with him and a survivor of about three, all I can say is, I am deeply sorry, and much safer. Cordially,

—WILLIAM F. BUCKLEY JR.

I asked Johnny, "Did you have those suits made to order?"
He said, "Yes."
"Where were you at the time?"
Really, Johnny's a charmer. He's helped many of us with our careers. And I thank him.

—HENNY YOUNGMAN

Let me tell you about Johnny Carson. In my lifetime, I've been interviewed by many guys. Some try to draw the humor out, and some I won't even discuss. John is probably the best, or equal to the best. As for fame and fantasy, he's far and above everybody. But I still look at him as a big star and with awe.

—BUDDY HACKETT

There's never been a show or a person who has affected stand-up comedy or as many stand-up comics' lives as Johnny Carson. I predict he'll be back. Maybe on another network . . . but he'll be back.

—LOUIE ANDERSON

# Acknowledgments

To all of those individuals listed here, and to those I may have inadvertently missed, I am grateful for your help and encouragement. Each time I pick up this book, I will recall your kind assistance—and in some instances, some arm-twisting I had to employ.

Foremost, I would like to thank Johnny Carson for giving me the chance and allowing me to reprint some of his hilarious routines; I'm sure he can recall an individual or two who gave him a break early in his career. And my plea to him: Please, Johnny, write a book about *The Tonight Show*—I'll be the first to buy it.

I'd like to offer great thanks to the many folks who agreed to be interviewed for this book. To Steve Randisi, my research consultant on both this and the original edition, I am thankful for your insight, time, and energy to make this better than I could imagine. Big thanks go to the folks at Cumberland House Publishing: Ron Pitkin, Mary Sanford, and the rest, who have provided a terrific home for some of my dream books about popular culture, film, and television. And to Carol Brady, my favorite librarian, who nurtured my interest in books when I was a youngster who could hardly see over the counter—her smile always brought me back.

Also, I would like to offer applause to: Ken Beck, Tom Brown, Bruce Button, Mickey Carroll, Bob Costas, my parents Gerald and Blanche Cox, Paul and Ruth Henning, Dayna Hooper, Ramona Christophel-Jones, Kevin Marhanka, Gary Meyer, Scott Maiko, John Michel, Scott Michaels, Jim Mulholland, Tin Meeley, Michael Pietsch, John Pertzborn, Peter Petrucci, Herbie J Pilato, Pam Reichman, Dan Roebuck, Helen Sanders, Ray Savage, Sandy Mailliard-Rotter, Jeff Sotzing, Billie Freebairn-Smith, Dave Strauss, Julie Sullivan (NBC legal department), Carey Thorpe, Dan Weaver, Elaine Willinghan, Mark Willoughby (Collector's Book Store/Hollywood), Dave Woodman, Bill Zehme.

Special thanks to those extraordinary writers who contributed their talents and unique insight in the guest forums for this book: John Lofflin, Joe Rhodes, and Neil Shister. To you colleagues, I tip my hat.

For assistance with photographs and a variety of images, I thank: *TV Guide*, Larry Ward, Personality Photos, Wide World Photo, Globe Photos, Doc Severinsen, Ed

McMahon, NBC, Joan Embery/Zoological Society of San Diego, Globe Photos, Don Locke, Art Trugman, and the entire NBC graphic-arts department.

For complete details about obtaining *The Tonight Show* on video and DVD, browse the official Johnny Carson website: www.johnnycarson.com.

# HERE'S JOHNNY!

# INTRODUCTION

It was fairly late in the game when Johnny Carson finally had the "Great One," Jackie Gleason, on his show for the first time, in 1985—just a few years before Johnny abdicated his throne as King of the Night. (I know, Johnny probably hated and still hates that royal phrase, which was pinned on him ages ago, but it was true for thirty years: He was king.) There were a handful of guests Johnny had truly wanted on the show but who declined, performers like Cary Grant, William "Hopalong Casssidy" Boyd, and Britain's Benny Hill, to name a few. But he finally got Gleason, and Johnny was obviously pleased that night, if not jittery, in the presence of one of his television idols. Johnny admitted to being an "unabashed fan" of the famous man in the moon, and Gleason didn't let him down. It was a beautiful, standout slice of television.

As for me, I felt the same kind of privilege and joy writing this book. I'm proud to admit I've been an unabashed fan of Carson for as long as I can remember.

When this book was written ten years ago to commemorate Johnny's thirty years of service as the champion of chat, I never thought I could reach the big man personally for an interview, but to my amazement, it happened. I was a young reporter then, awestruck and in my mid-twenties, you see, and I dreamt big. My parents gave me that. Some of the things I've reached for in my career, thanks to God, have come true and some

dreams have not. (Bob Hope, George Burns, Milton Berle, and Benny Hill are a few of the legendary folks I have been fortunate with.) I never got a conversation with Gleason or an interview with Lucy, but I snared a few moments of Johnny's time, and as a reporter, what more could I ask for? It doesn't get much better, in my estimation. The president of the United States might have been easier to reach at that time. No matter that the interview was brief, or that I fumbled around for the right words in my shock from his phone call, it was during a time when he was speaking to no others about his career, so I was fortunate. Certainly privileged. Most definitely grateful.

This book is meant to pay homage to his career, and it is not, and never was, meant to dissect his personal life and unravel the nastiness of his divorces or the tragedies and grave moments in his life, the fodder for tabloids. This is not meant to be a comprehensive compendium of his thirty years at NBC or his seventy-some years on this earth . . . that would be rather difficult to cram into one book. Rather, I hope this serves as a meaningful collage, a scrapbook maybe, of the years we all invited this Nebraskan gentleman into our homes so many times. He was the perfect guest, and who doesn't want to remember visitors like that?

Johnny took over *The Tonight Show* four years before I was born, and somewhere along the line he became a fixture in my life just as he had for millions of others around the country. That's why his exit from television in 1992 was such a sentimental—even sorrowful—event. He was always there for us, even in reruns, he was there to lean on while the country moved through wars, political administrations, triumphs, and taxes. Like midnight itself, he returned, and we, as viewers, counted on it. I had watched him in my bedroom, in the living room with my parents, in my college dorm room, in bars and basements, in hotel rooms, and in friends' dens. He was there. And then he wasn't.

A little percussion duet in 1976 with Ray Bolger, who played the Scarecrow in the classic film *The Wizard of Oz.*

My fascination stems from my childhood, when I stayed up much too late to watch Johnny. That's why I liked Friday nights: no begging. And as a fan of *The Tonight*

Johnny poses among some career mementos displayed in his front office in 1983. (Courtesy of Associated Press)

*Show*, the next best thing to genuinely experiencing the show in all its glory was to attend a taping. It's something thousands have done over the years. You went, you stood in line, you saw the show, and you left with some part of Hollywood in your pocket.

For most people, attending one of Johnny's shows meant you went prepared with a weird little ditty in the back of your mind just in case Johnny stepped into the audience for "Stump the Band." Or you hoped the "Edge of Wetness" camera zoomed in on your face and embarrassed you for the world to see. That would have been the ultimate, because time on camera meant you attained the greatness Andy Warhol once predicted for all of us—that personal fifteen minutes, or in this case, seconds.

Years ago, when I was eighteen and on a trip out west, a friend took me to a taping. Buddy Hackett was Johnny's guest, filthy and funny to the point you wanted to pee, and that's all I remember about the roster. But what a perfect night for me. That might have been the spark for this book. No matter that my late spot in line landed me in the nosebleed section of Studio One, way up there in that steep seating. There was nothing like visiting the welcoming house of Johnny: his couch, his curtains, his music, his décor, and him. It was smaller than I envisioned. You hear Ed McMahon's booming voice announce the man and then all eyes are fixed on the center of that colored curtain, waiting for a little movement and then his hand to draw it back as he entered the room.

Johnny always stepped out with a twinkle in his eye and a wide grin, happy to greet us as much as we were excited to see him. It really made you think. *The Tonight*

*Show Starring Johnny Carson* was the last of the great television events and maybe one of the last outposts of television where spontaneous comedy was possible. TV is hardly new, hardly spontaneous, hardly inaccessible now. There are so many shows on cable today and ways to make it on the tube that the medium itself has lost its singularity. *Oh you're on television tonight? So what? Isn't everybody?* Just walk outside, cameras are perched everywhere. It's no longer special to be "on television." There are no more spectacular showcases like those Ed Sullivan gave us, no more *I Love Lucy* filmings, no *Cavalcade of Stars* or *Hollywood Palace,* no larger-than-life Jackie Gleasons; Jack Benny is gone, and now Carson has stepped down, and ten years later, we still feel it. Television in a grand manner is gone forever, I'm afraid.

I was always a fan of Carson. I was a midwesterner, a kid who wanted to pry still more from the experience than just watching the show. The next time I was in Los Angeles, I attended a taping, and by way of a friend I was allowed backstage, where I wandered with my eyes wide open, all the while trying to appear like I knew what I was doing and that I belonged back there. My theory has always been that if you look like you know what you're doing, nobody asks questions.

Following the show, I met Doc, Tommy Newsom, and some of the band members. I took some pictures and quietly looked around a bit more. I eyed Johnny's coffee mug—a prop man had just washed the ceramic cups at a little sink backstage and set them on a cloth to drip dry. No, I thought, I can't take it. What if I get caught? The angel on my shoulder won this time, but I admit, I was tempted.

Johnny had returned to his dressing room immediately after the show. I peeked around corners for him, but he was gone. Then, minutes later, I spotted him coming down a hall and then some stairs toward me. He was in jeans and a brightly colored Polo, surrounded by four guards as he joked and made his way to his shiny white Corvette parked just outside the door. I later regretted not calling for his attention, because I'm sure he probably would've signed an autograph, but at the time I just stood by in awe and watched, as if watching a member of the royal family pass me in the hall. (I don't think it was typical that he be escorted by guards. Who knows what was happening behind the scenes during that time?)

Finally, my venture led me to Fred de Cordova in the hallway, a smartly dressed Hollywood type, tall and tanned, very well spoken. His clothes were impeccably fitted—

HERE'S JOHNNY!

a tan sport coat with perfectly pleated pants—and he carried a mixed drink in a clear plastic picnic cup. When I spoke to introduce myself, I startled the omnipresent producer and he dropped his drink on the carpeted hallway floor. He asked me if I was okay, which I thought was unusual. (I was horrified I'd caused him to drop his cocktail.) I assured him I was fine and we chatted for a moment. He was so polite and made me feel like everything was okay. No damage done.

My visit backstage that time was actually a mission. It was to try and interest de Cordova in booking longtime show business veteran Joe Besser, once a member of the Three Stooges, as a guest some evening. I thought it would've been perfect. Johnny was a fan of the old-timers from vaudeville, radio, and the vintage eras of comedy. In fact, he'd even done impressions of Besser's trademark sissy whine, "Not so looouuuud!" so recognizable from the Jack Benny radio show. Johnny welcomed lots of old veterans on his program. Besser was long forgotten, but he was enjoying a resurgence in the American consciousness by way of his association with the Three Stooges.

Longtime *Tonight Show* producer Fred de Cordova took a seat with Johnny in 1988 to plug his autobiography, *Johnny Came Lately*. De Cordova retired along with Carson in 1992; in September 2001, he died at the age of ninety. (Courtesy of Janet de Cordova)

Ask anyone who knew me as a kid and they'll confirm that the Stooges were a passion of mine; but more than that, the Three Stooges were becoming extremely hot at this time, and Besser, a fellow St. Louisan and a pal of mine, was one of the surviving members of the slapstick trio experiencing a comeback as well. Besides, I thought, Fred de Cordova had directed Besser in the film *The Desert Hawk*, with Jackie Gleason, some years ago. I had done my research. Surely it was a cinch to get him on the show some night.

No interest. De Cordova was polite, but really no interest. That floored me.

Even after a few letters, for some reason *The Tonight Show*, in all its show biz wisdom, did not wish to play host to a Stooge. What a shame. Not long after this, the Three Stooges received their long-deserved star on the Hollywood Walk of Fame in 1983. Well over two thousand fans greeted Joe Besser, along with a string of celebri-

# Trademarks

You might recall having seen Johnny . . .

1. Grab the knot of his tie and straighten it.
2. Apply his index finger to his upper lip when talking seriously.
3. Tap his pencil on the cigarette box or the rim of his coffee mug.
4. Flip a pencil in the air and catch it—sometimes.
5. Keep his hands in his pockets while his chest is inflated during the monologue.
6. Hold his hands behind his back, throwing his chest out (while standing for the monologue).
7. Scratch the back of his hand as though it itched.
8. Crane his neck.
9. Yell "Whoopee!" after his golf swing and the audience was applauding his monologue.
10. Shoot his index finger into the air like a gun.
11. Scratch the back of his ear.
12. Scratch his temple.
13. Lick his thumb when turning pages during a desk routine.
14. Tweak the bottom of his nose.
15. Hold up his hand, waving the audience, which has been roaring unceasingly, to a halt ("No, no . . .")
16. After the monologue, give the "come hither" gesture with his hands at his waist, sparking more applause.
17. Twitch one eye when he's noticeably annoyed.
18. Occasionally raise his voice an octave as if in transformation from puberty. "You know . . ." (clearing his throat).
19. Wink (as if to say, "I'm just teasing," "You're doing fine," or "Terrific.")
20. Swing an imaginary golf club to signal the end of the monologue.

*"We'll be right back, folks."*

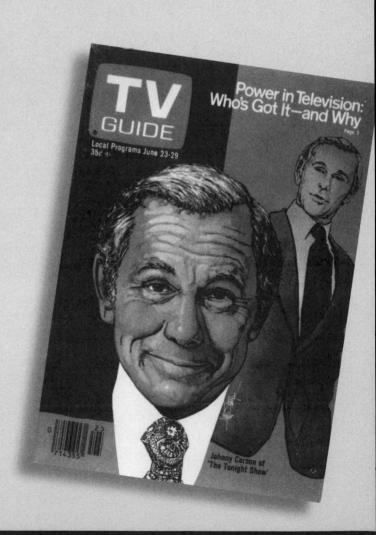

One of Carson's most
recognized trademarks:
straightening his tie.

In *TV Guide,* critic Jeff Jarvis astutely observed that Carson
"reflected the nation's culture and consciousness—which
means he set our standards—not only in comedy but also
in politics, marriage, divorce, music, fashion, the work
ethic, and failure. There is no successor to Johnny. And
because all America no longer watches the same show
every night, there may never be another Johnny. Come
May 22, 1992, the closest thing we'll have to a national
barometer will be the Weather Channel."

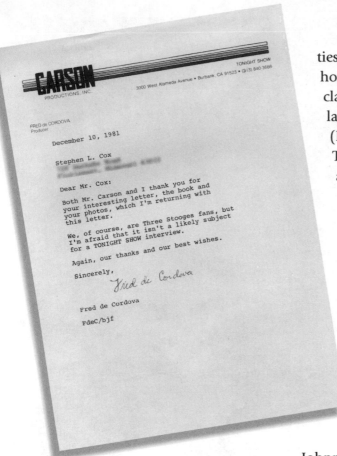

ties there for the induction. Besser accepted the honor on behalf of the deceased members of the classic comedy trio, and this was, at that time, the largest crowd gathered for a "Star Ceremony." (Eventually, Michael Jackson's crowd topped it.) These high priests of low comedy were enjoying a renaissance in the 1980s, but they were paid no respect from *The Tonight Show*. It really confounded me.

That didn't diminish my affinity for the show and I continued to watch when I could. Later, in 1989, just as I graduated college with a degree in journalism, I was well into writing my second book, all about the midgets who performed as the enchanting Munchkins in the movie classic of all classics, *The Wizard of Oz*. For this book, I had tracked down all of the surviving midgets (thirty of the 124 who worked in the 1939 film) and it seemed to me that Johnny might have some fun interviewing an original Munchkin. No one had heard from these diminutive folks in fifty years, which is why I wrote their memoirs. Their tales of Judy Garland and MGM studios were begging to be told, not to mention the fact that they eagerly wished to denounce the overblown Hollywood myth that labeled them drunks. (A blotto Judy Garland perpetuated that whopper on national television when she appeared with Jack Paar one night, and the surviving little people were left for decades to suffer with it.) Unfortunately, I couldn't interest de Cordova in the idea.

Oh well, life went on and so did the show. With an unceasing itch for nostalgia, I became increasingly fascinated with the history of *The Tonight Show*. This book is the scratch to that itch. It is an extension of my curiosity about the show and its remarkable place in history, the guests who shined, and Johnny's legacy. Hopefully, this will serve as a unique time capsule for you as well, ready to help you relive the days of old show business.

■ ■ ■

I won't lie and say this book was a painless endeavor. The nearly insurmountable difficulty was getting people to talk about Johnny Carson. At the time, he was still a viable property at NBC, a force to reckon with if it came to that, and performers knew it. Some didn't care, but most of the people I approached did. If I were to randomly ask anyone on the street why Johnny appeals to them or what shows stood out in their memory, it would prompt twenty minutes of recollections and favorite guests and routines. No problem. But ask some of the performers who sat right next to him, shared a cigarette with him during commercial break, or even broke bread with the man, and you might as well forget it.

Shelley Winters was suddenly out of town. Don Rickles decided it might not be a good idea. No answer from Bob Newhart. Robert Blake was reticent, his publicist informed me. Joan Embery was extremely hesitant. Jay Leno felt it would be "inappropriate" for him to comment as he was preparing to take over the show. (I couldn't have disagreed more.) Singer and actor John Davidson, a frequent guest host for Johnny, turned pale and backed away when I approached him about an interview. Sure, he admitted that appearances on the show were fabulous for his career, but he refused to be quoted saying it. Steve Allen's secretary wanted sample chapters. Dick Carson, Johnny's brother, did not respond to my handwritten plea personally given to him by his barber. (I tried just about everything to get interviews.) Magician Dean Dill, "the personal instructor to Mr. Carson," who had appeared on the show, would not expound on Johnny's sleight-of-hand talents. Instead, the part-time magician/barber had a pseudo-agent call me. He proceeded to quiz me as if I were a witness at some scandal-driven Senate hearing.

The list expanded, and finally, when all was said and done, I found that those who appeared to feel comfortable and confident in their relationship with Carson—as distant or close as it might have been—spoke to me for publication.

It was a sticky time, of course, because there was a year's worth of shows left and no one dared anger the King of the Night. So many of those I interviewed—whether they were still in touch with Carson or not—continued to walk on eggshells when it came to talking about the man. They chose words carefully and definitely made it clear they did not want to jeopardize a good thing. Everyone knew Johnny had been soured over the years by sensationalistic books about his personal life, and let's not even get into the tabloid treatment he fell victim to repeatedly.

Half of my time preparing this book in 1991 was spent explaining the project: This book delves more into Johnny's work and *The Tonight Show* than into his very private existence. This book celebrates three decades of excellence in television. Besides, Johnny has even said that he doesn't mind criticism of his work. But start digging dirt and his ears prick up, and all systems are shut down. I think that if I had even smelled of scandal, the drawbridge would have been locked.

I was warned that Johnny was "an elaborately wired security system" who rarely granted interviews and at this juncture was busier than ever. Although many writers have attempted to capture the essence of Carson over the years, no one has really done so with accuracy. I don't think anyone can. Only Johnny can provide that perspective, and it's doubtful he'll ever write his memoirs. He has always been a Hollywood mystery, the most private public figure, and it may have been this mystique that kept viewers coming back night after night for thirty years. With all of this staring me in the face, how was I supposed to crack the code and get in there with the inner circle to assemble a book on Johnny and the show? I was determined to make this book work. In assembling a pictorial of *The Tonight Show*, I wanted to surprise myself by unearthing some wonderful artifacts and present them as a gift. This was not intended ten years ago as a eulogy to Carson and his show, and it is not now.

You know what? All I had to do was ask. Some people closed their door, but many invited me in for coffee and maybe a cigar. I researched and wrote, twisting some arms for interviews, and I tried to compile a nice assortment of sentiments and recollections. Then, as Johnny's term drew to a close, the media went into a frenzy the likes of which America had never seen. Seemingly every periodical slapped Johnny on the cover and created their own star-studded tribute. Special editions filled every newsstand. News outlets counted the months, then the nights, hours, and minutes, and well-wishers emerged from every direction. I couldn't believe the about-face I was witnessing. Many of the same stars who had been mysteriously "busy" when I begged them for an interview rushed to toast Johnny in the press and offer their reminiscences, jumping on the broadcasting bandwagon to get their name in print, lest they be forgotten. Where were they a year ago?

By this time, my book was on the presses, but I had no reason to regret the wonderful contributions I'd managed to gather from the best—lots of great names, from Dan Aykroyd to Henny Youngman.

With some tenacity, I did my best with the resources at hand, and for those who were eager to assist with energy and honesty, people like Jonathan Winters and Buddy Hackett, I have newfound respect. All the while, Johnny allowed things to happen, opened some doors, and helped this young writer out just as he had generously helped so many young performers on his show over the years.

Truly, Johnny had more important things to deal with during his final year at NBC, but he still managed to help me. I understood that he and his troops were winding down and there was a swirl of sentiment and other emotions quite palpable at *The Tonight Show* and I tried to stay out of the way. His final year was a tough one, with the deaths of his son Ricky and his close friend Michael Landon, his final bow, and a horizon to head toward. After thirty years, what the hell was this guy going to do? When I asked him that question in 1992, he had no answers as of yet.

■ ■ ■

And so, it has come to this: Ten years have gone by, and we've all gotten older. I've looked for Johnny on television, but he's kept to himself and his family, and to his poker buddies. Even guests who frequented his show fifty times have not heard a peep or received a holiday greeting, but that's okay. He's entitled to some privacy after putting his life out there for all those years. He likes retirement, he'll tell you.

God only knows what he thinks of the state of television today. I'll offer this: The world of broadcasting has completely changed since Johnny was in the driving seat. He gave us class on *The Tonight Show*; he displayed an excellence that has not been equaled. Today, much of television is, as Steve Allen sharply opined, in the "garbage dump." The unspeakable is spoken, the unviewable is shown. There's very little class left on the tube. Johnny never came out from the curtain and went straight for the audience to slap hands, give high fives, and yell out "Yo! Yo! Yo!" He never required people to eat bugs. He never reminded us constantly just how wealthy he had become. It was not mannerly. No wonder Johnny distances himself from the medium. Not even NBC's recent seventy-fifth anniversary special could lure him back to prime time.

Johnny hasn't set foot in a television studio in the intervening years, preferring to indulge in an ultra-comfortable retirement overlooking Malibu with his wife, Alexis. He has spent "quality" time with family, enjoying some of those Tea-Time movies on his big screen. He's traveled the world, played tennis, flown airplanes, roamed Africa, watched television grow into a monster, brushed up on his self-taught Swahili, loved life, and of late, is

In an early television guest appearance, Johnny stopped by *The Jack Benny Show* in 1955 to seek advice from his mentor and playfully trade a few jabs. Later, Carson considered having Benny co-host *The Tonight Show* with him at NBC, but the elder funnyman was not anxious to do a live, unscripted show every night. On Carson's tenth anniversary show Benny said: "For years and years I've been Johnny Carson's idol. Then all of a sudden, the whole thing switched and Johnny became my idol. And do you want to know something? It's not nearly as much fun this way!"

still learning to play with his new toy—a customized yacht he christened *The Serengeti*. He's still at the helm, this time at home and abroad.

So cheers, Johnny! I hope this book isn't tossed overboard.

# Talking with Johnny

This time the tables were turned.

"Hello, Steve?" the voice greeted me as I ate my dinner. "This is Helen in Johnny Carson's office. Mr. Carson has a few minutes to speak with you now if you'd like."

*Like?* I couldn't believe it. I wouldn't have been more startled if the president of the United States had been calling. Nearly paralyzed for a moment, yet trying to remain conscious of my moves, I ran to another room, switched phones, set up at my desk, and took a breath before I began to speak with my late-night idol. The Silver Fox. King of the Night. Johnny. I had actually dreamed of this, but fully expected that he'd decline my request.

It was a summer evening in August 1991, about 4 P.M. Burbank time, and in the midwest it was dinner time. Johnny Carson was in his office preparing for his 5:30 curtain. I'd explained to him in a fax that preceded this phone call that I had a few riddles that had emerged in my research about his career and the show. Reiterating this to him, I noted my wish that this book be favorable to him.

"Well, that'll be new," he snapped light-heartedly.

*It worked!* I couldn't believe it. I asked him a question and he answered. Yes, that's how those things work, and I'd interviewed many people on the telephone, but having Johnny Carson on the other end of the line was so surreal, everything seemed to be moving in slow motion as shock almost overwhelmed me. I maintained, I really did.

Foremost, I assured him that I had no interest in digging up dirt about his personal life; I just wanted to inquire about a few things. "All right, go ahead," he said.

He was polite, quiet—a demeanor, I'm told, he usually maintains in interview situa-tions—and he was serious. This felt more like a conversation and I relaxed a bit as I went ahead. Still, I know I was hurried and tongue-tied. I imagined him sitting at his desk or his office couch, scanning pages of his monologue spread in front of him, his head cocked with the telephone squeezed between his ear and shoulder.

Where is Barbara Walters when you need her? I could have used one of her psychobabble queries: "If you were a carnival ride, which one would you be?" Instead, my mind raced through a hundred topics I could have approached, but mostly I held to the agenda stated in my letter. After all, I must have done something right, because I had been informed by his closest associates that he was accepting no interview requests. Fred de Cordova flatly told me an interview would not happen, but that made me persist even more. Why not? What have I got to lose? You don't ask, you don't get. So, I asked. And my fax to him by way of his personal secretary was slightly different: I had addressed it to Mr. John Carson at NBC, opting not to call him Johnny as everyone does. Whether that made a difference or not, I don't know, but it seemed the right thing to do. My request for a few minutes of his time was a legitimate one.

We discussed a variety of topics before I thanked him for his time. But the first thing I wanted to know about was his narration of *Stuart Little,* a stop-motion animated film I watched in grade school. This was decades before the *Stuart Little* motion pictures featuring Michael J. Fox's voice as the little mouse that is adopted by a human family. I remember it so well, sitting in a darkened room with my classmates, watching this 16mm projected story up on the big white screen. Based on the E. B. White children's book, this version, as I recall, was done in a style similar to Claymation. It's a fond childhood memory of mine. He recorded the narration in 1966, the year I was born, I told him.

"Somebody came to me from PBS and they were going to use it in schools, which they did," he began. "I just did it for a lark. I knew the story, of course. The producer came to me, I can't think of his name, and we did it in about a day. I think it won some kind of an award from the educational system or something."

I wondered if he was familiar with E. B. White's other books, like *Charlotte's Web,* and if he appreciated his work.

"Yes, very much so. I think his book *Elements of Style* is one of the best books written." I happened to have a copy right at my elbow, worn and ragged from my college days. It's sort of a nonfiction bible for writers, an instruction manual actually. I knew Johnny was extremely well-read, but it surprised me that he would know about *Elements of Style.*

Johnny is a fan of another person whom I also greatly admire. It's no secret Jack Benny was, maybe still is, his comedy idol, and I asked him to single out something Benny had taught him.

"Oh, that's easy," he said. "Editing and timing. Sure, how to edit sketches, and timing."

Was there another comedian who had greatly influenced him?

"It's hard to single out one," he said. "I grew up in the radio days. There are a lot of people I admired. Fred Allen for his wit. I admire Benny. I admired Hope in those days. A lot of those comedians. I am a Laurel and Hardy fan. I suppose when somebody starts, they unconsciously or consciously steal a little bit from everybody, and then later on you evolve your own style. But when you're starting, everybody grabs a lit-

Johnny with Stuart Little, the stop-motion animated character adapted from the charming E. B. White children's story. Carson narrated the sixty-minute *NBC Children's Theatre* production of "Stuart Little," which aired in color on March 6, 1966.

tle bit. Jackie Gleason admitted that he took a lot of his stuff from Oliver Hardy, but eventually it became Jackie Gleason."

I mentioned that I had detected a bit of Don Adams in him and him in Don Adams. He thought a moment.

"I think that's true," he said, but not with much certainty. "And that probably goes back to Groucho Marx. You know, the kind of satirical throwaway line." This, among other explanations he offered, revealed a rare, analytical side of Johnny that's rarely seen on television. He was a

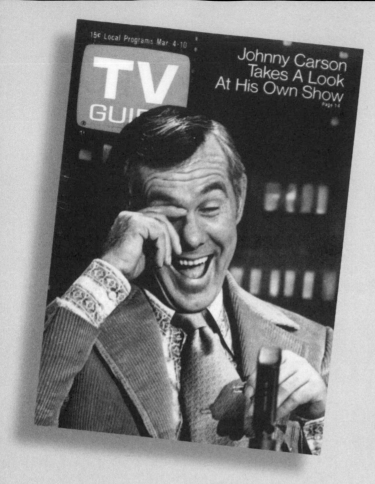

student of comedy, I knew this. Now he was the professor, able to analyze and interpret the art as many comedians are simply not able to do.

Moving swiftly to other topics, I inquired why he hadn't done some of the more popular routines in recent months, like the "Tea-Time Movies," Aunt Blabby, or Floyd R. Turbo.

"We haven't done Turbo in quite a while," he said, choosing this character to expound on. "Once you cover so many, you have to find the right subject. It's not enough to just go out and do him to be doing him. He has to illustrate a point of view, and we went through a lot of them. Whether it was the National Rifle Association or socialized medicine or women in the army or whatever."

I secretly speculated that as a comedian now in his mid-sixties with the frosted top,

and a few more wrinkles around the eyes, he no longer wanted to put on the kooky costumes, raise his voice an octave, and throw on a wig as Aunt Blabby. Or Art Fern, or El Moldo. It was now a difficult image to conjure, Johnny lying on a gym mat with Richard Simmons experimenting with new exercises, twists, and jumps.

Most likely, Carson knew I would inquire about his imminent departure months away. Above all, I wanted to approach this topic, so I reminded him of the time he quoted Jimmy Durante saying, "Let the audience let you know when to exit." I asked: "Are you assuming the audience is telling you it's time?"

"Basically, what I think he meant was, when the audience doesn't *show up,* it's time to pack it in," he said, with that likable Nebraska chuckle in his voice. "The audience will let you know when it's time to quit. That's not why I decided to retire from *The Tonight Show.* I didn't want to get to that point. I'd rather leave while the show was still hot. And it's time. There are other things to do."

Any plans? Vegas maybe?

"Oh, I may go in concert," he said. "I haven't been in concert for ten years, and that's always an option. There's other specials I might want to do. Maybe comedy in politics or something, when the timing is right."

Anxious not to lose my connection before I verified what I thought must be his finest line, I played straight man. I asked him what he wanted for his epitaph. Without hesitating, he answered, "I'll Be Right Back."

And on the final night, when he steps through that curtain for the last time, will he tell the audience he'll be right back?

"I don't know," he said, briefly quiet. "I haven't figured out what we're going to do for the final show yet, or even if we'll have a studio audience. No, I don't know. We're not going to do it in prime time. It will be the same time slot. We started there, and that's where we should finish."

■ ■ ■

**Postscript:** I lived in the heart of the midwest, St. Louis, when I was researching and writing this book in 1991. The research came in different forms, like taping nightly episodes of *The Tonight Show* and reviewing endless hours of past shows. I was privileged to pick through scrapbooks supplied by fellow Carson fan Steve Randisi, a film and television historian who lives on the East Coast. During this process, I flew to Los Angeles a few times to conduct interviews and photograph certain individuals and elements. I had a definite deadline—Carson after all was retiring in May 1992—and it was a mad rush to contact as many celebri-

ties as I could reach and gather the data I needed to cover a thirty-year span.

Doc Severinsen was an integral part of assembling my research back then. Somewhere along the line I had been given his home telephone number, and after I pestered him a few times in his off hours, he alerted his secretary: "For God's sake, just get this guy what he wants." I'm sure he was relieved to get me out of the way, and he remained playful about it all. Doc was great. So was Don Locke in the art department—an enormously talented artist who couldn't have been more supportive of the book.

Now, it's a touchy thing to name-drop. I don't want to become annoying in this personal narration by doing this, but it's almost impossible to discuss this program and not bring up celebrities who popped by NBC or gave of their time for an interview. I never took for granted how great it felt; I have to

Carson was once described as the "Teflon-coated comic who defies age and audience drop-off."

admit, it was always a thrill meeting some of these celebrities, to be able to say hello and discuss Johnny Carson or *The Tonight Show* with bigger-than-life legends like Jimmy Stewart or Jerry Lewis. So bear with me if I gush or fail to display the natural subtlety and disarming charm Johnny possessed when he would discuss his friends—who just happened to be well known.

For me, when Johnny would reminisce about the old veterans of entertainment, it was like a friend relating the stories, because he was as much a "fan" as all of us. It brought him down to earth. (It was rare for him to bring up his personal life, or the personal lives of others, but I remember one night Johnny went into great detail about being invited to an intimate party during the 1960s at a friend's house; he went mostly to meet one of his idols, Jimmy Cagney, who was supposed to show up that night. Johnny didn't hesitate to explain how anxious he'd been to meet the great actor who was now almost an old man. The party took place in a sunken den, with a bar, music going, people eating and mingling. Cagney, in an impromptu moment, began singing "I'm a Yankee Doodle Dandy" for a few in the group, and doing a little tap dancing. The memory was a special one for Johnny.)

While writing this book, I was fortunate enough to create a few special memories of my own. This was a privilege for me and I would thank God each time I drove out of the NBC parking lot in the evening long after the crowd left, waving to the security guard. I guess I was playing out a dream, imagining I was one of those guests who appeared on *The Tonight Show.* I got to be so immersed in the research and videotapes and conversations and writing, I actually once dreamed one night that I was a guest with Johnny. It was one of those bountiful, tactile dreams full of senses and detail, and

better yet, one that I can still recall. I remember waking up, reliving the memory, and concluding that it was as close as I'll ever get . . . it was a terrific guest appearance, though, you should have been there.

Generally, this book was a magical playtime for me, all under the guise of work. (Does it get any better?) I wouldn't say I had carte blanche to the show's center of operations, far from it; I didn't work there. But I had limited access, and it was not squelched, thanks in part, I'm sure, to Carson. He could have nixed my activity fast, but he didn't. Or, he just didn't care. Either way, it worked out.

The best part of writing a book like this is the hunt, the journey into the research and the delight of discovery. A lot of this took place right there around Studio One, and I relished every opportunity to visit and either watch the process from backstage, trying to stay invisible and soak it in, or from a beautiful vantage point—Doc Severinsen's personal seats, generously arranged by his efficient secretary, Dayna Hooper. Some nights were just incredible and I certainly took the time to say hello to some of the stars I'd always wanted to meet. One night, I stood all alone with Clint Eastwood in the darkened backstage area. He was wearing a polo shirt with a sport coat over it, very approachable, actually. I looked up at this tall guy and talked with him, and nobody bothered us. We talked about—of all things—a midget named Billy Curtis who had costarred with him in one of his best films, *High Plains Drifter.* It just struck me how un-celebrity-like and easygoing Eastwood was, and how crazy it was for me to be standing next to this icon, looking up at his weathered face and holding a conversation with maybe the greatest outlaw from the movies.

This book also afforded me the opportunity to bring my parents to a show when they were visiting Los Angeles, and that was a personal treat for me. Meantime, I was preparing to move to California, and in January of 1991 I trekked across the country to la-la land, leaving behind the tornadoes and snow.

It seemed like an eternity, but when the book was finally published, I was immediately sent two copies by my editor—one was for me, and the other was quickly mailed to Johnny. For weeks and weeks, I just wondered what he thought. I heard nothing.

During the final month of shows, I contributed to *TV Guide*'s special edition saluting Johnny, as well as the massive tribute published by the editors of the *Hollywood Reporter*. Along the way I attended a few choice tapings and met with some of the folks who had contributed to the book, presenting them with copies. I was there the last time Bob Hope appeared, and I sat next to him on his dressing room couch, projecting my words a little as I thanked him for his kind words. (He was hard of hearing.)

"This is great," he said, flipping through the book, scanning the pictures. "Where am I?"

Buddy Hackett seemed somewhat nervous in his dressing room on his final appearance. He was trying to calm down, still dressed in one of those jumpsuits and wringing his hands, almost at a loss for what to do on the show that night. I think it was hitting him that this was his final appearance with his pal John. His suit was impeccably pressed and hanging on the back of the door, as he usually put on his best clothes as the last thing he did before emerging from his dressing room. Buddy was kind and we chatted briefly before I left. He was thankful for the book and congratulated me. And then I watched the pro from the audience that night as he turned on the comedy switch. As usual, the audi-

ence was convulsed in hard laughs from Hackett, but also saddened when his tone turned serious and he thanked Johnny for his kindnesses over the years.

During these stops, I thought of approaching Johnny backstage, but my courage dimmed and I didn't take the opportunity. Maybe it was best, as things happen for a reason. The timing just never seemed right.

But one afternoon I headed over to NBC and as I walked through the small parking lot around 3 P.M. I noticed Johnny's white Corvette parked in the number one spot, just outside the door. I thought to myself, "Wow, wouldn't it be great if Johnny was nearby." No one was around.

All of a sudden, however, he emerged from the car that I had thought was empty. He grabbed a small black case and this time something clicked, because we ended up walking up a little ramp into the studio at the same time. I couldn't help myself and I extended my hand.

"Hi, Mr. Carson, I'm Steve Cox."

He did a double take. I knew I didn't need to explain that I was the guy who wrote the book. I was fairly confident he'd received it. And I was right. I think he had an idea I'd be older and it startled him. I was twenty-five at the time with a round face that made me look twenty. I'll always remember the brief stunned look in his face, and the genuine smile that wiped it away.

"Steve, it's nice to meet you," he said, and we shook hands. "How's the book selling?"

All I could think to say was, "Great . . . thanks to you."

"Well, we're winding down. Enjoy the show," he said, then he wished me luck, gave me that quick nod and wink, and he was on his way. I went in another direction and then slowed down somewhere in the hallway to unravel in my mind what had just happened because I felt like someone had just hit my funny bone—you know, sort of that weird feeling that isn't triggered often but it's pleasurable in a strange sort of way. I couldn't believe the King gave me the wink, meaning just one thing: things were good. That wink he sometimes delivers is from the old school of charm, a facial expression rarely used today in this politically correct climate, lest someone take it the wrong way. In this rare trademark gesture, this simple friendly signal, volumes are spoken—whether it be to a friend, one of his sons, or the waitress serving him his turkey burger.

Later, Johnny sent me a very kind note thanking me for the book, and that little treasure is . . . just that.

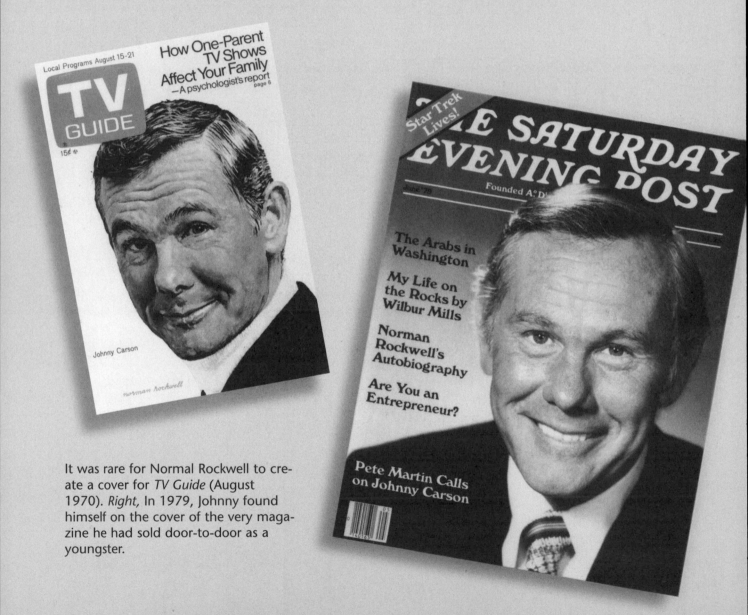

It was rare for Normal Rockwell to create a cover for *TV Guide* (August 1970). *Right,* In 1979, Johnny found himself on the cover of the very magazine he had sold door-to-door as a youngster.

# 1

# THE EVOLUTION OF THE TONIGHT SHOW

*I don't want to sit there when I'm an old man. I don't envision sitting there in my sixties. I think that would be wrong.*

—JOHNNY CARSON, *ROLLING STONE*, 1979

On the occasion of Johnny's fifteenth anniversary show, NBC president Robert Mulholland appeared on the live special and congratulated the host: "It's good to be here. This show, as you know, means a lot to NBC. Not only to the people who work here, but to all the people who watch NBC across the country. This is only fifteen, and we'll go for fifteen more if you will."

Carson thought aloud, "Fifteen more, let's see . . . I would be eligible for the Motion Picture Home."

No one knows whether Johnny had that visionary night in mind when he informed an NBC affiliates convention in May 1991 that he would be leaving a year later, his final show to be broadcast on May 22, 1992. Just shy of thirty years actually, Carson was packing it in. What followed his announcement was a flurry of activity, lots of confusion, and just one year for the nation to prepare for this loss.

There was some doubt as to whether Johnny would actually leave. He had threatened to quit the show several times before in the wake of contractual disputes and other matters. Way back in 1979, he

Comedians David Letterman, Garry Shandling, and Jay Leno joined Johnny for his twenty-sixth anniversary special. (October 1988)

had told the Associated Press: "After seventeen years, I'm getting a little tired of it. I don't think I can bring anything new to it and it gets a little tougher all the time to do it, and I want to keep the standard of the show up."

HERE'S JOHNNY!

The standards over the decades remained lofty. Johnny had some of the best comedy writers in town, and his delivery and timing aged like wine and improved— or we became so accustomed to him that it didn't matter. Audiences were forgiving; even his flubs were funny.

Johnny changed his mind many times during those thirty years with NBC, always pulling solutions out of his hat to overcome his fear of continuing. Johnny shaped the show, shortened it, moved it, but all the while he steadily kept it thriving as a consistent entity of quality network programming with more than pleasing ratings. In exchange, he collected a more than pleasing paycheck with lots of perks. He told *TV Guide* in 1981, "When I was thinking of quitting once, I got a wonderful letter from Kenneth Tynan, who was a big fan of mine. It was very flattering, and he said, 'You know, Picasso didn't do much besides paint, and Astaire was pretty content to dance most of his life. . . .'" Carson gave in to the obvious. He clearly loved what he did, though the job may have become routine at times. So he stuck around a bit longer.

This time, however, Johnny had made up his mind and felt the time was at hand. Thirty years was an obvious milestone. This was not a ruse to hike his salary, or a ploy for added ratings. He was quitting, handing over the show to NBC. Was this a complete retirement for him? He assured us at the time that he would be staying in television in some capacity; however, ten years later, Johnny has yet to find the right venue.

■ ■ ■

Three decades raced by while Johnny sat behind the desk and entertained us in so many ways, he was more than just a mainstay to late night audiences. During his tenure, seven presidents passed through the White House and the world population increased from three billion plus in the early 1960s to five billion plus when he retired in 1992.

Ultimately, Jay Leno was chosen as Johnny's successor. It was a painful decision that *TV Guide* reported in June 1991, shortly after Leno's appointment: "NBC executives Warren Littlefield and John Agoglia flew from Los Angeles to New York so that they could personally tell the iconoclastic host of *Late Night with David Letterman* that they had chosen Leno as Carson's replacement. Letterman was reported shocked at the news. His shock turned to anger, then hurt."

At NBC, the powers making the decisions felt that Leno, permanent guest host since the autumn of 1987, was the logical choice. His tenure already established him with younger audiences, which would hopefully result in a smooth transition. However, one behind-the-scenes figure at NBC revealed Letterman was "angrier than anyone had ever seen him." Another report from an Associated Press story quoted a source describing Letterman as "fit to be tied."

The general public was not aware of the fighting and scheming going on behind

Impressionist Rich Little portrayed Johnny Carson and actor Daniel Roebuck (with a chin prosthesis) was Jay Leno in the 1996 HBO TV movie *The Late Shift*. (Photo by Lynn Houston/HBO)

closed doors at the network and backstage at *The Tonight Show*. Employees were largely divided into two camps: Johnny's exiting family and Jay's incoming bunch. It was a messy parting on some levels for the Carson staff. It was a messy beginning for the Leno newcomers. And it was the sneaky and underhanded stuff of books and movies of the week, starring Dave, Jay, and Johnny. So twisted was the behind-the-scenes transference, most reporters just mildly touched upon the network's squabbles. One writer, Bill Carter tried to dissect the backstage backbiting in his 1995 bestseller, *The Late Shift: Letterman, Leno, and the Network Battle for the Night*. His controversial book (later adapted into an HBO dramatization) was an inside account of the high-stakes, backstabbing rivalry that surrounded the pressurized decision to award Jay Leno the *Tonight Show* throne rather than David Letterman. One reviewer put the complicated story into precise perspective: "Leno's management quite literally stole *The Tonight Show* for him. Dave was hoping to be let in through the front door, but Leno's camp broke in through a window."

If you had to place a bet back then, the odds would have undoubtedly been on Letterman, who, by most accounts, seemed the more logical choice since he was, you might say, Johnny's protégé. Both men were slender, clean-cut, wholesome Midwestern humorists; their styles paralleled each other's in many ways, and the transition probably would have been smooth with Letterman. Moreover, it seemed that Letterman's years following Johnny every night were thought of by some as a "warm-up" for the big show; as if Letterman had spent all that time in the on-deck circle waiting for his turn at bat. But politics behind the scenes washed all of that away. Despite the fact that Letterman was a wildly popular late-night host who had certainly put in the time, he was not given the opportunity, and Jay Leno took his place behind the desk.

Within weeks of Letterman's notification, he seemed to mellow and even made a few jokes about the situation on his own show: "You know what this means to us?" he asked his sidekick, Paul Shaffer. "We get 'Stump the Band' and I'm negotiating for 'Aunt Blabby.' Keep your fingers crossed. We don't know if they'll be handed over or what. . . ." A few months later, Letterman appeared as Johnny's guest and the two made light of the news stories.

*Carson:* There were rumors you were gonna firebomb NBC.
*Letterman:* Well, I hate waitin' in lines, but I'd do it.

Was Letterman just putting up a class act by appearing with Johnny or had he truly gotten over the hurt? It didn't show in his face as he continued: "No, I'm not angry. Not angry at NBC. Not angry at Jay Leno. . . . Now if the network had come to me and said, 'Dave, we'd like you to have this show' and then a week later they said, 'Dave, we don't want you to have this show,' you could be angry. I was never, never angry.

"Now, would I like to have this show? Oh yeah! And from what I know of you, a guy can make a pretty comfortable living doing this show."

The exposure—and the handsome paychecks—were not always the case. But late-night television had come a long way on NBC—the network that lured viewers to the television at bedtime.

## A Shot in the Dark: Broadway Open House

Nightclub comic Jerry Lester believed a late-night television show could be lucrative as well, when NBC programming genius Sylvester "Pat" Weaver (who also created the *Today* show) contacted him in 1950 about pioneering a show. This program would be on late, quite unusual for the limited television audiences during the period, but Weaver was confident that viewers would indeed stay up and tune in if there was something to watch. It's unimaginable now, but in the late 1940s, television's infancy, there were just test patterns or static on the tube following prime time programming. TV simply signed off at night. Yes, there was a time.

Weaver was a televisionary who knew what he wanted and hopefully had his radar set on what the audience wanted. He imagined a lighthearted format, rather than serious—a format almost every host since then has tried to emulate. Jerry Lester, he felt, was the perfect host to start things off in this late hour timeslot. Lester was a multi-talented entertainer. He could sing a little, deliver jokes, set up humorous stories, play a little trombone, and even juggle a bit. But then again, TV didn't require too much because it was fresh territory, and audiences probably would have watched almost anything at that hour—that's how hungry America was for more televison.

*Broadway Open House*, TV's granddaddy of all informal talk-and-variety television shows, premiered May 29, 1950, on NBC and lasted until August 24, 1951. It was sponsored by the Anchor Hocking glass company (which produced beer bottles). The show's run may have been brief, but the implantation was significant and historical. It would become a landmark in television, the forerunner for the rest. *Broadway Open House* was TV's answer to the test-pattern blues. And audiences bit.

Comedy writer Morey Amsterdam, who went on to fame as comedy writer Buddy Sorrell on TV's *The Dick Van Dyke Show,* was the alternating host of *Broadway Open House* in 1950.

After the nighttime show took hold, *TV Forecast* magazine named it first place in comedy and variety:

> The bouncy, roly-poly Jerry Lester, who took the show over for three of the five nights each week, was considered the real spirit and brains of the show as well as its chief performer. It was he who decided what was right and not right, who was to go on and for how long. It was he who hired a big blonde model, Jenny Lewis, and gave her the famous name of Dagmar. The Chicago-born Lester, a puckish veteran of stardom in vaudeville, radio, nightclubs, and Broadway revues, knew he had a good thing with *Broadway Open House.*

Comedy writer Morey Amsterdam was the alternate host of *Broadway Open House* on Monday and Wednesday nights, while Lester emceed the other three. There was not

Jerry Lester, the nightclub comic who became TV's first late-night host.

much of a format, said Amsterdam in 1991. "It was like a little stock company. We had our own people on the show. We wrote our own sketches but ad-libbed most of the show." Amsterdam's forté was his ability to be quick with jokes, and he was an accomplished cellist and songwriter (he co-wrote the Andrews Sisters' quirky calypso hit, "Rum and Coca-Cola").

Regulars on the program included musical director Milton DeLugg, Dagmar, Dave Street, Jane Harvey, the Mello Larks, Bob Warren, Elaine Dunn, Jack Leonard, Buddy Greco, Ray Malone, the Honeydreamers, Dell & Abbott, Maureen Canon, Frank Gallop, and Barbara Nichols.

Amsterdam described one of the program's biggest burdens in those days: "There was no such thing as videotape. We went on live, and kinescopes were distributed. We had to have a studio audience. Where in New York, at midnight, are you gonna find a studio audience? Radio was big now, so I went out in the halls and a whole line would be waiting to get into *The Fred Allen Show.* By eight o'clock, everyone was on their way home."

Amsterdam thought of a solution. "So I went to a bus company and I told them, 'You know, television is new and everybody wants to see what a studio looks like. . . . Tell your people when you take 'em to the nightclubs and the hot spots in New York, the big thing is to see a television show! We filled it up with people visiting on buses."

Musical director Milton DeLugg admits he had little faith in television as a burgeoning medium, but he says that when *Broadway Open House* opened up late-night viewing possibilities, the show instantly became a "remarkable hit. It was the only thing on at eleven at night." The program lasted an hour, with commercials. When it became hot, the entire show took to the road and broadcast live from other cities, such as Detroit. The program's base, however, was NBC's Studio 6-B at Rockefeller Center in New York. (*Note:* This historic studio was the home for Milton Berle's variety show, *Texaco Star Theare,* and at one time it was the base for the quiz shows *Break the Bank, Twenty-One,* and *Name That Tune,* as well as Jack Paar's *Tonight Show.* Eventually 6-B became the stage Johnny Carson would occupy for his

Television's landmark late-night variety show, *Broadway Open House,* a forerunner of *The Tonight Show,* featured: (L–R) announcer Wayne Howell, emcee Jerry Lester, bandleader Milton DeLugg, and sexy comedienne Dagmar.

*Tonight Show* until 1972. Almost immediately after Carson relocated to the West Coast, the studio was employed for broadcasting local news on WNBC-TV, and to date, it remains a news studio.)

DeLugg's band on the show consisted of himself on the accordion, with fellow musicians on the piano, guitar, bass, drums, and trumpet. "The accordion was received wonderfully then," he says. "After a few years, it was not considered too noble an instrument. It's a shame. Everybody did put-downs on it." Eventually, DeLugg's band had a few hits popularized on the show and finally placed on the Hit Parade: "Hoop De Do," "Orange Colored Sky," and "Be My Life's Companion."

It was a simple show and very loose, explains DeLugg, the only surviving main cast member from *Broadway Open House.* "NBC had a limited network, but they distributed kinescopes to the affiliates," he says. "The kinescopes were terrible, very grainy. We all thought we were funny then, but I've seen some of those old shows and we were terrible. You'd be shocked. We look like a bunch of high school kids trying to put on a show.

"We used to sit down a couple of hours before the show went live and try to figure out a premise for the show," he recalls. "You know, Ray Malone will dance into the ash can or something. The show took off and made celebrities out of nearly all of us."

On a typical night, the cast and any guests would gather

The granddaddy of them all, *Broadway Open House,* ran just one year, but carved out a lasting tradition with late-night viewers. The variety show proved that audiences were hungry for television well into twilight time. (Courtesy of Steve Randisi)

around a couch and tell stories and introduce musical bits or light comedy set-ups. Co-host Morey Amsterdam, who stood just five-foot-four and weighed considerably more than he did when he later costarred on *The Dick Van Dyke Show* in the 1960s, was the butt of a few fat jokes on the show.

"He and I used to do the warm-up" says DeLugg, "and I used to say, 'I don't want to get you mad, Morey, but you're getting a double chin.'"

"It's my necktie," Morey would answer.

"Well your necktie needs a shave."

Okay, so the comedy wasn't sophisticated, but it was entertaining. The real sensation of *Broadway Open House* was Jenny Lewis (real name Virginia Ruth Engor) who became known simply as "Dagmar." Writer Wambly Bald described in 1957 the "phenomenal rise of Jenny Lewis . . . junoesque blonde with outstanding natural endowments . . . first given $25 per performance just to sit on the high stool and decorate the set. Then she was given a few dumb-blonde lines to say, and the public went wild. The name Dagmar became synonymous with sex appeal at its grandest. . . . Her fan mail was enormous. In a matter of months, she was getting $1,250 a week."

Reportedly, Jerry Lester, who claimed to have discovered Dagmar, began to envy her rising popularity on the show, which led to a feud between the two and ultimately the demise of the entire program. Dagmar's ditsy delivery caught on and she began receiving mounds of fan mail. Lester denied any jealousy, but Amsterdam and DeLugg both labeled Lester an "egomaniac," citing his demands as the primary reason the show was halted.

"Jerry was a talented comedian," Amsterdam noted of his former co-host. "He said to me one day, 'Starting next year, I'm gonna do the show just once a week. Then I'll do it once a month. And once a year. And they'll be waiting for me.' He was out of his mind."

The show's producer, Hal Friedman, indicated in a 1957 interview that egos began to clash and the spontaneity had vanished within a year. "In the beginning," Friedman said, "the show shaped up as a well-balanced unit . . . just a running order and a premise every performance. As soon as individual performers stood out from the others, the balance was destroyed."

And so, the tale of TV's first late-night program is a fleeting one. The program never hit its stride, but it certainly opened windows to let the fresh, cool night air keep those TV tubes burning.

## ■ POSTSCRIPT

Jerry Lester kept performing in nightclubs, and he became a regular on the NBC series *Saturday Night Dance Party* (1952) as well as *Pantomime Quiz* on CBS (1953). He continued to act in television (*The Monkees,* 1967; *Barnaby Jones,* 1973) and retired to Florida with his wife in the 1970s. He was reunited with regulars from *Broadway Open House* in the 1970s for a taping of the *Tomorrow* show with Tom Snyder. Jerry Lester died on March 23, 1995, in Miami, Florida.

Morey Amsterdam was a show business institution. As a young concert cellist, he switched to gags and became a vaudeville-trained comedy writer and entertainer. From there he moved into radio, nightclubs, television, and films. For years he wrote special material for others (including Rudy Vallee, Milton Berle, and Clark Gable) and later delivered the punch lines himself. In the 1940s, Amsterdam had his own CBS radio show, and he was a regular on one of television's first quiz/panel programs, *Stop Me if You've Heard This One,* for NBC in 1948. Amsterdam never stopped working in television, the voice-over field, and comedy writing. He wrote several books, including *Keep Laughing,* and *Morey Amsterdam's Cookbook for Drinkers (or Betty Cooker's Crock Book).* He'll be best remembered as the insult-spitting comedy writer, Buddy Sorrell, on the popular *Dick Van Dyke Show* in the 1960s. Morey died on October 27, 1996, in Los Angeles.

"Dagmar," the buxom blonde who became one of TV's first sex symbols, died on October 9, 2001, in Ceredo, West Virginia. She was seventy-nine. Jenny Lewis performed with the famed comedy team Olsen and Johnson in their Broadway show

*Laughing Room Only* in the mid-1940s before moving on to television. She was an overnight success on *Broadway Open House,* and she hosted her own NBC show, *Dagmar's Canteen,* directly thereafter. She was a regular panelist on ABC's TV show *Masquerade Party* in the mid 1950s. She continued to appear in nightclubs and summer-stock theater and retired in the 1970s. Married three times, she outlived all of her husbands, including actors Danny Dayton and bandleader Dick Hinds.

Milton DeLugg went on to direct musical segments for many NBC television "house specials" during the 1950s and eventually took on the chores to supply the music for Macy's Thanksgiving Day Parade, the Orange Bowl Parade, and the Junior Miss Pageant. He returned to television briefly as the bandleader on *The Tonight Show* in 1966, when Skitch Henderson left the show. DeLugg even recorded an LP with the *Tonight Show* band in 1966. An accomplished composer, one of his most famous television themes is "Rollercoaster" (the theme to *What's My Line?*). DeLugg joined forces with producer Chuck Barris in the late 1960s and supplied music for *The Dating Game, The Newlywed Game,* and *The Gong Show.* DeLugg lives in Los Angeles and has no plans for retirement, he says.

# Enter: Steve Allen

## ■ Tonight!

In the 1950s, a young bespectacled performer named Steve Allen had started to make a name for himself as an adept ad-lib comedian and musical entertainer in Los Angeles. He hosted a local television presentation on the West Coast, which Allen says was a "dress rehearsal" for the *Tonight!* show. Allen moved for bigger and better television opportunities on the East Coast, where *The Steve Allen Show* actually began as a local presentation in June 1953 on WNBT-TV, the flagship station in New York. Eventually, the show was retooled and became a network offering re-titled *Tonight!* on NBC. Beginning September 27, 1954, Steve Allen's new late-night show was expanded to 105 minutes on the air, nightly.

During this period, the basic format of *The Tonight Show* as we know it was established by the indefatigable comedian. NBC handed Steve Allen the reins and let him loose to create and develop a show the way he wanted. *Tonight!* opened with a monologue (with Allen standing, or sometimes seated, accompanying himself on the piano), a segment where Allen would go into the studio audience, and a simple set with a desk, chair, and a couch for guests was initiated. Allen inspired the likes of Johnny Carson and David Letterman with his loose style. He was the first to take the camera out of the studio for his "Man in the Street Interview" segments and also invented a skit called "The Question Man," which was the precursor to Johnny

NBC's *Tonight!* with host Steve Allen broadcast live in New York from 11:20 P.M. to 1 A.M. "This show will go on forever," Allen groaned to the audience on his first night. Allen was referring to the late hour, but he might as well have been predicting the series' longevity. "You think you're tired now, wait till one o'clock in the morning rolls around." Allen's show set the standard for what is still broadcast on late-night TV: the opening monologue; the familiar talk show set with a desk and city skyline mural behind it; the improvised bits and sprints out into the streets of Manhattan—the trademarks were all built here.

Carson's "Carnac, the Magnificent." Within a year, Allen was riding high on the popularity of his hit and newly married to actress Jayne Meadows (sister of Audrey Meadows).

There were guest stars on *Tonight!* with Allen, in addition to semi-regulars such as Gene Rayburn (who went on to host the popular TV game show *The Match Game*), Steve Lawrence, Eydie Gorme, Andy Williams, Skitch Henderson and his Orchestra, Hy Averback, and announcer Bill Wendell. Some of the fresh performers who appeared with Allen early in their career were Louis Nye, Don Knotts, Tom Poston, the Smothers Brothers, Bill Dana, Don Adams, Jim Nabors, Tim Conway, and Jackie Mason, to name but a few.

As Allen's popularity grew, so did his value to NBC. Allen had many projects going on simultaneously, and he eventually starred in a weekly prime-time series for the network as well. For several months in 1956, Allen was hosting the ninety-minute *Tonight!* show as well as an hour-long Sunday evening prime-time comedy program, *The Steve Allen Show,* and he somehow found time to star as the King of Swing in the dramatic motion picture *The Benny Goodman Story* for Universal. Allen was caught in a web of hectic schedules, conflicting engagements, and just plain exhaustion, so he

HERE'S JOHNNY!

cut back his late-night chores to Wednesday through Friday until he left *Tonight!* A series of guest hosts filled in the remaining days until the brilliant TV pioneer Ernie Kovacs accepted the position as permanent guest host for Allen's nights off.

"For most of his laughs," wrote TV historian Bart Andrews, "Steve Allen relied on his guests. They were his springboard to humor. Once one of them showed up with a few live ducks in a wading pool, so Steve went wading too.

"When two old ladies in his *Tonight!* audience kept talking noisily to each other during the performance, Steve turned the problem into a plus. He recalls: 'I think the heart of all humor is something going wrong. So I slanted all my talk that night to these two old ladies. I could have had a page throw them out, but instead I made them a part of the show.'"

Allen boldly introduced to his audience a string of new talent, including Lenny Bruce, Shelly Berman, and Jonathan Winters. Above all, with his wide-ranging improvisational skills that are still greatly imitated and adapted by David Letterman, Allen pulled in a sizable audience during his tenure as host, and he became a television superstar.

Actor Tony Randall recalls Steve Allen's show with fondness as he describes one of his guest-hosting stints: "In those days, it was live, and the show was two hours and fifteen minutes long," he explains. "I was playing in *Inherit the Wind* at the Broadway Theater on Forty-first Street, and *Tonight!* was from the Hudson Theater on Forty-fourth Street. My curtain came down at 11:15 and the *Tonight!* show began at 11:15 P.M. There was no way to get a limo or cab through those streets at that hour when all the theaters were letting out. There was only one way to do it, and that was to run, literally run, through the streets. The announcer, Bill Wendell, would cover for me until I got there," Randall says, laughing. "A couple of times they had the cameras out there on the streets so the audience could see

Steve Allen and bandleader Skitch Henderson rehearse an outdoor bit in New York City for *Tonight!*

me running. I'd be running as fast and as hard as a man could run."

Steve Allen decided to give up the nightly show and suggested to NBC some suitable replacements: Jack Paar or Ernie Kovacs. On January 25, 1957, Allen hosted his final *Tonight!* show and decided to concentrate on his Sunday evening prime-time variety show (which lasted until 1960). Allen's show battled the steady ratings of Ed Sullivan, and by comparison was a formidable match for Sullivan.

## ■ POSTSCRIPT

Steve Allen, the multi-talented renaissance performer, died on October 30, 2000, at the age of seventy-eight. He left behind more careers than can be counted. He put on so many hats during his career (disc jockey, comedy writer, television host, actor, author, motivational speaker, documentary narrator, composer, and lyricist among them) that he never actually became famous for any one thing. Undoubtedly, he secured his place in the history books as a broadcasting pioneer, and as the creator and first host of *The Tonight Show.*

Allen had a lifelong love affair with the entertainment business. His work was ubiquitous. He appeared in Broadway shows and soap operas, composed songs, wrote plays, contributed to charitable causes, and hosted several television shows including the Emmy-winning *Meeting of the Minds* for PBS. Allen assisted innumerable ambitious students in the field of communications, not only with advice, but with his talents and experience. He wrote dozens of books, both fiction and nonfiction, and his thirty-eighth book, *Hi-Ho Steverino: My Adventures in the Wonderful Wacky World of TV,* was an autobiography covering fifty years of experiences in the medium. Allen was always an advocate for free speech, often commenting on political issues such as capital punishment, nuclear policy, and freedom of expression. During his last years, Allen was an outspoken activist attempting to help clean up the airwaves. He blasted tabloid TV for "taking television to the garbage dump."

## THE INTERIM

### ■ TONIGHT! AMERICA AFTER DARK

Despite the fact that Steve Allen had suggested his show continue with either Ernie Kovacs or Jack Paar as his replacement, when Allen departed his late-night spot in

# Tonight Show Timeline

May 29, 1950–August 24, 1951: *Broadway Open House* (with alternating hosts Jerry Lester and Morey Amsterdam). The first late-night talk/variety show, NBC.

August 27, 1951–September 24, 1954: *The Steve Allen Show* on NBC late night.

September 27, 1954–January 25, 1957: *Tonight!* (starring Steve Allen)

January 28, 1957–July 26, 1957: *Tonight! America After Dark* (various hosts)

July 29, 1957–March 30, 1962: *The Tonight Show* (starring Jack Paar)

April 2, 1962–September 28, 1962: *The Tonight Show* (interim with various hosts)

October 1, 1962–April 1972: *The Tonight Show Starring Johnny Carson* (emanating from NBC's Studio 6-B, in New York City)

January 1967: The show is shortened to ninety minutes in length.

May 1, 1972–May 22, 1992: *The Tonight Show Starring Johnny Carson* (emanating from NBC's Studio One, in Burbank, California)

September 1980: The show is shortened to sixty minutes in length.

September 1983: Joan Rivers is named permanent guest host.

Fall 1987: Jay Leno becomes permanent guest host.

May 1991: Johnny announces his retirement.

May 25, 1992–present: *The Tonight Show with Jay Leno*

January 1957, the time slot was filled by an experiment, which utterly flopped. *Tonight! America After Dark*, in retrospect, was ill-conceived and diffuse, and more of a magazine show than what its predecessors had established as welcome entertainment in the wee hours.

The show featured a group of correspondents and local show hosts who broadcasted from different cities. The original lineup included Hy Gardner, Bob Considine, and Earl Wilson in New York; Irv Kupcinet in Chicago; and Paul Coates and Vernon Scott in Los Angeles. Music was provided by the Lou Stein Trio.

The show more resembled NBC's early-morning *Today* show in format, with a mixture of entertainment and hard news coverage. It was dumped by NBC on July 26, 1957, after ratings had plunged.

# The Era of the "Open Nerve"

## ■ The Jack Paar Tonight Show

Things took a drastic turn when young CBS game-show emcee and talk-show host Jack Paar took hold of the new version of NBC's late-night show. Paar debuted on the show July 29, 1957, and American television will probably never see another host grab the country with such passion and spirit.

Paar broadcast from NBC's intimate Studio 6-B, and his program was eventually taped earlier in the evening for later broadcast. Monday nights offered guest hosts, which included Johnny Carson on at least one occasion. The show's title changed a few times: It became just *Tonight* (minus the exclamation point), and later it was officially re-titled *The Jack Paar Tonight Show*. Paar's first task was to win back the ratings and sponsorship that Steve Allen had worked so hard to build. During the *Tonight! America After Dark* interim, audiences had left the room. Paar also had the job of selling himself in this time slot, as he was not a known stand-up comic or actor. The television audience had skyrocketed in number, and Paar nervously knew he faced an uphill climb.

About Jack . . . many, many things can be extrapolated regarding this unique, intricate television personality who seemingly always had his dukes up. Carl Reiner describes him like this: "Jack Paar was an open nerve. Everything Paar said had a vitality to it because you didn't know if he was going to explode or fall apart or anything. He was very vulnerable, where Johnny Carson was very closed."

Above all, Paar wishes to categorize himself, admitting he's a conversationalist. "I don't think of myself as an interviewer. That's something I did just to fill time. I was just as happy if I were alone on the show."

"Steve Allen had a different kind of show," Paar said in 1991. "The idea of *The Tonight Show*, in my view, started with me, in that it became conversation. Before that,

The charming, popular, and emotional Jack Paar, host of *Tonight* during its Camelot years, 1957–1962.

John F. Kennedy appeared on *The Jack Paar Tonight Show* during the primary campaign for the presidential nomination in 1959.

Steve did sketches and bits and music. And Steve, however witty he may be, he's not a conversationalist I don't think, in the terms that I was."

Paar was highly emotional on his late-night program. His audiences never knew what to expect when tuning in, or attending a taping. He was a master of the insult, but he smiled when he jabbed. As writer Cheryl Lavin put it, when audiences watched Paar, they might wonder, "Whom would Paar attack? Who would walk off the show? Would he do another episode of beat the press—or would it be Mr. Weepers tonight? There was a built-in excitement based on his unpredictability."

*Newsweek* described the show as "Russian roulette with commercials."

His theme, "Everything's Coming Up Roses," would fill the studio, and his announcer Hugh Downs would say, "Here's Jack." Paar's delivery might be a delightful stammer through a monologue or a painstakingly descriptive tale of the day. He might relate his latest trip to the dentist, or a chance meeting with an old friend, or an amazing exchange with a little kid. His chats were real, rambling, personal, and most importantly—like the medium of television itself—intimate. "Daughter Randi got her first bra today," he'd say. And then he'd cry. He cried a lot.

"I am emotional," he said in an interview from his home in Connecticut where he has been fully retired for more than twenty years. "If you were talking for nine hours a week—don't forget I did an hour and forty-five minutes live, not like they are doing now . . . an hour on tape with twelve or thirteen writers. I had two, possibly three, writers at one time.

"And there you are for an hour and forty-five minutes at night. Naturally, if you're creative and humorous, you talk about things you know about. Things that happened to you with your daughter, with your dogs, with your friends. Or my experiences with the Kennedys or the Nixons or the Fords. I think the emotional thing was highly played up. It's not to say there weren't emotional comments. But that's the way I am. Now and then."

He was a pretty good name-dropper, with credentials to do so. Paar began with a crew of regulars, but only two remained to the end: announcer and sidekick Hugh Downs and bandleader José Melis (Paar's former army buddy). Welcomed guests who dropped by the show from time to time included Dody Goodman, Elsa Maxwell, Zsa Zsa Gabor, Hans Conreid, Peggy Cass, Charley Weaver, and Mary Margaret McBride, to name a few.

His guests were usually also great talkers, entertainers, wits, and thinkers. Minds such as Oscar Levant, Richard Nixon, Selma Diamond, Burl Ives, Hermione Gingold, and a young senator named John Kennedy and his brother Bobby even appeared on the show. Fans of Judy Garland could always rely on an amusing storytelling session with the legendary singer. Paar was one of the few to draw that ability from Garland, who also favored audiences with a song or two.

He liked unusual guests—not professional studio personalities with rehearsed conversation. He also hated anyone unjustly hogging his camera. Once, comic Jack E.

One of Jack Paar's favorites was actor Cliff Arquette, appearing here in character as his comic alter-ego, Charley Weaver, reading the humorous letters from Mamma. "Charley Weaver had done more for the success of the *Tonight Show* than anyone who was ever on it," stated Paar in 1959. Arquette (as Charley Weaver) was a radio comedian who became a fixture on television in the 1950s and 60s, and a regular on the original *Hollywood Squares.* His son, Lewis Arquette, became an actor and several grandchildren also followed in his footsteps: Rosanna, Patricia, David, and Alexis Arquette.

Leonard insulted Paar for nearly ten minutes on the air. Then Paar stopped him with this line: "Jack Leonard got a lot of laughs tonight. And you'll be seeing a lot more of him. But not on my show."

Paar also introduced a variety of talented entertainers on his show, budding performers who jumped at the chance for national exposure: Phyllis Diller, Bob Newhart, Carol Burnett, Barbra Streisand, Jonathan Winters, Bill Cosby, and the Beatles—yes, the Fab Four. He didn't introduce the Beatles as an appearing group on stage at NBC's Studio 6-B, but he did feature them in a videotape of unusual acts hailing from England. (And this was prior to their sensational debut with Ed Sullivan, which threw American teens into a frenzy. He's proud of that edge he has on Sullivan, slight as it may be.)

There were front-page feuds between Paar and members of the press (Walter Winchell, Dorothy Kilgallen); between Paar and other entertainers (Mickey Rooney, Steve Allen, Ed Sullivan); between Paar and his employers (regarding a variety of concerns like censorship and the program's length). No one was safe, it seemed. And yet, everyone in America tuned in. His ratings went through the roof. When he began, he broadcast over sixty-two affiliate stations that carried his show. Eventually he doubled it. His feuds always helped the ratings, because audiences would return to this late-hour soap opera, and loved to experience the next installment of Paar. His infamous walk-offs were usually the topic of conversation the next day.

In 1958, he threatened to quit because of the rigors of hosting an hour and forty-five minute program. He urged NBC to cut the time, but the network refused. "I'm doing more television than Gleason, Gobel, Allen, and Berle combined," he told the press. "I don't want more money, I just want less time." In 1960, Paar walked off his show abruptly because of a censorship dispute with NBC over a "water closet" (European term for bathroom) joke he had told. NBC's Broadcast Standards department determined the story was in bad taste and edited the tape before it aired. This enraged Paar. He returned after a month and expressed regret, but the news had made headlines. By 1961, his walk-offs became less surprising. In September of that year, Paar and Peggy Cass traveled to Berlin to tape several shows one month after the erection of the Berlin Wall. During the program, Paar stood by the Brandenburg Gate as soldiers were stationed in the background and America got a true taste of what was really happening in Germany. Some of the press accused Paar of heightening East-West tensions and the incident triggered a U.S. Defense Department inquiry. Paar was aggravated and gave notice he was leaving the show.

When Ed and Johnny teamed up prior to *The Tonight Show,* neither one had any idea they were on the cusp of more than thirty years together in television.

His final broadcast as host of *Tonight* was aired on March 29, 1962. The forty-three-year-old host, a massively popular American personality by that time, cried three times as he left his show, and ultimately left America wondering how he could ever be replaced.

# Interim II: Revolving Guest Hosts

## ■ The Tonight Show

Johnny Carson became the appointed successor to Jack Paar, but prior to jumping into the water he was forced to complete his existing contract with producer Don Fedderson and the ABC-TV game show *Who Do You Trust?* Meantime, a succession of hosts filled in during the transition. The announcers were Hugh Downs (who stayed until August, then became host of NBC's *Today* show), Jack Haskell, and Ed Herlihy. The orchestra was led by Skitch Henderson, who stayed on the show for a few more years. Hosts during this period included: Art Linkletter, Joey Bishop, Bob Cummings, Merv Griffin, Jack Carter, Jan Murray, Peter Lind Hayes, Mary Healy, Soupy Sales, Mort Sahl, Steve Lawrence, Jerry Lewis, Jimmy Dean, Arlene Francis, Jack E. Leonard, Groucho Marx, Hal March, and Donald O'Connor.

The format was relatively unchanged, and the six-month hiatus while awaiting the arrival of Johnny Carson was uneventful, at best. The network reported the ratings were steady, but most Americans were, by then, ready for change, ready for something durable. And they got it.

The First Show: Johnny Carson and Ed McMahon dove into what would become a thirty-year television phenomenon when they broadcast their debut *Tonight Show* from New York City. "I wish we had a copy of that one," Carson admitted. "The network didn't keep tapes because it was too expensive and there was a storage problem." To date, only an audio portion of this program and a few photographs are known to exist. In fact, just scattered kinescopes and tapes of *The Tonight Show* exist from the entire decade of the 1960s.

# The First Show

*Date: Monday, October 1, 1962, 11:15 P.M.–1 A.M.*
*Broadcast from NBC Studios, Rockefeller Center (Studio 6-B)*
*Announcer: Ed McMahon*
*Music: Skitch Henderson and the NBC Orchestra*
*Appearing: Groucho Marx, Rudy Vallee, Joan Crawford, Tony Bennett, Mel Brooks, the*
*    Phoenix Singers*
*First Guest: Rudy Vallee*

**Groucho Marx's Opening:** Don't be alarmed, I'm only going to be out here for a few minutes. The fact is, I happened to be walking past, and Johnny Carson sent his suit out to be cleaned and pressed. It didn't get back yet, so he asked me if I'd come out here.

This is a kind of jump from what I was talking about, which was nothing, but they're doing some very interesting experiments now, scientific research, at the University of Chicago. I think they have a lot of time for this now because they've abolished football there. They don't play any of the big universities. They have what they call 'intramural games.' They play against each other every Saturday. Last week, the girls won. So this gives them a lot of time for scientific research. Now, I don't mean because they play the girls, I mean they do a lot of research in Chicago, at the university.

Perhaps I can explain it better this way: They did an interesting experiment last year on a very important subject. It's something we should all know something about. They put a female mouse in a little maze that has a trap door on it, and there's also a male mouse. Then, they have another cage that's filled with food. Mouse food, whatever that is, I don't know what mice eat . . . maybe they eat other mice. It's probably cheese, or something like that.

Now the male mouse hasn't had any contact with the female mouse in some time. I don't know exactly what the time is with mice. Anyway, any information for me is purely academic. They had the male mouse, the female mouse, and cheese—whatever they eat at Twenty-One. You know, I had a cheese sandwich there last

Groucho Marx talked with the studio audience, or rather toyed with them, and introduced Johnny Carson to America as the new host of NBC's *Tonight Show* on October 1, 1962.

## close up

**TONIGHT SHOW'S
25th ANNIVERSARY
9:30 PM ③ ⑭ ④**

### A SILVER JUBILEE

Johnny Carson celebrates his 25th year at the helm of "The Tonight Show" with (what else?) a prime-time stroll down memory lane.

As usual, he'll be reminiscing with Ed McMahon and Doc Severinsen, and he'll screen clips—including vintage Carson levity from '62. Other highlights feature . . .

**Comic legends:** Appearances by Groucho Marx (1965), George Burns (1975), Bob Hope (1982), Red Skelton (1986) and Jack Benny (1973).

**Comic "newcomers":** "Tonight Show" debuts of Steve Martin (1973), Jay Leno (1977), David Letterman (1979), Garry Shandling (1981) and Eddie Murphy (1982).

**Musical memories:** Selections by Pearl Bailey (1964), Judy Garland (1968), Louis Armstrong (1970), the Jackson 5 (1974), Diana Ross (1975), Buddy Rich (1979), Benny Goodman (1980) and Luciano Pavarotti (1980).

*In the beginning: Joan Crawford (1962)*

**Presidents-to-be:** Conversations with Richard Nixon (1967) and Ronald Reagan (1972).

Also: a 1982 impression of President Reagan by Johnny; a 1968 "Dragnet" spoof with Carson and Jack Webb; Ed Ames' now-legendary 1965 tomahawk throw; and Fred Astaire's 1976 vocal of "Life Is Beautiful"—his own composition, which later became a "Tonight Show" closing theme. (Live; 90 min.)

week, and it was two and a half dollars. And then they charge you extra for the bread and the cheese.

Where was I? I had a female mouse in one trap, cheese and a male mouse in others. It remained this way for three days, and then they opened up the two cages simultaneously. They then opened the cage with the male mouse and let him run around. Now, I'm going to ask you, because I'm interested in your reaction to this, which do you think that the male mouse went for first—the cheese or the female mouse?"

[Audience: "The cheese!"]

The cheese? You're wrong. Your contact with sex must be less than mine. I'm not trying to be funny, and I don't think I am, but this is fundamentally true. It's the law of retaining the sex of the human being or mice or whatever it happens to be. So the first thing is that sex is the most important thing of all. If it wasn't for that, the whole nation, the universe, would disappear. Might not be a bad idea, either.

So they go for that first, and then they go for the cheese. In some homes, this isn't much different. I think the men in the audience tonight, when you go home, ought to try it themselves. Put your wife in one cage and some cheese in the other, and see which one you're going to go for. . . .

And now the permanent star of *The Tonight Show:* Johnny Carson!

**Johnny's First Words as Host:** Boy, you would think it was Vice President Nixon. My name is Johnny, and I didn't have trouble getting a suit—I was out buying some cheese.

**Highlight from the Monologue:** Ladies and gentlemen, thank you. Seriously, Groucho, I want to thank you so much. This is kind of an emotional thing for me because I have known about this show for a long time.  And with the newspapers and magazines, I've probably now been interviewed 150 times in the last nine months.  As I say, you work up to it. We came over here this afternoon, met the guests that were on the show and you get kind of charged up. I don't mean to be maudlin about it, but I know that tonight a lot of people, a lot of my friends, are watching all over the country. I only have one feeling as I stand here knowing that so many people are watching . . . I want my na-na.

Ed, Skitch, and Johnny in 1966.

An animated moment during of one of his earliest *Tonight Show* monologues, circa 1962.

# 2

# THE MONOLOGUE:
# "THAT'S GOOD STUFF"

*The monologue truly is the pride and joy of his appearance on the show. I think it developed from the God-given ability to read a newspaper and see one day before the American public what their attitude would be the next day.*

—FRED DE CORDOVA, APPEARING ON
*LATER WITH BOB COSTAS*

It's true, Johnny's sense of gauging the public's opinions and mood was incredibly acute. Maybe we were fooled. Were we the followers and he the leader? Maybe he dictated the public's attitude; he had this influence, you know. The power of the medium was wielded with the mighty hand of Carson, no doubt in that. He'd been called television's most powerful man in the business and with good reason. He'd proven the notion many times, from the infamous toilet paper incident to the annual paycheck he received, Carson possessed great charm.

The power was in the words. And most of the words came lumped at the beginning of the show in a segment known simply as "the monologue." The word became synonymous with Carson for a time. He didn't invent the television monologue;, Bob Hope preceded him in that distinction, and probably a notable performer or two predate him. The ingredients in Carson's monologue were part his and part the creative wit of his team of writers who would hand him pages of material earlier in the day. Whatever the source, Carson molded the material into a seven-minute speech that informally kept America apprised of current affairs for nearly thirty years. At times, more viewers absorbed those monologues than presidential fireside chats and state of the union addresses.

Johnny is a magician, that we know. But just where did the jokes, the observations, the stories, the ad-libs, the zingers, and the newsy and gossipy updates all come from? And how were they delivered with such finesse for so long?

You need to know this: His delivery was his own, but it truly was an amalgam of Jack Benny, Bob Hope, Harry Truman, John Kennedy, Don Adams, Jackie Gleason, Tom Poston, Will Rogers, and a few others. Still, at least 50 percent of it is pure Johnny Carson. His editing and timing he learned from Jack Benny on radio, he said.

Johnny was a Nebraska kid drawn to the cabinet radio that sat in the Carson living room and was played often for the family to enjoy. Johnny was there lying on the floor with his chin in his hands, lost in a comedy world provided by the airwaves and the unique talents who knew how to put it across with sound only. Johnny idolized the radio comedians and followed their careers; years later, he was just as in awe of them when he became friends with them. His respect for these talents from radio spilled over into his television years and Johnny truly loved inviting many of them on his program, partly out of fascination, but more than that—because they were damned good. People like Jack Benny, Edgar Bergen, Bob & Ray, Mel Blanc, George Burns, Milton Berle. And above all, Johnny had respect for the veteran comedians, the "old-timers" he might have thought at one time. And then, all of a sudden, Johnny was past the stage of observing from afar, and somewhere along the line he jumped the hurdle and joined the ranks of the comedians. Call him a protégé, but he was trying to carve out his own spot in the business on local television, then national television, game shows.

Now, the old timers are all gone, the legends and pioneers have just about all passed, and Johnny is our elder statesman of television comedy. One writer dubbed him the "president emeritus of American humor." Where that transition from fan to veteran took place, it's hard to pinpoint. But certainly, the standard of comedy Carson upheld in his regular monologues deserves honor.

Fred de Cordova put it this way in 1988: "He has an innate ability to see

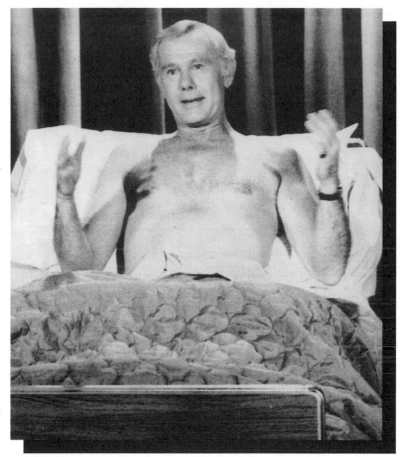

Beginning his seventeenth year, Johnny was wheeled out in a bed to deliver the monologue propped up with pillows. "I thought I'd try something new," he said. "People seem to catch me while they're in the horizontal position, so I thought I'd do the monologue while I'm horizontal."

humor, sarcastic sometimes, just plain funny other times, of what the foibles of the world are. He can mold that into an observation that later becomes of serious importance."

A cute observation in Johnny's monologue on December 19, 1973, may have been in jest, but that didn't lessen the urgency it created when throngs of Americans flew into a panic. This was the year of the great toilet-paper shortage, if you'll remember. Johnny was talking about shortages in the country and he said, "But have you heard the latest? I'm not kidding, I saw it in the paper. There's a shortage of toilet paper."

The *New York Times* reported, ". . . thus began the second chapter in what may go down in history as one of the nation's most unusual crises—the toilet paper shortage. [This was] a phenomenon that saw millions of Americans strip every roll of bathroom tissue from thousands of grocery shelves."

Johnny returned from several weeks of vacation in February 1985 with a winter beard, trying to give his face a rest from shaving.

The shortage was full of humor and fear, and it was a rumor run wild that caused a buying binge and mass case of hoarding across the country. Shoppers were checking out with $40 toilet paper purchases in some cities. Carson never realized he would create a consumer calamity when he made the remark, which actually had a shred of truth to it. The gag was rooted in a "paper shortage" report put out by the federal printing office. After news reports debunked the trailblazing rumors, consumers calmed down and stopped their T.P. frenzy.

The level of influence Johnny had on the American public was probably more than even he could imagine. Politicians were known to become quite angry at his political jabs, and no one was ever safe, not in the White House or any branch of the government. Johnny's observations could sting at times, and that's why the public loved them. But not all of the public.

Entertainer Wayne Newton became so infuriated by a string of suggestive gay jokes Johnny made about him in the early 1970s that he finally hit the roof when he watched Carson deliver this line one night: "I saw Wayne Newton and Liberace together in a pink bathtub. What do you think that meant?"

The next day, Newton stormed the *Tonight Show* offices at NBC, walked right past Johnny's secretary, and interrupted a meeting between Carson and Fred de Cordova. Ol' de Cordova shot out of there quickly, leaving Johnny alone with Newton and his manager; the singer verbally chewed out the host, told him the jokes were not funny to him, and asked him why he was an apparent target. The Las Vegas heavyweight went so far as to threaten physical harm. Carson assured Newton that he didn't realize the jokes were aggravating him.

According to Newton in his memoirs, *Once Before I Go,* Carson was shaken and apologetic and ceased all jokes about the singer. "He never again told Wayne Newton jokes. In fact, I even did his show after that. When I was on his show and talking to him, Carson would constantly look past me at Freddy de Cordova. We had no eye contact at all. This happened a couple of times. I felt so uncomfortable that I told my manager I wouldn't do the *Tonight Show* any more unless there was a guest hosting it."

HERE'S JOHNNY!

Generally, Carson did not want to transform the show into a forum for his own motives, political or otherwise. He was, to the public anyway, apolitical because he threw spears at all parties. Setting the record straight in the *L.A. Times,* he said: "I think it's dangerous to get involved politically with any one candidate. I keep it very open with everybody. I've made jokes about presidents . . . Kennedy, Nixon, Ford, Carter, all the way through. People can't say what my politics are."

Mostly, Johnny's material in his monologues came from his writers. When he joined the show in 1962, along with the contract came a staff, a studio, a secretary, a network to back him . . . and a staff of writers. He thanks God for them.

Granted, Johnny Carson is a natural wit and often displayed how quickly he could rescue a joke while at the desk or when things went south in the monologue. That was his expertise: digging out of a hole in the funniest of ways and arriving at the surface perfectly clean. Even on rare nights when Johnny didn't bat a thousand, he could rescue himself with a mere expression. Writer Bill Cosford said it was his "most acclaimed skill—his ability to extract humor from all but the most desperate on-camera situations." When a joke fell flat, he not only retrieved it, he juggled it for laughs. Golf swing. Yadda yadda. And the show was on its way.

Johnny had a theory that the show was like a bone yard—everything must be used. Comedian Steve Martin observed, "In one of my early appearances on *The Tonight Show,* Johnny and I got to talking about something which led him naturally into a very good impression of Goofy. The audience laughed and during the break, Johnny leaned over to me and said, 'When all else fails, you must use everything you ever knew.' He was right."

That didn't mean he had to burn up everything the writers put before him. He was selective, and some of his writers felt he did not rely on their material enough. And for some sour nights, the blame can be put on the audience. The excitement was usually in the studio, in the crowd, but not always in full force, and not always physically evident. Regardless of the show's pace, his emergence from the colored curtain was usually greeted with long, steady, wild applause, especially after a week or two in absentia.

Usually, he'd open with a quick shot to settle the whooping crowd:

Thank you . . . Look, I . . . c'mon folks [raising hand] . . . Sorry, but I was warned never to take applause from strangers. But be honest, after two hours in line, you would applaud a box of stale Wheat Thins.

Or maybe this one after his wedding in 1972:

Listen . . . you really must stop, because I have to have the Applause sign back in my honeymoon suite . . . Now, Ed, I want to talk to you. I don't like to do this on coast-to-coast television, but enough is enough. We've known each other for fourteen years. I have great affection for you, but it was not necessary to stand in my room on my wedding night going "Hi-yoooooo!"

Or this one from the '90s:

I know . . . I know your type. You're good at foreplay, but how will you be after we consummate the monologue?

Following a few amenities, the actual printed word would kick in. Just below the camera's eye was a long wooden barrier used to prop up giant cue cards (white poster board) stretching out in front of Johnny. (Stenciled on the back of the custom made wooden barrier was "Tonight Show Joke-Board") The cards were lined up so he could effortlessly jump from one topic to another, not necessarily in the order of the cards. That was all part of his editing. If the "Liz Taylor's Wedding" jokes weren't working so well, he'd proceed to the next. Sometimes the cards needed to be changed by the "cue-card boy" and if he had to wait for the next card, the timing was ruined. On these cue cards were sentences, sometimes just cue words, written boldly in black magic marker. Most nights if you looked, you could see Carson, with his keen vision, glance down at the cards to pick up the next topic. He never squinted, but sometimes he would take a quick peek when he turned to Ed.

Then the meat and potatoes was introduced. No one but Johnny and the writers knew what might be said, not even Ed McMahon—which explains why his hefty, barrel-chested laugh was sincere most of the time. It was sort of like Santa with a few beers in him. He actually enjoyed Johnny's humor, and not because he was at work and *had* to enjoy Johnny's humor.

Even the writers were not sure exactly which jokes were going to be used each night, said one of Johnny's most prolific writers, Pat McCormick.

Their mechanics were this: The team of writers met during the day, but not always for a brainstorming session. Sometimes it was playtime, but the work still had to get done. McCormick explains: "We'd meet as a group. Some guys just did monologue work. I did routines and desk spots, and monologue. We'd pitch a consensus of stuff and write up the ones we liked. We'd get his approval on the routines first. Johnny had his own ideas, too."

For the monologue, the writers separated to their hideaways and produced. They'd write, they'd toil or scream. They would do whatever they had to do to put their share of humor on paper, good or bad. Sometimes the oddest things submitted just worked. The amount totaled maybe thirty or thirty-five jokes, typed. Written, if you were really in a hurry. Faxed, if you were out of town.

Then, by 3 P.M., with the individual writer's name at the top, the jokes were handed to the Man and he gathered the papers, convened to his office, and whittled

Johnny is pummeled to the floor by Australian comedian Rod Hull and his overgrown puppet Emu. (1985)

Discussing a sketch backstage in this snapshot taken in 1977.

Comedy writer Pat McCormick occasionally put on a costume for *The Tonight Show,* or removed clothing, like the night he streaked Johnny during the monologue. Here, McCormick is the Easter Bunny, Jaws, a spring chicken, a Thanksgiving turkey, Cupid, and the NBC peacock (center). (Courtesy of Pat McCormick)

his monologue. From a team of six or eight writers working each day, he may have used eighteen or twenty of the jokes. It always varied. The only way to find out your "score," if you were keeping track, was to watch the shows. Pat McCormick was one of the few writers who waited until the five o'clock hour to watch the magic.

"I got into doing that, kind of a habit," McCormick said in 1991. "I'd see him just before the monologue and maybe tell him a joke or two [usually off-color]. Not everybody did that. You'd kind of figure it out," he said of the backstage etiquette around the host, just before showtime. "I'd stand by in case he wanted to talk. But you didn't force it on him."

Describing Johnny's monologue, *TV Guide* writer Bel Kaufman offered:

This is often the best part of the show; it's the voice of Middle America. He comments on topical and local events, criticizing what is currently safe and popular to criticize: the postal service, British royalty, air pollution and our own government, which he claims is his best source of humor. His political comments are irreverent without being rebellious or abrasive. They are not to be underestimated. His bite is often sharper than his barb; his barbs are pointed, but not poisonous. His accurate gauge of the country's political climate keeps him from taking risks; he avoids extreme positions.

■ ■ ■

Repeats notwithstanding, the monologue was always happening "here and now," because it was written the day of the show, just hours before taping and the broadcast. Monday nights with a "Best of Carson" repeat became rough to swallow. Nothing is staler than yesteryear's news.

There was a friendly competitiveness among the writers. It was all about their gems that Carson held to the light for shine on television. McCormick didn't deny the game. "The competitiveness was to look at the count," he said. "I did pretty well most of the time. Like anybody else, I had streaks."

When the California earthquake of 1971 hit and rumbled the visiting Carson crew at NBC, McCormick's opening line for Johnny eventually became a classic. Johnny came out and said, "Due to today's earthquake, the 'God is Dead' rally has been cancelled."

"I did the earthquake monologue almost solely," McCormick said proud as an NBC peacock. "The next day, Johnny thanked me for it."

It was rare that one of Johnny's writers also became on-air talent. McCormick, who occasionally put on a costume or two during his decade as a *Tonight Show* writer, also specialized in certain comedy sketches for Johnny. He handled many of the Art Fern spots and he also suggested the heavy-handed soap opera parody, "Edge of Wetness," a routine in which the camera scanned the studio audience and zoomed in on individuals while Carson read utterly insulting and embarrassing narratives about the fictitious townspeople of "Sludge

Accompanied by an "officer" to deliver the monologue, an embarrassed Johnny attempted to comically explain his charge of drunken driving, which had been splattered across the newspapers in 1982.

Falls." The comedy bit was originally a routine that McCormick had written for Jonathan Winters for some television specials in 1964, and Carson adapted it very successfully for *The Tonight Show.*

# The Art of Bursting Bunkum

*by Neil Shister*

What I liked best about Johnny Carson is what, in general, I like least about other people—his steadfast refusal to commit himself to virtually anything other than his own stagecraft, which, in its best moments, means stepping in and out of social confusion with equal parts impulsive abandon and icy detachment.

For what seemed an untold number of years, Johnny Carson made me laugh. (I don't date Carson in standard chronology, but rather by the phases of my life we've shared, and I can vividly recall several eras back rushing home from the college library to catch his monologue.)

He hasn't intellectually stimulated me, nor caused me to think new thoughts or see the world in a different light, but simply— and regularly—has made me laugh. Often out loud.

More than anything else that readily comes to mind, he had been the consistent presence in my adult life. It's not that I followed him devoutly. There were huge stretches when I didn't tune in, months when I didn't watch. But he was always there to come back to, the way one resumes contact with a trusted friend, holding down the fort with irony that can salvage even the worst days like a brandy nightcap.

In person, so tales go, Carson is sullen, reclusive, intensely private. He's given to spending time at parties barricaded in a corner, nervously tugging the knot in his tie. He has been through several marriages, is reputed to have once had a drinking problem, and can, on occasion, be positively surly.

I find none of this disconcerting. On the contrary, it adds to his on-camera charm, the fact that his unflappable, accommodating cool is masking a considerably less sociable nature. My Carson, the one who peered forth at me in some intimate moments, was something of a rogue, one who spoke with a slightly forked tongue but got away with it because of his disarmingly innocent manner.

There is to Carson still a quintessentially American quality, distilled no doubt from the Nebraska heartland he hails from. Years ago, in his six-bedroom Bel Air home hung a portrait of the man painted by Norman Rockwell. It was a perfect match: the idealist of the American scene portraying the televised embodiment of the ideal American personality, a title Carson has earned, if only through longevity.

That quintessential quality is, I'd hazard, cynical civility. It's a willingness to let each person speak his mind, coupled with an unwillingness to take all that is said at face value. The old Missouri "show me" stuff.

But Carson, to get back to his refusal to go public with his politics, didn't debate on the air, didn't force his guests to prove their points. In his monologues, he scathed assorted newsmakers. (In 1973 he mentioned that Richard Nixon was unworried about the gas shortage, adding, "That's understandable, of course—everything's downhill for him.")

But he did this in such a random way that some shrewd observers regarded his remarks as an astute barometer of public opinion, not the concerted assault of an identifiable ideologue.

No, what Carson did was puncture bunkum with deadpan humor of polished economy. In a moment of upward-rolling

*The Tonight Show* troupe in the 1980s: Doc, director Bobby Quinn, Johnny, producer Fred de Cordova, and Ed.

eyeballs or a startled shake of his head as if he were dozing off, he expressed stunned disbelief or disagreement. This was his nightly genius, this talent for building a laugh off an unwitting straight man seated on his right, while still maintaining the facade of the dutiful host displaying his best manners.

He made conversation on camera the way, say, Picasso might have doodled: less as an end in itself than a prelude to something grander. In Carson's case, that meant a topper, a joke spontaneously pulled out of the air that suddenly gives order to an

unstructured dialogue. One didn't watch Carson to hear what others had to say (too often they tended to be show-biz glitter types of the most passing interest) but rather to watch Carson work.

Perhaps what finally most fascinated me about Carson was the certainty that I could never do what he did, to be so rigorously "on" over such a sustained length of time. He reminded me of how Joe DiMaggio has been described, a ballplayer of such raw talent that he could make the toughest plays look easy. Even when a line in the monologue fell flat, he sidled away from it with a hint of self-deprecation calculated to pan a comic payoff out of his own predicament.

Carson's was a singular presence on the screen. In his natty suits and trimmed haircuts, he represented, to me, the perfect corporate-type go-getter gone ever-so-slightly bad. He was intimately acquainted with the "system" and its self-effacing discipline—but he was clearly not *of* it, having escaped while never decisively turning his back on its decorum.

*Neil Shister is a former* Time *magazine correspondent and TV critic for the* Miami Herald. *He was publisher and editor of* Atlanta *magazine before accepting his current position as vice president of the custom-publishing division of Hill and Knowlton, Inc., in Chicago.*

A certified scuba diver, Carson dove into a human aquarium in the NBC variety special from Florida *Johnny Carson Discovers Cypress Gardens.* (September 9, 1968)

In early 1962, Johnny Carson was finishing his duties with his ABC quiz show and simultaneously preparing to assume the job as host of *The Tonight Show.* "Actually I could have taken over *Tonight!* right away," he told UPI reporter Jack Garver. "But I also would have had to continue *Who Do You Trust?* until next fall under my contract. I'm skin and bones already. Can you imagine what I'd look like in a couple of months doing ten shows a week, five of them being 105 minutes each? I'm very appreciative of the fact that NBC was willing to wait. It's nice to be wanted."

"Stump the Band" usually meant Johnny threw out the routine that night; questions from the audience written on a little blue cards meant the same thing. One of the less frequent routines was El Moldo, a half-wit psychic played by Carson, donning a cheap black wig and a black cape. El Moldo would sit center stage, while Ed would choose random participants from the audience. El Moldo tried to cosmically ascertain what was on the mind of the participant, or an item Ed had chosen to be deduced. It was the Amazing Kreskin gone awry:

*Ed:* El Moldo, would you guess [participant's] hometown?
*El Moldo:* Yes, I'm working on it now. Concentrate . . . I see . . . Chicago.
*Ed:* No!
*El Moldo:* I didn't say you live there, I said I saw it! How quick they are to jump down El Moldo's throat. . . . The word city is coming in very strong . . . You are from Kansas City? [wrong] Oklahoma City? Rapid City? Sioux City? Dodge City? You once drove a Dodge through a city?

■ ■ ■

Some of Johnny's favorite routines involved his rapid-fire delivery of tongue twisters that he could spit out like a machine gun. The most famous, perhaps, was his deadpan parody of *Dragnet* with guest Jack Webb. It was called the Copper Clapper Caper, a quick exchange of tongue twisters that progressed and got more difficult for both Carson and Webb as they got into the routine.

As the story went, there had been a robbery at the Acme School Bell Company. Claude Cooper, a kleptomaniac, had copped Carson's clean copper clappers that were kept in the closet.

*Webb:* Who first discovered the copper clappers were copped?
*Carson:* My cleaning woman . . . Clara Clifford.

During a series of News Update routines, Johnny portrayed a TV anchorman delivering these beauties—quickly and without flaw:

But first . . . is there a royal divorce in the works? Will Prince Chuck chuck Di? Will Di chuck Chuck? Or would Britains rather die and upchuck than give Chuck and Di up?

. . . And later we'll have film from our roving reporter, Pete Polk, who went to Pikes Peak to take a peek at Pike, then to peek at Topeka, Topeka State Park, then to Pocatella to take a poke at Pocatella then to Tacoma, Potomac, Paduca, Tucumcari . . .

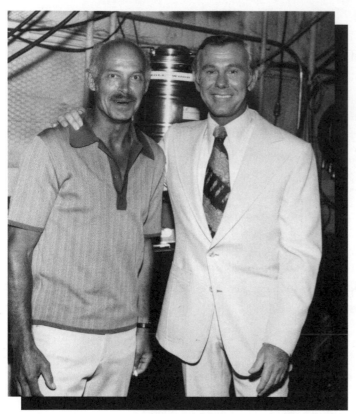

Johnny poses backstage with his pal Jack Grant, long-time prop man for *The Tonight Show.*

All of the credit for a decent monologue or routine cannot go to the writers, McCormick maintained in 1991. "Like his writers, Johnny was aware of everything going on," he said. "He's a very good editor. He might hand us back a routine or jokes and say, 'Not quite there yet.' And reject it temporarily. He's open to all kinds of things. He's not averse to doing something wild."

Neither was McCormick. That was his reputation. Audiences may just know him as a former judge on *The Gong Show* or scattered sitcom appearances on shows like *Get Smart, Sanford and Son,* and *The Golden Girls,* or the tall goof dressed up as Cupid or the NBC Peacock in routines with Johnny. It's hard to believe that McCormick is a Harvard graduate. Other writers who have worked with him describe him as crazy, wild, and completely unpredictable.

Former *Tonight Show* talent coordinator Craig Tennis said, ". . . any story you hear about Pat McCormick is probably true, provided it's too gross to tell outside of a men's room, and even then, it's probably been cleaned up. Pat is without a doubt one of the best comedy writers in the business, even if he is rather consumed with the humor of bodily functions."

A few Pat McCormick tales:

"According to legend," said Tennis, "when his baby was christened, Pat presented the nude child on a silver turkey serving platter, all surrounded with parsley."

To a rookie writer on the show who wished to remain nameless, McCormick prescribed cure for crabs: "You shave exactly half of your pubic hair. Then take a match and light the other side on fire. And when the crabs come running out of the fire—stab 'em."

Former *Tonight Show* writer Greg Fields described meeting McCormick as shocking. "The first day I was there, I went into the bathroom and I was in the stall," he says. "Now McCormick's tall, like 6'8". He came in there, and I didn't know it. He just put his head over the door, and he was looking down at me. I looked up, and it was the most frightening sight I'd ever seen. I just screamed."

And then there was the infamous *Tonight Show* streaking by McCormick in the early 1970s. Remember the seventies? Ray Stevens's popular song, "The Streak"? The nudie who traipsed across the stage as David Niven was presenting an Oscar on the Academy Awards telecast? Parading around nude became a national rage.

For weeks Johnny had jokingly speculated that *The Tonight Show* might be streaked and how funny that might be. On a Thursday night's taping, McCormick, wearing just a cowboy hat and a Johnny Carson Halloween mask, ran across the stage in front of Johnny during the show. All McCormick remembers is the particular shrill screech of one woman, audible above all of the audience reaction, and how he's never heard the same high-pitched sound since. ("Maybe she recognized me," he adds.) Said McCormick of the stunt that ended up almost costing him his job:

> Naturally, from going to the set and looking at the cards, I know the last joke. So I didn't interrupt the monologue. As soon as I heard the last joke—and I'm standing there on the side in an overcoat. Nobody took any notice of it because they never knew what I was gonna do anyway. I wanted this to be a real streak.
>
> I thought it was a perfectly normal thing to do. I did not anticipate whatsoever that some New York lawyers at NBC would get all excited and annoyed by it. I ran toward the band, and the Johnny Carson mask I had on went over my eyes, and I couldn't see where I was running. People in the band said I was coming at them like a walrus. . . . A guy on the other side was holding the door. For a second, it gave me the terror of not being able to get out.

Producers inserted a black band across McCormick's privates and the bit was aired that night. When the network offices at NBC in New York saw this, they were blistered and moved to have McCormick fired. Carson, knowing it was just a gag, went to McCormick's defense. "I always appreciated that," McCormick said. "He's been a good friend."

Of the material that McCormick submitted to Johnny over the years, there was one instance when the routine didn't set well with the host, and the concept was ultimately turned down. It was during a period when a new pope was being installed as the Catholic Church's new spiritual leader. "It was preempting NFL Football," McCormick recalled. "My idea was for Johnny to be the pope and he would deliver the scores in Latin. Carson liked the skit, but because of certain reasons, we had to bow to that. He's pretty good at not doing religious stuff too often, unless it's a screwball cult or something.

"I think he was right," McCormick said. "He was one of the few voices of our times. There's nobody like that anymore."

■ ■ ■

Greg Fields was a kid from Kentucky who came out west with almost no money. He was living in a one-bedroom apartment with a bed that pulled out of the wall when

Johnny and his younger brother, Dick, who directed *The Tonight Show* from New York, are shown here in this rare snapshot discussing the show during an afternoon rehearsal.

he blindly submitted some material to the head writer at *The Tonight Show* at the suggestion of a friend. Six weeks later, someone called him back and said they thought his Carnacs and Floyd Turbo essays were good and he was hired. He felt he fit right in.

"Johnny always thought, the worse you looked and the drunker you looked, the funnier you probably were," says Fields, whose appearance back then was admittedly sloppy, hardly Hollywood. "Any writer who looks like he's got his life in order is probably not a very good writer. And as long as you can produce, you can dress and act like an idiot out here."

Fields began at a salary of $1000 a week, which nearly sent him into shock. He was still riding to work on a bus and gambling most of his savings away at the track, and none of his friends or family back home could actually believe he was writing for Johnny Carson.

"He was my hero," Fields says. "In Kentucky especially, he was God." Fields admitted he was naïve when he began writing for his idol. One day at NBC, a studio worker asked him to help carry some heavy piping to the next soundstage. Being new, Fields thought he better assist, fearing a refusal might cause a commotion. Johnny's head writer, Ray Siller, spotted Fields and pulled him aside quickly.

"Hey, what the hell are you doin'?" Siller asked him. "You work for Johnny, you know. You don't have to do heavy lifting!" Siller laughed as he walked away from the rookie. In essence, the writers were Johnny's boys. He could pick on them, but nobody else.

Fields points out that writing for Carson was one of the best jobs in town. It was a great place to begin—or end, for that matter. The salary was great and a graduate of the Carson comedy crew could almost always go elsewhere and find work, whether their departure was by choice or not. In Fields's case, he left after almost two years when Johnny was "cleaning house," he says. Fields went on to contribute to many shows, such as *Solid Gold, The Pat Sajak Show,* and *In Living Color,* and later he wrote the storyline for Rodney Dangerfield's best film, *Back to School.*

Fields further detailed his *Tonight Show* gig: "If there was nothing going on in the news, you'd see writers bullshitting, trying to come up with stuff. Pee-wee Herman masturbating in a porno theater—every writer was on that. That's something to write about. It's the slow news times that kill you."

Oddly enough, Carson had mercy and made no on-air comments about the 1991 Pee-wee arrest. During a commercial break on *The Tonight Show* while the Pee-wee incident was news, Carson opened the field for questions from the audience. "What do you want to talk about, anything?"

The audience yelled out, "Pee-wee! Pee-wee!"

He hesitated, smiled, looked at Ed. The audience was chanting "Pee-wee! Pee-wee!" Finally, McMahon sided with the audience. "Just one joke?"

Carson broke down. "Okay. But if you tell anyone I said this, I'll deny it. There's a few jokes going around. Evidently, Pee-wee's gonna represent himself in court . . . because if he does, he thinks he can get himself off."

Johnny's decision to confine the Pee-wee cracks solely to commercial breaks was a compliment to his editing skills. He knew every show, every host, every stand-up comic was using it as fodder. And it happened just like that. Carson was just about the only host to avoid the topic. If the writers submitted Pee-wee jokes at the time, or any jokes that were omitted by Carson, it was all right, says Fields. "The whole idea, like any show, is to please the guy with the ball and bat. Make him happy. And even if Johnny picked the jokes and they didn't do well, that was okay. Because this is the king picking them. This isn't Arte Johnson saying, 'I don't like that.'"

Fields continued: "When I first got my job on *The Tonight Show,* I was twenty-four, and I used to think, Johnny never comes around. He never asks me to go have a drink. Johnny never calls me on the weekends. What an asshole. And then, I got out there the

# A Few "Tea-Time Movies"

*Announcer: It's time once again, friends, for the Mighty Carson Art Players. One of the mainstays of daytime television is the late-afternoon movie. It's usually hosted by the happy-go-lucky bigmouth who's very happy to bring you the film feature, but a lot happier to bring you more commercials than you can find up Eighth Avenue. And now, your host . . . Art Fern.*

*"Mmm . . . hello there, Southland Viewers!"*

Hoot Gibson, Dean Stockwell, the Lane Sisters, and Cesar Romero in *Andy Hardy Gets a Girl in Trouble.*

Fuzzy Knight, Allen Jenkins, and Helen Twelvetrees in Otto Kruger's immortal classic *Ma & Pa Kettle Host an Orgy.*

Bob Steele, Spring Byington, Regis Toomey, and the Mormon Tabernacle Choir in *The Merry Widow Has a Change of Life.*

The Jackson Five, the Four Tops, the Three Stooges, the Doublemint Twins, and Furball the Wondercat in *Tarzan Breaks His Loincloth.*

Bobby Breen, June Frazee, Lash LaRue, and Beulah Bondi in *How Ya Gonna Keep 'Em Down on the Farm After They've Seen the Farm?*

Douglas Fairbanks Jr., Junior Gilliam, Stu Gilliams, Stu Erwin, Irwin Corey, and Spurt the Wonderskunk in *Gidget Takes on Fort Ord.*

Jack Lemmon, Jack Haley, Hayley Mills, the Mills Brothers, Dr. Joyce Brothers, and Spawn the Wondercarp in *Dracula Gets Bombed on a Wino.*

Bess Flowers, Fifi D'Orsay, Guy Kibbee, and Cora Witherspoon in *Ma & Pa Kettle Join the Black Panthers.*

Spanky McFarland, Al McKrueger, Olga San Juan, Erich von Stroheim, and Fuzzy Knight in *I Was in Heat for an Artichoke.*

Benson Fong, Anna May Wong, Peter Chong, and Monatius Kummich in *Dr. Kildare Lances a Hickey.*

Ed Platt, Earl Flatt, Jack Sprat, Fats Domino, and Mervyn LeRoy in *How to Lose a Chinese Fortune (or Charlie Chan Drops His Cookies).*

Eddie Foy, Myrna Loy, Clyde McCoy, Troy Donahue, and Mae Bush in *Joyce Brothers Finally Gets Hers.*

Buxom blonde Carol Wayne was "The Matinee Lady" with Johnny as "Art Fern" in a recurring comedy sketch known as the Tea-Time Movies.

next few years and worked for every other star and realized he's the nicest guy to work for. For as much power as he had, he could've busted everybody's balls, but he didn't really do it. He didn't abuse his power. And these other little Hollywood pipsqueaks really do it."

Nostalgia ripples through every word. He's a Carson fan from way back, ever since his grade-school teacher wrote for Carson's autographed picture in the early 1960s and later presented little Greg with the photo as a gift. He's kept it all these years. Even when he worked for the man, he never updated that old picture with a new one. He met Carson and talked with him maybe ten times during his stay at NBC, and he says he never walked into Johnny's personal office. But he's a fan, through and through, after all these years, with respect for Carson's stamina.

"He went out there almost every night," Fields says, "and it's like mental gymnastics. To see jokes at two o'clock and go out there at five? For a sixty-six-year-old man, it was unbelievable. So many others can't do it. Jay Leno's tried most of his jokes out six or seven times."

For Fields, and for most Americans, *The Tonight Show* with Johnny was "the last vestige of show business," he says. Well, show business in a grand tradition, anyway. "You could feel the five hundred people tense up and get really excited," he says of the studio audience most nights anxiously anticipating the wizard's appearance from behind the curtain at show time. "Most of the audience have never seen him in person. I loved to stand by that curtain and just watch their faces. It's what show business used to be. When people came into town, they'd want to see a real show, done in an hour, and see the biggest star. This is the guy they've watched most of their life."

Tiny Tim, one of the most bizarre performers to burst from the sixties. He was launched into stardom by *The Tonight Show.*

# 3

# MEMORABLE
# MOMENTS

# THE WEDDING OF TINY TIM

By today's standards, the sight of Tiny Tim performing or walking down the street would hardly be shocking or prompt any stares. There are more interesting freaks to consider nowadays, more bizarre gender-bending creatures who have eclipsed his star. But in the 1960s, the late Tiny Tim was a departure from reality on many levels.

Following the televised wedding, Tiny Tim toasted his nuptials with milk and honey on *The Tonight Show* in December 1969. Johnny, Ed, and the guests uncorked champagne.

Between 1968 and 1979, this peculiar performer appeared on *The Tonight Show* sixteen times. One of them made history.

The highest-rated *Tonight Show Starring Johnny Carson* featured the broadcast of the wedding of novelty performer Tiny Tim, aka Herbert B. Khaury, and his seventeen-year-old fiancée, Victoria May Budinger—whom Tiny called "Miss Vicki." The heavily publicized ninety-minute show from NBC studios in New York on December 17, 1969, started as usual with Johnny's monologue (peppered with wedding do's and don'ts and some honeymoon jokes); the guests included Phyllis Diller, Florence Henderson, and Nick Lucas. (Tiny had requested Rudy Vallee to be present as well, but the old crooner declined.) The fifteen-minute wedding at the tail end of the show, however, was the center of attention and grabbed an astronomical 85 percent share—whopping by any standards. The ratings for this show were only surpassed by Johnny's farewell on May 22, 1992.

Talent coordinator Craig Tennis was responsible for booking Tiny on Carson's show long before the idea of the televised wedding had ever been contemplated. Said Tennis, "Just having him walk through the office on his visit—a white-faced Baby Huey with a shopping bag and the ukulele neck sticking out of it and his mincing little gait—was enough to send everybody in the offices into shock, and enough to make me feel a little leery, too."

Tiny had begun making appearances on *The Tonight Show* in 1968. Andrew

Edelstein, author of the irreverent guidebook *The Pop Sixties,* described Tiny's "pop" into fame: "This hook-nosed, stringy-haired, ukulele-playing character was the world's foremost androgynous entertainer. [Tiny] was a fixture of low-rent Greenwich Village nightclubs for years before he burst into the national consciousness in the summer of 1968, blowing kisses on *Laugh-In* and trilling turn-of-the-century tunes in his falsetto voice on his LP *God Bless Tiny Tim.*"

Craig Tennis knew that booking Tiny was a risk, because Tiny might have already spent his fifteen minutes of fame on *Laugh-In* and the novelty might have worn thin. Only audiences could dictate. It would "either go down as the most disastrous moment in ten years of broadcasting on *The Tonight Show,* or it would score as something monumental." No one had any idea of the eventual landmark Tiny would create.

To Carson as well as the national audience, the sight of this tall, awkward man with the falsetto singing voice and long curly hair plucking a ukulele and singing "Tip-Toe Thru' the Tulips with Me" was beyond comprehension. Was he a genius or a fool? Was he talented or just silly? On Carson's couch, he was the quiet geek in school. He was shy, dainty, extremely polite, and he spoke in a soft, Michael Jacksonesque voice, covering his mouth like a schoolgirl when he giggled. Imagine Boy George in 1969— just not as bold. Carson always played it straight, never condescending; Tiny never felt exploited or like he was being thrown to the wolves on national television. Can you imagine David Letterman being let loose on Tiny Tim? Don Rickles might have torn him into tiny pieces.

On one memorable *Tonight Show* spot, Tiny gave his bizarre rendition of "Living in the Sunlight, Loving in the Moonlight," a catchy little tune made famous by Maurice Chevalier in 1929. "You don't do it like Chevalier," Carson quipped. The audience erupted as Johnny's innocent facial expression—a mixture of bewilderment and embarrassment, pure Nebraska—told the story.

One night after Tiny Tim had made several appearances on the show, the wild idea of broadcasting his nuptials emerged. Tiny mentioned to Johnny that he was getting married to "Miss Vicki." Tiny and his young bride-to-be, of Haddonfield, New Jersey, had met at Wanamaker's department store when she was getting a copy of his book, *Beautiful Thoughts,* inscribed. Carson inquired if Tiny would like to have the ceremony take place on the show, and Tiny's hands fluttered as he responded, "Oh, could we?"

It was *the* wedding to see on national television. NBC blanketed the airwaves with on-air promotions, pre-show interviews, and lots of ancillary hype around the country. None of the 268 studio tickets were disbursed to the public; it was an invitation-only show with guests of the bride and groom making up much of the studio audience.

"Tiny Tim must have requested me," said guest Phyllis Diller, herself a wacky, fright-wigged product of the '60s. Of course, Diller, the cackling comedienne known

# Carnac the Magnificent

*"Oh, Great Sage . . ."*

*Announcer: I hold in my hand an envelope; a child of four can plainly see these envelopes are hermetically sealed. They've been kept since noon today in a mayonnaise jar on Funk & Wagnall's porch. No one—but no one!—knows the contents. In his mystical, magical, and borderline divine way, Carnac will now ascertain the answers, having never heard the questions.*

It was sort of like psychic *Jeopardy*. The bumbling telepath-in-a-turban could "divine answers" from a white envelope held at his forehead without seeing the questions. Methodically, the envelope was torn across the end, and Carnac blew into the it and pulled out the question. And if the crowd booed the Great One in his mighty wisdom, he might curse in response: "May a kangaroo punch on your erogenous zone" or "May a love-starved fruitfly molest your sister's nectarines" or possibly "May your youngest son run the spit-shine concession at a leather bar." One night it was, "May a nearsighted sand flea suck syrup off your short stack."

## Answers (Questions on opposite page)
*"Silence, please . . ."*

1. Moonies
2. A cat and your wife
3. Lollipop
4. Preparation H and take-home pay
5. Dairy Queen
6. The American people
7. Sis Boom Bah
8. A B C D E F G
9. Mr. Coffee
10. The Loch Ness Monster
11. Mount Baldy
12. The zip code
13. A linen closet
14. 20/20
15. "Thank you, PaineWebber"
16. Coal Miner's Daughter
17. Real People
18. NAACP FBI IRS
19. I give a damn
20. Hasbro
21. Spam and Jim Bakker
22. Ovaltine
23. Bungy diving and a date with Geraldo
24. Hop Sing
25. All systems go
26. 10-4
27. persnickety
28. "These are a few of my favorite things"
29. Hell or high water

*Announcer: "I hold in my hand . . . the last envelope."*

30. A pair of Jordache jeans and a bread box

1. Name a religion that drops its pants.
2. Name something you put out at night and someone who won't.
3. What happens when someone stomps on your lolly?
4. What can you depend on for shrinking?
5. What do you call a gay milkman?
6. Name the loser in the 1976 presidential race.
7. Describe the sound you hear when a sheep blows up.
8. What were some of the earlier forms of Preparation H?
9. Name the father of Mrs. Olsen's illegitimate baby.
10. Who will they find sooner than Jimmy Hoffa?
11. How do you play piggyback with Telly Savalas?
12. What do CIA agents have to remember to go to the bathroom?
13. What do gay Irish guys come out of?
14. What will a gallon of gas cost by next year?
15. What might a girl say at a stockbrokers' orgy?
16. Where can you pick up a nasty soot rash?
17. What do lonely inflatable people buy for companionship?
18. How do you spell naacpfbiirs?
19. What did it say in the beaver's will?
20. How does Tito Jackson get work?
21. Name two things that'll be in the can for the next eighteen years?
22. Describe Oprah Winfrey in high school.
23. Name two things that end with a jerk on your leg.
24. Name a prison for one-legged people.
25. What happens if you take a Sinutab, a Maalox, and a Feen-a-mint?
26. How do a big guy and a little guy split fourteen bucks?
27. How do you get paid when you're picking snicketies?
28. What do you say to a doctor who's wearing a rubber glove?
29. Name two things you really don't want in your underwear.
30. Name two places where you stuff your buns.

**Answer:** Green Acres
**Question:** What does Kermit have after Miss Piggy kicks him in the groin?

for her wild wardrobe, was anxious to appear, but she was afraid it might be impossible. "I remember distinctly, I was in New York doing *Hello Dolly!* on Broadway. I said, 'No, I can't make the show' because they taped at 5:30 P.M. and in the theater, you have to be there a half hour before curtain. I didn't see how I could possibly manage with New York traffic, even then.

"Honey, they sent a police escort," said Diller. "By then, I was so confused, I had forgotten that at the wedding everyone was to be formal, including the crew. I arrived in a short, shiny dress, and Shirley Wood, the talent coordinator, took her long purple wool dress off and I put it on."

Hordes of press covered the event, some inquiring about the sanctity of the ceremony, but NBC and the show's staff insisted there would be no toying with this fully legal wedding ceremony. Critic Jack Miller, in the *Ontario Spectator*, noted, "If Tiny himself wants to make a sideshow of this, that's his business—and there remains the suspicion that he's the biggest put-on to hit the U.S. since those Japanese peace delegates in 1941."

Nonetheless, media swarmed the studio that evening to cover the best-attended wedding of the year. Preparations for the event were detailed: ten thousand tulips were provided by Aberdeen's Flowers of Chicago. The seven-foot wedding cake, prepared by a Wilmington, Delaware, bakery, was on display a day before it arrived at the studio in New York. The bride wore a $2500 Victorian gown, the groom a black silk velvet frock coat with top hat and cane.

The Reverend William Glenesk officiated while Johnny, Ed, and guests—all decked out in formal attire—witnessed. After the ceremony and applause from the audience, Tiny Tim prepared milk and honey for himself and his bride to toast, while Johnny popped open a bottle of champagne. Then Tiny sang two songs to his beloved. The first one was titled, "The Wedding Song for Miss Vicki." In his high-pitched voice, he sang:

Oh won't you come and love me, O pretty Vicki mine,
Oh won't you come and love me, and be my Valentine,
Like violets and roses, our spirits will entwine,
Like violets and roses, our bodies will combine.

Then Tiny sang another tune, called "You Were There." Nick Lucas, who had recorded "Tip-Toe Thru' the Tulips with Me" in the 1929 early Technicolor musical film *Gold Diggers of Broadway,* was flown in to reprise his version of the ditty. This was a full show.

The press reported the wedding kiss was "the couple's third osculatory contact" and following the wedding, Tiny and Miss Vicki were planning to observe three days of abstinence. It was a tradition derived from the prophet Tobias in the Old Testament. Said Tiny: "Not even a kiss. I plan to give the Lord the first fruits of my marriage. If only more people followed the ways of Saint Paul and King David."

Although millions of viewers attested this union, it seemed destined for doom almost immediately. Weeks after the show, the minister who married the odd couple sued the producers of *The Tonight Show* for $500. The Rev. William Glenesk, acting as his own attorney in Brooklyn Small Claims Court, filed the suit, claiming producer Rudy Tellez promised him the usual $265 scale appearance fee, but also said he would pay Glenesk's membership fee into the television and radio union AFTRA

The televised wedding of Tiny Tim and Miss Vicki attracted a record 21 million viewers in 1969.

with another invitation to appear on *The Tonight Show* attached in the agreement. Tellez denied the promises, and the suit was later settled. Outside the courts, the minister explained why he was pressing for additional money: "I had to make a serious ceremony in a circus situation before thirty million people," he said, "and that's hard work."

Alas, the marriage of Tiny and Vicki ended in separation and eventual divorce in 1977. (The couple had one daughter, named Tulip, and separated not long afterward.) But by then, one of the most bizarre events on television was already written into the history books. Phyllis Diller said in 1991 that Tiny Tim's star dimmed not long after the historic *Tonight Show* wedding. "Tiny was at his peak in 1969 and we're talking about a freak. I saw a recent appearance, and what he did he would have been pegged as [the acts of] a crazy person.

"He gained about eight hundred pounds, you know. He sang, and during the number, he simply fell to the floor and you could see his bare stomach while he writhed on the floor during the song. Tiptoeing is one thing. Writhing is another."

There's no question that Tiny was a peculiar fellow, with odd and obsessive-compulsive habits. For years, he traveled with plenty of fresh packages of Viva absorbent paper towels and stocked them in his hotel rooms. He did not trust the cleanliness of hotel towels, so he routinely dried off from a shower using yards of paper towels. He preferred wearing adult diapers rather than underwear because it was more sanitary. He applied a variety of lotions to his body: Vaseline Intensive Care on his torso and Oil of Olay on his face, usually six times a day. He never ate meat or cheese, and he drank salsa from the jar.

## ■ Postscript

Tiny Tim was married twice more, to Miss Jan in 1984 (ending in divorce in 1995) and to Miss Sue in the fall of 1995. During all those years, Tiny's career and his personal life seemed to jump around aimlessly, but somehow he always seemed to pull himself together and go on the road for more work, sometimes finding it at the strangest venues. At one point, he was considered to host a kids' television show, and went as far as taping a pilot, but Tiny was terrified of children and knew it wouldn't work out.

In the 1980s, Tiny had gained considerable weight and eventually doctors warned him that his heart was bad shape and urged him to stop traveling and performing. Tiny liked it too much, however, and he needed the money, so he kept going. In September of 1996 he was to perform at the Ukulele Hall of Fame but collapsed before plucking the first tune. He fell forward off the stage and down another two feet onto a concrete floor, hitting his head. He was hospitalized and convalesced briefly, but died weeks later of congestive heart failure. Tiny was laid to rest with a ukulele in his hand, and tulips around his white casket. Writer Scott Michaels describes Tiny Tim's final performance, a sad ending that took place at a gathering of the Women's Club of Minneapolis.

> He had been hired for this performance because Miss Sue's stepmother was a prominent member. The day of the gig, Tiny was not feeling well and did not want to go, but he also felt he could not disappoint any fans. He was dizzy and he fell trying to get into the limousine that was sent for him.
>
> Tiny almost fell coming up the marble staircase at the meeting hall, and Miss Sue tried to support him. She asked him how he was feeling and Tiny told her he hadn't taken his medicine (he had a habit of this). There was a lovely dinner, but Tiny didn't eat much. After the meal, Tiny was introduced backstage to the bandleader who was not impressed. Not aware that Tiny was to perform that night, the bandleader refused to have his band back Tiny on stage, claiming the musicians didn't know his songs. Tiny politely inquired, "You don't know 'I'm Looking Over a Four Leaf Clover'?" Still, the bandleader refused to have his band play.
>
> Regardless, with ukulele in hand, Tiny was ready to perform at 9 P.M.; by 10 P.M. he still had not been called to the stage. Tiny's wife was about to take him home when the bandleader called a break, without introducing Tiny. It was a terrible insult to him, as it would have been proper for the

guest vocalist to be introduced at the end of the set, while the crowd is still warmed up. The crowd filtered out of the room leaving just a few people. It was a deliberate insult by the bandleader. The lady who ran the affair went up to the microphone and introduced Tiny to a near-empty room. He got up and stood at the microphone. The cords were tangled around his feet and his ukulele was out of tune.

Tiny sang and people were applauding him. Sue went to take his arm because of the uneven footing and she could see he was shaking. He waved and blew kisses to the audience, something he always did at the end of his show. Sue took Tiny's arm and asked if he was all right. He stood there and looked at his wife and said, "No, I'm not." Those were his last words. Tiny collapsed on the stage. The ambulance was there in a matter of minutes and they worked on him; he was taken to the Hennepin County Medical Center where doctors worked on him for another hour before they declared him dead. He was sixty-four years old.

Tiny once speculated that his appearances on both *Laugh-In* and *The Tonight Show* would most definitely be an essential part of his obituary someday, and he was right. As with so many artists whose work is never fully appreciated until they vanish, Tiny will be, at the very least, a bold footnote on the decade of the '60s. Who knows whether there will be a huge resurgence for him? Tiny had already amassed a strong cult following over his last ten years. He even attracted groupies who tracked his performance schedule and genuinely loved his eclectic style. Tiny was always grateful for fans and any following they devoted to his music and his personal life; his friends say he probably would have loved the biographical *E! True Hollywood Story* produced in 2000.

Tiny was sure that much of his fame was due to *The Tonight Show*, and he proudly acknowledged that in interviews. When he found out that Johnny Carson was leaving *The Tonight Show*, the beholden performer retrieved one of his earliest ukuleles from storage, carefully packed it up with a note, and shipped it him. Johnny was moved by the sentimental gesture and grateful for the keepsake.

# Michael Landon's Final Show

Johnny fidgeted more than usual. His forehead tight with tension, he nervously introduced the next guest:

I think most of the nation and the world probably know by now that on April 8th, Michael Landon was diagnosed as having inoperable cancer of the pancreas and liver, and that would stun everybo—anybody. But like Michael Landon, he met the problem head-on. He invited the press to his house and told them the situation. He did that mainly to avoid the

Michael Landon jokes with his pal Johnny in the early 1970s. Landon made a brave final appearance on *The Tonight Show* just weeks before his death of cancer.

rumors, the speculation, the misinformation; and to try to avoid sensationalism by the tabloids. And for the past month, he has continued to face this battle with humor, honesty, and a personal sense of dignity that characterizes the man. Would you welcome . . . Michael Landon.

History was in the making as Landon walked jauntily out from the curtain, as prepared as possible both physically and mentally, for this appearance. The camera panned the audience as they spontaneously stood to honor the actor with a hearty round of applause. He hugged Johnny, moved around the desk, and hugged Ed. The studio audience was at capacity, leaving a trail of hopefuls outside NBC. Some were crying because they did not get in.

Landon's ovation hummed strongly until the actor raised a hand to halt the applause. He wore a bright turquoise shirt with light beige pants—the same colors he

HERE'S JOHNNY!

# A Few More Stars

Lore has it that Arnold Palmer appeared on *The Tonight Show* one night and Johnny Carson asked him if his wife did anything special to give him luck before his golf tournaments. Palmer nodded and explained, "She washes my balls."

"I guess that makes your putter stand up," Carson replied.

■ ■ ■

Actress Cybill Shepherd was quoted in a periodical saying she thought Johnny Carson was an interesting individual and that she'd love to have dinner with him. Carson invited the actress on the show and prepared an impromptu, catered dinner ("courtesy of the NBC commissary") with candles, china, and champagne. When Carson popped the cork on the champagne, it bubbled all over his desk; Shepherd took her linen, wiped the spill, and replied, "You should have spilled it on your pants, and I could have cleaned it up."

■ ■ ■

There are viewers who will swear they saw this. Urban legend or not?

The story goes that when Zsa Zsa Gabor appeared on the show with Johnny one night, she was sitting in the chair with her Persian cat in her lap. She said, "Johnny, would you like to pet my pussy?" To which Johnny replied, "Sure, if you move that damn cat out of the way!" In the 1980s, Jane Fonda was Johnny's guest one night, and she said, "I have to ask you about something," and recapped the Zsa Zsa story. Laughingly, Carson said, "No, uh, I think I would recall that."

■ ■ ■

One night, Angie Dickinson, a frequent *Tonight Show* guest, came on wearing a red, billowy outfit that caught Johnny's attention. He asked why she was wearing jammies, and inquired, "Okay, do you dress for men or for women?"

Dickinson stunned Johnny: "Well, I dress for women and I undress for men."

had worn on April 8, nearly a month prior, when he had summoned the press to his home to announce to the world that he had been diagnosed with cancer. He looked thin, especially along his jaw line, but he kept his brows raised. He looked tired but retained his humor.

Landon was a veteran of more than forty appearances with Johnny, his Malibu neighbor and tennis buddy from way back. Carson enjoyed Landon's friendship and his work, and Landon professed to never miss a *Tonight Show* when his pal was hosting. In fact, Landon had carte blanche to appear on the program.

Carson mused about the time the two were at the trendy Beaurivage restaurant in Malibu when Landon cunningly convinced him that he had backed over the restaurant owner's cat in the parking lot. Carson didn't want to return to the eatery a month later, but Landon insisted.

Carson had arranged for the waiter to serve a nice dish with a fake flattened cat on a silver platter. Landon was thinking too. When the two arrived, specially designed menus were handed to them with entrées stylishly listed in old English calligraphy. As Carson looked over the menu with Landon sitting across the table, he slowly noticed the new dishes: Tureen of Tabby . . . $8.75 (served with scallions, tomatoes, and cucumbers . . . in 30-weight oil) and Baked Fillet of Feline.

"I go to the next page and see 'Pussy Mousse à la Mercedes' . . . prepared right on the property," Carson said, laughing. "And then I get down to this one here, 'Pressed Pussy Provencal, served outside in the dark.'"

Trying to keep the mood light, Carson joked as usual with his guests that evening, also aware that it might be one of the last times he'd see his friend. Since Landon's illness had been made public, every news and talk show on the air had pined for his presence. Barbara Walters called requesting an interview, as did *60 Minutes*. Harry Flynn, a spokesman for Landon, was quoted in the *Hollywood Reporter* about the scheduled appearance: "He wanted to go somewhere he could show people he isn't all that sick. . . . He wants people to know he's hanging in there despite the deathbed stories appearing in the tabs. He wanted to go on a show and lighten up. It will not be maudlin."

Carson said he was flattered to make room for Landon—on any night. But on this night, May 9, 1991, the primary reason Landon mustered his strength, dyed his roots, and asked his pal permission to stop by the show once again was to publicly reprimand the tabloids who had exploited his illness. One tabloid had issued a dictum declaring he had four weeks to live. The *National Enquirer* led its front page with glaring bold letters: "Michael Landon: It's Over!" Such screaming sensationalism frightened Landon's family and angered the actor. Overtly stern, he turned to the audience at one point and said, "It's unbelievable that people can be that way. *That's* the cancer, you know. That's the cancer in our society."

Carson added, "I think that most people watching with a scintilla of intelligence realize that most of those things, like the *Enquirer*, and the *Star* . . . are garbage."

Some performers have said that Johnny Carson is a frustrated singer at heart. Actually, Johnny was pretty good with a tune, singing with some greats on the show like Pearl Bailey, Bette Midler, and the Andrews Sisters. *Left,* Johnny performed a perfect Willie Nelson and teamed with singer Julio Iglesias in a memorable number in 1984. *Below,* Bob Hope and Johnny croon an impromptu duet of Hope's adopted theme song, "Thanks for the Memory." (1982)

Landon said he also wished to clear up what he called "this tenth-child business." Setting up a punch line, he explained: "There's a headline in one of those incredible tabloid magazines about the fact that I want to have a tenth child so my wife will have something to remember me by. Here, I've got nine kids, nine dogs, three grandkids—one in the oven—three parrots . . . and my wife, Cindy, needs something to remember me by?"

The tension eased as the show progressed and Landon seemed to joke and laugh with hearty strength. Throughout the show, he exuded optimism and emphasized the importance of high spirits in handling disease. "I just want to say one thing," he said quite seriously. "For any of those families out there who have a relative who has cancer . . . they know how tough the fight is and how important the mental attitude is . . . and how you pull together and keep a very, very up attitude. Mentally, it's more than fifty percent of your medicine."

Before cameras, the two friends discussed a lot of topics: the illness, the press, and even the proposed cures that had arrived in bagfuls to the Landon residence. One treatment involved a series of coffee enemas, which Landon admitted trying. "I invited John over for a coffee enema, but he wanted cream and sugar and I'm not pourin'!" Carson quipped, "You better make sure somebody hasn't secretly replaced your coffee with Folger's Crystals . . . or it could be a long day."

Landon was forthright about his illness. "I really want to thank everybody. [I've received] a lot of great suggestions, and I'm using a little bit of everything.

"Although . . . there were some I didn't try. One guy wrote me and told me that the reason I got the Big C was that I did not get enough sex. See, he thinks it was only the nine times when I had the kids . . . well he gave me this regimen which would kill the average twenty-five-year-old.

"I've gotten tapes, books, you name it," he said. "Swim with a dolphin. You only have to do it once. Something about sonar from the dolphin—and *ping-ping!*—it goes away. What can I tell you? Here, I'm going to all these hospitals, and I only gotta go to Marineland!"

Landon moved over a seat to the couch while the next guest, fighter George Foreman, came out and joked with Johnny until the end of the show. At the end of the taping, Carson hugged Landon and the crowd was hesitant to leave the seats. The audience clapped and rose for the courageous actor as he waved to everyone and said "Bye" and walked behind the curtain. His family waited for him in the green room and the tension was still just as thick behind the scenes. Kind to his fans as always, Landon signed a few autographs and quietly said some goodbyes to some of Johnny's staff before leaving the studio.

Landon's appearance nearly doubled the ratings that night. It was the highest overnight rating for a *Tonight Show* in recent memory, claimed an NBC official. Landon later told his wife, Cindy, that he was pleased America was watching. His family

# "Weird Stuff"

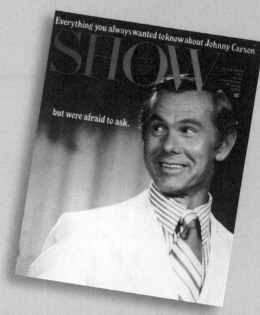

- *Splitting Hairs:* Johnny didn't actually host the show for thirty years as we all celebrated. Technically, his final show was just a few months shy of the actual October 1992 thirty-year mark. And with lengthy vacations and guest hosts . . . geez, did he actually host at all?
- Where Again? *The Tonight Show* was never "Frommmmmmm Hollywood . . ." as Ed McMahon announced in each night's opening. Starting in 1972, the show was taped at NBC Studios in Burbank, right near the mountains in Southern California's San Fernando Valley. (Hence, all of the "beautiful downtown Burbank" jokes over the years, a leftover gag from *Rowan & Martin's Laugh-In.*)
- Johnny Carson—one of the most recognizable men in America—has been featured on more than 350 magazine covers, including *Rolling Stone, Time, LIFE, GQ, AARP, Jet, MAD, People, TV Guide, US, Newsweek,* the *Saturday Evening Post, Look, Esquire* . . . you name it.
- The biggest and brightest stars shined on *The Tonight Show Starring Johnny Carson* over the years. However, some did decline to appear, including Cary Grant, Britain's Benny Hill, Jack Nicholson, Al Pacino, Robert DeNiro, William Boyd (Hopalong Cassidy), and John Gielgud, to name but a few. And believe it or not, Elvis never appeared on *The Tonight Show* either.
- The Golf Swing: Johnny always closed his monologue with his signature slow motion chip shot, a trademark he began in his first year as host—and it stuck. He's famous for this patented move, yet Johnny's never been much of a golfer at all. Tennis is his game.
- William Reynolds of St. Catharines, Ontario, decided to produce a line of portable toilets with a catchy name. Sometimes referred to as "Johnny on the Spot," this new line of porta-potties was going to be christened "Here's Johnny."

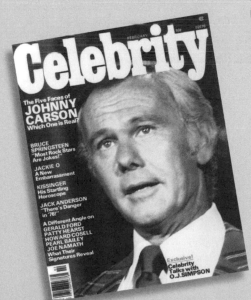

Upon learning of the marketing scheme, Johnny Carson investigated the matter. In reply, the registrar of trademarks decided to allow Reynolds to use the phrase for his business of renting portable outhouses. Carson appealed.

The Associated Press reported on March 12, 1980, that a Federal Court of Canada judge ruled that "Here's Johnny" is just too readily associated with Johnny Carson and *The Tonight Show* to be allowed as a trademark for portable toilets. The bright idea was officially down the drain. "Therefore," it was reported, "the phrase could not be registered as a trademark without Carson's permission." Before rendering his decision, Justice Patrick Mahoney had accepted as evidence a random survey "in which 63 percent of those polled connected 'Here's Johnny' with Carson or his show."

watched that evening on television as well, so pleased with how it all turned out, and thankful he had the energy to do it.

On Monday, July 1, 1991, Michael Landon died at his home in Malibu with his family around him. He was fifty-four. His appearance on *The Tonight Show* turned out to be his final television appearance.

Johnny released a statement about his longtime friend: "This has been a devastating week for me and my family. Michael called last Monday expressing his deepest sympathy on the death of my son, Ricky. The courage and sensitivity he showed in our conversation, in comforting me while he was in great pain, attests to the quality of this man and his character."

## MORE MEMORABLE MOMENTS . . .

■ Probably the clip that has gotten the most mileage on *Tonight Show* anniversary specials is the famous Ed Ames tomahawk-throw from 1965. At the time, Ames played Mingo the Indian in the television series *Daniel Boone*. Appearing with Johnny, he was demonstrating the art of precisely throwing a tomahawk. The target: a large wooden plank with the silhouette of a human figure drawn on it. Ames joked at first, quickly took aim, and "plunk!" The tomahawk landed directly in the crotch of the silhouette. Ames, laughing, claimed it was a mistake, and Johnny wouldn't let him hide his embarrassment by exiting the stage or quickly removing the tomahawk; Johnny grabbed his arm, pulling him back out in front to the screaming audience for a few more jokes. "I didn't even know you were Jewish," Johnny joked. (This bit has been parodied on *Saturday Night Live*. Dan Aykroyd, as Ames, hacked away at the silhouette's crotch until it was kindling. It was a sarcastic comment on the overused warhorse clip.)

Elizabeth Taylor couldn't resist creating a splash when she made her *Tonight Show* debut with Johnny during his last weeks as host. (February 21, 1992)

■ During an interview with Bob Costas, host of NBC's *Later*, Ed McMahon reflected on his days as the Alpo dog food spokesman on *The Tonight Show*, delivering live commercials during the commercial breaks. One story stuck out.

> I had this dog that was so great . . . his name was Patrick. He was an English sheepdog and had those white, furry eyes. He was so in tune with what he was doing. He was Mr. Show Business. He would sleep in between the seats in Studio 6-B on the concrete where it was cool. When he heard my voice in the back of the studio, he stood up and walked to the commercial area because he knew we were gonna rehearse. I had a small amount of Alpo in the bowl, and I'd put it down and do the spiel for a minute. One night, for some reason, when I put the Alpo down, he came in, took one smell of the Alpo, and walked out. Here I am, I've got a bowl of Alpo, one minute, and no dog. Johnny, bless him, comes in on all fours and pretends to eat the food and lick my leg.

■ Baseball great Pete Rose emerged from the curtain in 1991 for a rare interview following his imprisonment for gambling on the very sport that had made him famous. Rose said first thing, "Nice to be here . . . and Doc, thanks for not playin' 'Jailhouse Rock.'" Then he told Johnny it was his first appearance on the show. "All these [baseball] records I got . . . you gotta go to prison to get on this show!"

■ How sweet it was in 1984 during an especially classy evening with the Great One. It was the night Jackie Gleason stepped onto the *The Tonight Show* stage for the first time. Surprisingly, Gleason had never stopped by the show to chat with Johnny, primarily due to the fact that Gleason was based in Miami and traveled mostly by train. While in Hollywood filming what

Brooke Shields shows Johnny the new Brooke doll in 1982.

Middleweight champion Marvelous Marvin Hagler appeared in 1986.

In one truly classic moment, singer Dolly Parton made her first appearance on her birthday, January 19, 1977. Johnny brought up the topic of the singer's sizeable breasts. "Have you always been that healthy?" he asked. Once the subject was brought up, Parton wanted to establish, once and for all, that her figure was not artificially enhanced. "Let me tell you, they're real . . . these are mine," she said. Johnny blushed and admitted, "I'd give about a year's pay to take a peek under there."

HERE'S JOHNNY!

became his last movie, *Nothing in Common,* with Tom Hanks, he heartily accepted Johnny's invitation, and that night you could see the host was visibly excited to introduce him.

Natty as usual, Gleason came out from behind the curtain in a light gray tailored suit with a red carnation on the lapel, shiny cuff links, and a diamond pinkie ring. The comic genius of television (Gleason, that is) smoked seven cigarettes during the extended interview, while Johnny broached subjects such as *The Honeymooners,* pioneering television, aspects of comedy, and even his reputation for emptying the flask a time or two.

Gleason said: "I'm not advocating that everybody should drink—it just worked for me. And of course, the gentleman on my right [McMahon] has had a taste or two."

The rotund comic was a bit shaky at the time, unknowingly living with cancer; Gleason couldn't stay for the rest of the show and carefully exited the stage with a gracious kiss and wave to the audience while the band played his theme. Wouldn't it have been great if he had kicked up one knee and left through the curtain with his signature "And a-waaaaaaayyyy we go"?

Carson, an "unabashed fan" of Gleason, and one who has emulated him frequently over the years, concluded with this: "He's remarkable. . . . That gentleman has never received an Emmy, if you can believe it, from the Television Academy in this business. And the Academy ought to be towed out twenty miles and dropped in the ocean. Something's wrong there."

■ Charlton Heston appeared one evening in the 1970s with Johnny. The two thought they'd treat the audience to some "classical" orations from podiums on the stage. Stately postured and elegantly mannered, the two recited from their soul.

**Heston:**
There was a young lady of Norway
Who hung by her toes in the doorway.
She said to her beau, "Hey look at me, Joe!
I think I've discovered one more way."

**Carson:**
There was an old preacher named Spencer
Whose abstinence made him grow tenser.
So he called up a chick, who came over real quick,
For the rest you better check with the censor.

# The Tenth Anniversary Show

*Date: October 2, 1972, 11:30 P.M.–1 A.M.*
*Broadcast from NBC Studios in Burbank, California (Studio One)*
*Announcer: Ed McMahon*
*Music: Doc Severinsen and the NBC Orchestra*
*Appearing: Dean Martin, Governor Ronald Reagan, Jack Benny, Joey Bishop, George Burns, Jerry Lewis, Don Rickles, Dan Rowan & Dick Martin, Dinah Shore, NBC executive Don Durgin, and Carol Wayne*
*First Guest: Ronald Reagan*

Johnny's first big cause to celebrate on *The Tonight Show* was the occasion of his tenth anniversary as host; it was an all-star glitzy show with some surprises that included a nostalgic "reunion" of the comedy team Martin & Lewis. For many reasons, the program that night was unique: It was structured differently, more like a gathering. Johnny had certainly reached a television milestone as well as a career high point, and, believe it or not, both Dean Martin and Jerry Lewis accepted their invitations to appear with Johnny and toast him on the occasion. But that last little television event didn't happen—not for several years yet. When ol' Dino realized someone was masterminding a reunion of him and the monkey, the singer felt he wasn't quite ready for that, and he found it necessary to politely ask pardon . . . something about a prior engagement. Not to disappoint, Martin instead videotaped a special opening (across the hall, on the set of his show at NBC studios). With a drink in one hand, Martin stumbled through the show's opening: "No, this isn't *The Dean Martin Show,* but don't touch your dial because you've got a treat coming up. You've been watching Johnny Carson swing that golf club for the past ten years, and as a swinger myself, I can tell you he's made a lot of people happy. Now here comes Johnny Carson's tenth anniversary show, loaded, to coin a phrase, with a batch of real big stars. Ten years, that's a long time. I'll drink to that. Here's lookin' at you, Johnny."

After Dean Martin's intro and Ed McMahon's customary opening, Johnny commented in the monologue, "What a treat, being introduced by two drunks in the same night." Carson kicked off the show with the usual golf swing and joined Ed at a huge horseshoe-shaped set with lengthy couches that spanned the entire stage. Johnny was in the center as master of ceremonies. "Looks like you're about to read the will here," Ed McMahon said. Carson couldn't help but admit he felt naked without a desk, and it might have been the only time he departed from his comfortable desk and chair set in the history of the show.

**Highlights from the Monologue:** Ten years, can you believe that? I have trouble getting by the seventh year of anything.

. . . Gee a lot has happened in the past decade—three presidents, two wars, twelve different series starring Don Rickles.

. . . I saw Jack Benny arrive a few moments ago in front of the studio. You should have seen the people going to get autographs as he stepped off the bus.

**Best Exchange of the Night:**
*Joey Bishop:* I must say that no one could dislike anyone who can raise ten million dollars for a charity. (points to Jerry Lewis . . . applause)
*Jack Benny:* Well, I raised six million for musicians! (applause)
*Johnny:* I have a telethon coming up for prickly heat.

Johnny's tenth anniversary broadcast was an unusual, star-studded show. Surrounding the host: (L–R) George Burns, Joey Bishop, NBC executive Don Durgin, Dick Martin, Jerry Lewis, Carol Wayne, Dinah Shore, Dan Rowan, Ed McMahon, Doc Severinsen. Guests Don Rickles, Ronald Reagan, and Jack Benny also stopped by. Dean Martin's appearance was taped. (October 2, 1972)

**Heston:**
There was a young man with a hernia
Who said to his Dr. Galernia,
"When improving my middle,
Be sure not to fiddle
With matters that do not concern ya."

■ During a commercial for cellophane wrap, Ed McMahon was supposed to demonstrate its sealing ability by layering a piece over a wine goblet filled with wine and turning it upside down. No wine was supposed to spill or leak.

"I did something wrong, and I overlapped a piece of it or something," says McMahon, "because when I turned it over, the wine leaked out. . . .

"Here the commercial is blown, and it's all over for the sponsor. The audience is laughing, and I'm making a fool of myself. So I took a chance. I walked out front and over to the desk with another glass of wine, put it down, took the wrap, and put it on the glass. I sealed it very carefully this time and turned it upside down over Johnny's head. Thank God nothing dripped out. It could've been the end of a nice career."

■ Marty Ingels was a raspy-voiced comic actor beginning to make strides in television in the early 1960s, landing guest spots on a string of sitcoms like *The Joey Bishop Show, The Ann Southern Show,* and *The Dick Van Dyke Show.* Success seemed right around the corner when Ingels and John Astin costarred in a sitcom in 1962 called *I'm Dickens . . . He's Fenster.* But things came crashing down when the show was cancelled after the first season, his car was repossessed, and his wife left him. Ingels sank into a depression. When he appeared on *The Tonight Show* in 1964, he suffered a full-blown nervous breakdown on camera, sitting there on the couch at Johnny's right. Ingels had done his bit, and by now the next guest, Buddy Rich, was chatting with Johnny. The culmination of overwhelming pressures caved in on Ingels precisely at that moment, and a panic attack was building in him. Or a stroke. He wasn't sure what was wrong, but he knew he needed to get off camera because he was either going to throw up or pass out. Ingels says his hands were quivering, so he sat on them, and giggled a bit. Carson said, "There's Marty, going after a cheap laugh." Ingels stood up and nervously excused himself by saying, "Johnny, no one has ever used your private bathroom, and I've got to go." A bewildered Carson and audience watched Ingels feel his way past the desk and reach over to the curtain, which he grabbed and swung around to the other side and collapsed. Carson, who was not amused, thought it was shtick. Ingels was never asked back on the show. Says Ingels, "Johnny may have thought I ruined the show, but let's put it this way . . . it didn't work out too well for me, either." After his lengthy recovery from what turned out to be a nine-month breakdown, Ingels married Oscar-winning actress Shirley Jones.

■ One night, Zsa Zsa Gabor went a little far and turned the tables as she began quizzing Johnny about his love life and past wives. Zsa Zsa found out eventually that asking such questions and pushing him into a corner like that was

Ann-Margret visited *The Tonight Show* in 1978.

a no-no and the hot-tempered Hungarian was left out in the cold. She was not asked back. Commenting years later, she said, "I think [Johnny Carson] is a volf in sheep's clothing. If you made a mistake on his show, he made you feel like the vorld vas coming to an end . . . I think he's neurotic."

■ Rose Marie became famous as a child star (originally billed as "Baby Rose-marie") singing and entertaining on her own national radio show in the late 1920s when she was just a little girl. Rose Marie grew up and eventually became a Broadway performer and nightclub headliner. By the 1960s, though, everyone knew her face from her regular role as man-hungry Sally Rogers on *The Dick Van Dyke Show*. During the '60s and '70s, Rosie became a frequent guest with Johnny, but one night really stood out. She was the final guest of the evening, following Debbie Reynolds, George "Goober" Lindsey, Carl Reiner, and John Byner.

While introducing her, Johnny added that Rose Marie "was in show business before any of us." The audience groaned at what sounded like a funny, cheap shot at her age. Instantly, Johnny caught on. "No. What I meant was . . . let me . . . no no, you misunderstand." The audience kept laughing as Carson nervously wriggled his way out of the unintentional jab. "She started at an *earlier* age than any of us, that's what I meant . . . the words just tumbled out helter skelter." And they continued to, as he tried to spit out his intro: "Let me see . . . me . . . get out of this . . . will you welcome, Rose Marie!"

Rosie emerged from the curtain with a smile and Johnny kissed her. She sat down, turning to comedian John Byner beside her. "What did he say?" Byner hesitated, but added, "Well, uh, he said 'When they first built a stage, you held the hammer.'" The audience screamed as Carson bit his lip, laughing. More squirming.

The situation was hopeless. Rosie just sat stoic, staring at Carson while the audience continued to laugh. All of a sudden, the entire group of guest stars, including Ed, got up and walked off the stage in a moment of desperation. Perfectly timed, Rosie saluted the host and made her exit. Johnny was in hysterics. But with forty-three minutes to go, all he could think to do to stretch was slump into the chair, then get comfortable by removing his jacket, which triggered a striptease in front of the colored curtain while the band encouraged him with music. Stripped down to his pants, and feeling cold and naked, the bare-chested host sat back down at his desk. Rosie sauntered in and said, "Is that it?" Then the rest of the men, Ed McMahon, George Lindsey, Carl Reiner, and John Byner, re-entered with their lily-white tops exposed—all shirts were gone. It was a parade of man-bosoms the likes of which *The Tonight Show* had never seen.

■ George Burns was 96, closing in on 100, when he made his final *Tonight Show* appearance in November 1991. His movements were thorough, unhurried, and

sure-footed, and his mind was clearly still very sharp. The little man with dark round glasses who had played God in the movies dispensed his usual wisdom: "Fall in love with what you do for a living. Terribly important. I love show business. It's great to be my age to get out of bed and have something to do. I can't make any money in bed." And always the consummate entertainer, Burns was itching to sing and did a terrific job with an intricate little ditty called "Monkey Rag," accompanied by his pianist, Morty Jacobs. Then he mentioned Johnny's approaching retirement. "I've been on with Steve Allen, Jack Paar, and you . . . you're all leaving. I'm the only one left," he said, puffing his cigar.

Burns was no stranger to mild sexual innuendos, because on him it was cute, so Johnny

Johnny as Baby New Year in 1977.

Academy Award–winning actress Shelley Winters was outrageous and daffy, occasionally putting Johnny on the spot.

decided to bring up women. "Can you tell me at what age you became interested in girls?"

Burns replied, "I did it myself."

There was a long pause as the audience, and Carson, tried to figure out whether they had heard right. Did that little old man just make a reference to masturbation? Burns immediately filled the void: "I didn't need girls."

"Now that's *really* safe sex," Johnny responded, rescuing with genuine timing and tact.

Then Burns kindly topped it. "I was very careful. I wore gloves."

■ Shelley Winters. Ahhhh, Miss Shelley Winters. Where do you start?

Johnny called her "one of our finest actresses." Over the years, he introduced her more than sixty times on *The Tonight Show,* from both coasts. She was there with him at NBC right from the beginning, always daffy, outspoken, witty, outrageous, and sometimes extremely charming. And then there were the terribly embarrassing moments.

With Winters, anything could happen. One night she sweetly serenaded Johnny with some special lyrics that went with his *Tonight Show* theme. When the disaster film *The Poseidon Adventure* was released, Winters strutted out on *The Tonight Show* overstuffed into scuba gear. She could talk endlessly about her ailments, her numerous sexual exploits ("I thought menopause was a pause between men"), her former roommate Marilyn Monroe, or her experiences with Marlon Brando. The portly actress feared no topic, not even her compulsive overeating: "Why does everybody have to be so thin? Food is wonderful. Food is a great experience. If I even *smell* spaghetti, I gain two pounds." And she dropped a few bombs on the show as well.

Sammy Davis Jr. was adored by Carson and the show's staff, not only because his visits were always entertaining, but also because Davis was one of the "super-stand-bys," always willing to appear in a pinch.

This one's been run on a few of the anniversary shows: Remember the night when actor Oliver Reed chauvinistically commented about a woman's "place" in the home? Shelley Winters, who had been the previous guest, suddenly exited the platform while Reed was talking to Johnny.

> *Reed:* I think a woman's place is looking after her man and chil-
> dren. . . . I think the man's place is to look after her, protect her,
> and provide her with a little warmth.
> *Johnny:* The old-fashioned concept, huh?

Just then, someone from the audience made a comment aloud and Reed looked up and said, "Shhhh! Quiet, woman!" All of a sudden, Winters reappeared with a full glass of water, walked up in front of Reed, and poured it over his head. She confidently walked off the set, and the audience was in hysterics; Reed just sat there as stunned as Johnny.

In 1968, an impassioned Shelley Winters wanted to make a political statement and did not withhold her opinion about her opposition to the United States' involvement in the Vietnam War. She mentioned that the dear little boy who played Beaver on *Leave It to Beaver* had been killed in action. Although Winters's heart was in the right place, actor Jerry Mathers, who was serving in the military at the time, was in fact alive and well. Immediately, the former child actor's family began receiving sympathy cards and condolences from around the country. (Even his TV brother, Tony Dow, sent flowers.) Unknowingly, Winters had sparked an urban legend about the death of Jerry Mathers, a misconception that spread for years until the surviving cast of *Leave It to Beaver* reunited for a nostalgic TV movie in the 1980s.

One night in the mid-1980s, Winters warned Johnny on the show that she was going to be including a story involving Johnny in a new book. She began by making a reference to a period in his life where he was between wives. This made Johnny stop in his tracks while his face turned red.

"Remember 'The Factory,' where the Playboy bunnies used to go?" she asked Johnny, who just stared blankly. "Don't act like you don't remember. I have pictures of this. Somebody there invited a bunch of us to a party on a boat. A moonlit sail to Catalina. . . . We were both rather sloshed. Well, I was drunk and I'm sure you were not exactly sober. Somehow, we got confused and I thought you were Jack Lemmon and you thought I was Angie Dickinson."

Johnny said, "You're thinking of *The Poseidon Adventure*."

*Below,* Johnny and Robert Blake switched places for a while on this July 1976 show with guest Burt Reynolds. Don't ask.

During the 1970s and '80s, actor Robert Blake found a new niche in Hollywood when he became a frequent guest on many TV talk shows, including *The Tonight Show.* Everyone knew Blake was a volatile type, which is perfect for TV talk. Known to be an intense performer and a cool conversationalist, Blake sat next to Johnny about seventy-five times between 1970 and 1985, welcomed back to discuss everything from his days as a child actor in the *Our Gang* comedies to Fred the cockatiel, his feathered friend from the TV police drama *Baretta.* It was common for the outspoken actor to casually chat with a lit Winston dangling from his mouth, sometimes a pack was rolled up in his short sleeve—like Tony Baretta himself. And when smoking fell out of fashion, almost taboo on camera, Blake would still play with an unlit smoke.

In a December 1972 appearance, Blake followed his friend, singer Sammy Davis Jr. (who eventually recorded "Keep Your Eye on the Sparrow," *Baretta*'s theme song), and talked to Johnny about his work in the 1967 motion picture *In Cold Blood*, an adaptation of the bestseller by Truman Capote. The movie, nominated for an Academy Award for best screenplay, was a factual documentary-style drama about the slaughter of a family in a small Kansas town by two delinquents, and the eventual search, trial, and execution of the killers. (It's an engrossing black and white film, directed by Richard Brooks, and today, it's probably more haunting than Blake could have ever imagined.)

To lighten things, of course, Johnny unhesitatingly did his cute impression of Truman Capote's effeminate, cartoon-like voice, but he switched to seriousness when he mentioned having recently seen the film on television.

"You were brilliant in that movie," said Johnny. "There was talk when that film came out, about five, six years ago, that you might get an Academy Award."

"You don't start off with no light stuff do ya?" Blake said in his best streetwise. "What can I say about that? If I had my choice of doing the job or winning the award, I would have done the job, and let somebody else have the trinket on their mantelpiece."

Sammy Davis Jr. interjected: "You did the job, man, and you got robbed. It was a beautiful, beautiful job."

Blake shrugged his shoulders, took in the applause, and started to tell it as he saw it. Which was, as usual, with brutal honesty. Simply, he said, the studio did not lobby for his nomination. And oh, how well he remembered exactly who took home the trophy for best actor that year—Rod Steiger, for *In the Heat of the Night.*

Blake confirmed for Johnny that the movie was filmed in the small, bleak Kansas town, on location at the actual murder site.

"Was Truman Capote on the set?" Johnny asked.

"He wasn't on the set," Blake said. "I didn't like him and he didn't like me. We got to know each other afterward. It was a little tense there in the trenches and I didn't need a lot of folks tellin' me, 'Well, that isn't the way Perry used to comb his hair. . . .'"

Sammy Davis jumped in again. "My wife and I saw the picture. What do you go through, as an actor, really doin' it?"

Blake hesitated for a second. "By the time I did it . . . I was so far into it," he said, "I mean, it was spooky for the crew and everybody to be there, saying 'Hey, that's where that poor little girl died' and all that. I was so far into it, I was pretty well bananas by then; they coulda stuck me under water and I woulda still been doing Perry, doing my duty like that. It was heavy.

"I had to go to the [psychiatrist] for a year or so to get my head unraveled after that. I had a lot of friends goin' in, man, before the movie started, saying 'Whatever you need, man, you got it.' Help all around," Blake said. "When the movie was over, there was nobody but me. Even to pay for the shrink to unravel my melon."

Call it good conversation or call it lighting the fuse, Johnny knew he was baiting Blake with this: "Truman Capote was on the show the other night and said that all actors, and the better the actor they were—and you're a good actor—the dumber they were."

"Well," Blake said, "you're lookin' at one actor he's right about, 'cause I'm dumb. Truman got a half a million dollars for the picture plus one third of all the profits and I got a one-way ticket to the funny farm. So I'm dumb! But I fooled 'em, 'cause I'm still here. . . .

"I didn't get no piece of the picture," he admitted. "I got a piece of paper that said, 'Get your car off the lot. Get outta the dressing room. And you owe us three thousand six hundred dollars' . . . when the movie was over."

Johnny was stunned. "Are you serious?"

"They loaned me some bread before I made the picture so I could feed my kids some corn flakes while I was preparin' for the epic," he explained. "Well, it wasn't clear it was a loan 'til the picture was finished, you understand.

"That's cool man, I'd a done it for nuthin'. I'd a paid them to do it and I was gonna do it anyway, and I was gonna kill anyone else who was gonna do it . . . so it didn't make any difference."

Odd Couple: Tony Randall told Johnny in 1977 that he suffered from tinnitus, an affliction that causes a constant ringing in the ears. It's so loud, Randall told him, that he might be able to hear it. "I can," Carson quipped.

# 4

# CELEBRITIES ON TONIGHT

# TONY RANDALL

It could have been a play, a film, a TV series, a charity event. Or maybe his memoirs. Tony Randall says he realized long ago that an appearance with Johnny Carson meant business.

"I'm always on the show to plug something," he said years ago, preparing for another visit on the show. "That's the reason to go on. It's Plugsville. I've never gone on except to plug something. That's why people go on for no money. It's the finest avenue there is to advertise something."

Sometime over the years, the fun kicked in, and Randall's visits on the *Tonight Show* became mostly for fun, just as he graduated to many extracurricular appearances on *Late Night with David Letterman*—just for the kick. Much of it was his spontaneity, though, that drew producers to the phone to call him.

For most people, when they think of Tony Randall, the image of Felix Unger pops up. Rarely does anyone consider him one of our television pioneers, but he is. He costarred in TV's *Mr. Peepers* with Wally Cox when the first situation comedies were being invented, broadcast live from the Big Apple. He's still in the business at age eighty-plus, and astonishingly, he has young children to support.

On with Johnny on more than 120 occasions, Randall stepped from behind the curtain each time more nervous than the last.

"And I'm never nervous," he professed. "I don't have any stage fright. None. Opening night I can go to sleep in my dressing room until ten minutes before my entrance. I'm blessed that way. But I'm always nervous before Carson."

That was due to his record of success with Carson. Every appearance was a pretty good one. Probably not a sour show in the bunch. The fear of not being funny on *The Tonight Show* plagued him through the years, Randall says.

"Before television got this big, if you had a movie, a play, a book, a record—the most you could hope for or the greatest thing that could happen was to get the cover of *Life* magazine," Randall explains. "That would sell. Today, it's television." And for years, above all, the best promotional tool was *The Tonight Show* with Johnny. "If you're looking at it any other way, you're misconstruing it," he says.

Still today, on television Randall eagerly and consistently plugs not a tangible thing or an item for purchase, but he tries to sell a lifesaving commitment: Stop Smoking. He'd said it many times on *The Tonight Show,* and with Carson, who had smoked for years, it became a running gag. While Randall sat there, smoke would eventually waft his way. Carson and Randall got a lot of mileage out of it. And it was funny to see Randall rant like Felix Unger.

Carson respected Randall's message and eventually quit smoking. During the 1960s, Carson openly puffed away, leaving a lit cigarette balanced on the edge of the glass ashtray on the desk. It was nothing for Johnny, or a guest, to take out a smoke during an interview and enjoy themselves, get relaxed and cozy, and then pinch out the flame while delivering a zinger. Carson adopted a no-smoking atmosphere in the 1980s, although status helped. If the likes of George Burns, Milton Berle, or Jackie Gleason were sitting next to him, Johnny said absolutely not a word while probably craving a smoke himself.

"I think every now and then Johnny quit," says Randall, who is openly bothered by smoke and equally vocal about it. "When I'd come on, he'd light up without a word, knowing that I'd say something. He provokes you, and it's so sly.

"You see, it's misdirection. He was a magician once; you're watching his left hand, but his right hand's doing it."

Conversations with Randall swayed from personal plugs to entertaining topics, all gracefully facilitated by Carson. Once, Randall remembers, singer Carmen Lombardo was on the show, and Randall, who imitates Lombardo singing "Boo Hoo," was pitted against the singer in an impromptu "Boo Hoo" competition. Carson gauged the audience's reaction by a hand-over-the-head applause meter. Randall says he saved that episode on videotape, a rarity since he detests watching himself on television.

One night, Randall revealed to Johnny that he suffered from a chronic physical ailment called tinnitus, which causes him to constantly hear ringing in his inner ear. "That show had remarkable consequences," he says. "I told him I had tinnitus and I'd gone to doctors and tried everything. There is no cure. Every doctor had said the same thing to me: Learn to live with it.

"I got hundreds of letters saying, 'You claim you've cured your tinnitus. . . . How did you do it?' You see, people don't listen. The American Tinnitus Foundtion asked me to come aboard and I've been active with them ever since."

All in all, Randall got his revenge on Johnny—with kindness. "I'd sit there after the show with my mouth gaping," he says of his nights on the show. "And every time, when the show was over, I'd say the same thing to him: Johny, you're the most brilliant man in the world. It seemed to embarrass him. I don't think he liked it.

"I remember Kenneth Tynan wrote that Johnny Carson was an authentic genius, and I've quoted that a number of times. He's an authentic comic genius and people should recognize that."

# Buddy Hackett

Whenever Buddy Hackett was on the show, while the home viewing audience was wading through pizza commercials and network promos, the studio audience at NBC would usually be lucky enough to witness an earful of Hackett telling an off-color story with his usual candor. It was one of the few times a guest at the couch would interact with the audience during commercial breaks and the band would rest.

# The Joan Rivers Feud

"The way Johnny found out about my new talk show was horrendous. I wanted to be the one to break the news to him."

—Joan Rivers, *People*, May 26, 1986

"I just felt she could have handled it differently, that's all."

—Johnny Carson, *Los Angeles Times*, July 6, 1986

It was a media firestorm before anyone had even coined the phrase. No doubt, the controversy over who would replace Johnny when he retired was fierce and unprecedented. But the war of words and publicists that erupted back in 1986 over the Johnny Carson/Joan Rivers feud definitely rivalled that event in intensity. It began when Rivers suddenly announced at a press conference that she would be launching a late-night talk show in September 1986. The new program would air at 11:00 P.M. on both coasts, giving it a half-hour jump on *The Tonight Show*, and backers at the Fox Broadcasting Corporation boasted that Rivers would tap an audience that was ripe for the picking: younger viewers.

"But what 'youth-oriented' has to do with Ms. Rivers is anybody's guess," wrote reporter Bob Wisehart. "She doesn't have the vaguest

idea how to attract the viewers she needs to succeed."

So what if Rivers decided to compete with Carson? Many other talk-show hosts tried to do the same thing. Joey Bishop did, and returned to *Tonight* to guest host for Johnny. Carson was sporting about competition and never discouraged anyone from mounting a show of their own. The opportunity had been given to many—and failed by most. Television's morgue was littered with cold hosts who had attempted to bump the king: Dick Cavett, Mike Douglas, Les Crane, Alan Thicke, Pat Sajak, Merv Griffin. The only close contender was Arsenio Hall.

The bottom line was that Carson was angry at Rivers for negotiating to renew her contract with the Carson company at the same time she was cutting her own deal with Fox. Carson was also upset by "how she handled the announcement." When she let America in on her new endeavor, she let her mentor in on it at the same time. As longtime *Tonight Show* producer Fred de Cordova put it: "A secondhand discovery that a member of your family has moved out of your home doesn't make for joy and celebration. . . . Her manner of saying bye-bye to Johnny and *The Tonight Show* was, in my opinion, somewhere between tacky and tasteless."

Staff at the *The Tonight Show* were shocked and surprised. To comprehend the impact this falling-out had on both Rivers and Carson, one must go back to 1965, when Rivers was a thirty-one-year-old "groveling outcast," as she described herself, "struggling through mud up to my waist to break into show business, going through humiliations nobody should have to endure."

Rivers's life changed on February 17, 1965, when she was slated to appear as a guest on *The Tonight Show.* She had been writing for Allen Funt on TV's *Candid Camera,* toying with nightclub gigs, writing material, and attempting to hit it big. When *The Tonight Show* finally gave her that long-awaited chance with Johnny, she was excited and nervous, and unconfident. She described her initial thoughts in her book *Enter Talking,* which she dedicated to Johnny Carson for "making it all happen." Rivers recalled:

I did not allow myself any emotion. I had been through the excitement before, been through the rush of adrenaline and the dreams, and knew the predictable end. Twice before I had been in the very same studio for Paar and twice I had been a failure.

The many faces of Joan Rivers—or, the early ones, anyway. Rivers began appearing on *The Tonight Show* in 1965 and eventually became "permanent" guest host from 1983 to 1986, sitting in for Johnny more than ninety times.

That night, Carson wiped his eyes from the tears of laughter, and told her, "God, you're funny. You're gonna be a star." Rivers says the words did not register at all. She only heard them later when she watched the show with her parents. Her thoughts did not include a fantasy that this would be the beginning process of her adoption into the *Tonight Show* family. But that's exactly what was brewing.

Rivers says that night was "the moment when my life began, when seven years of

rejection and humiliation paid off, when I got past all the people who were saying I was too old and would never make it." As Rivers describes her relationship with Johnny from then on, it was a "curious" one.

They saw each other rarely socially. In front of the camera, they clicked, but during commercial breaks when the camera's red light went off, they had nothing in common. Carson would sit silently drumming his pencil on the desk, and she'd say, "Gee, doesn't the band sound great tonight?"

"And yet the relationship has been deeply precious to me," she said in 1986. One of her fondest memories of Johnny Carson, she told *TV Guide* reporter Mary Murphy, happened off the air: "In appreciation for an appearance he made on her pilot in 1968, Rivers sent Carson a gift—her baby daughter, Melissa Rosenberg, wrapped in a white blanket. Melissa was carried into Carson's office at NBC accompanied by a note that said: 'I weigh 4 pounds 3 ounces. I eat very little. Please bring me up Jewish.'"

Carson took the baby in his arms, and she immediately fell asleep. Carson was afraid to wake her so he held her in his arms for two hours. "How's that for a sweet guy?" Rivers asked.

Through the years, her appearances were steady and they were all good shots. Her style differed greatly from Carson's, which was the reason he enjoyed her on the show. Her brand of comedy, her monologues, were popular with audiences, and a younger crowd emerged from the stable of talent that Johnny was building. The Rivers wit was seldom without sting. ("Elizabeth Taylor was so fat they had to grease her thighs to shove her through the Golden Arches at McDonald's" . . . "God didn't mean Jewish people to exercise and bend over, or He'd have put diamonds on the floor.") One of her favorite targets was Great Britain's royal family. Especially the Queen.

"Sure she's strident," Carson described Rivers to *L.A. Times* writer Paul Rosenfield. "What she does is in total contrast to what I do. I am not going to ask Joan Collins her age. Joan can get away with that. It makes sense for her. But seven or eight weeks a year is one thing. It would be difficult for Joan to do this full-time, and she knows it. She admits this—she's said herself that her style would become too obvious if exposed every single night, fifty-two weeks a year."

Carson was right, and ultimately Rivers was correct also. When she decided to curtail her position as *The Tonight Show*'s first permanent guest host—a position she'd held since August 1983—she was commanding terrific ratings, a hefty paycheck, and exposure to beat 'em all. She also knew she would be taking a chance. So did Fox Broadcasting.

Rivers professed to be loyal, and she "swore" she'd never go up against Johnny. Things at NBC and Carson Productions in 1985 were not all well, she says, a year before her announcement; Johnny's contract was solid for two more years, hers was only for one. "That shook me to the very roots of my confidence," she wrote in a letter about the feud that was printed in *People* magazine. "It could only mean one thing—the powers were uncertain about my future." Moreover, Rivers held in her hand an NBC interoffice memo that listed possibile successors to Johnny in

case he did not renew his contract. Her name was nowhere to be found.

She thought she should seek employment with a steadier outlook, and in essence, began hedging her career to counterbalance the employment, so as to limit any risks. But after all, she was in show business. Nothing's steady. Everything's a risk. That's the breaks, baby! Even with a contract, nothing is certain.

When Fox Broadcasting approached Rivers about launching a show of her own opposite Carson, she decided to consider the offer for her own survival. She accepted, and much later rejected the NBC offer she received—submitted too late in the process, she explained.

In his memoirs, *Johnny Came Lately*, producer Fred de Cordova described the events surrounding the dropping of the Rivers bomb.

> Monday, May 5, 1986, Joan (and Edgar on extension) called me at home at 7:00 P.M. Tearfully, she had "something to tell me": she had made a deal with Fox to do a talk show. It would start in October. It would be on the air opposite Johnny. She was calling me first and would shortly call and tell Johnny and Peter Lassally, in that order. I was stunned. All I could say to Joan was, "You're kidding!" She told me how dear I was to her—Edgar said the deal was for three years and there would "always be a candle in the window" for me. I repeated, "You're kidding!" Then I called Johnny immediately. He had just received a call from Brandon Tartikoff telling him that Joan had, indeed, made a deal with Fox and a press conference was scheduled by her for the next day. While John and I were talking, he was told that Joan was on the other phone. He said he wouldn't take the call—it was "a little late in arriving . . . about three months late."

Since that phone call, and another when she did reach Johnny—but he hung up when

Joan Rivers was guest host for the Halloween *Tonight Show* in 1985, with guests Pee-wee Herman (dressed as a vampire), Phyllis Diller (as sex therapist Dr. Ruth Westheimer), and Cassandra Peterson (Elvira, Mistress of the Dark).

she addressed him—she has not spoken with him at all and they have not made up. Rivers, to this day, is confounded by his actions, and Carson has simply dropped the subject.

Eventually Joan's show, called *The Late Show,* did not score the ratings Fox had hoped, and Rivers's three-year contract was shortened while lawyers settled with Rivers for the remainder. Rivers's life took another sharp turn when her husband of more than twenty years, Edgar, committed suicide and her career began to fall apart.

In the early 1990s, with a new face thanks to plastic surgery she makes no secret about, Rivers picked herself up, tucked herself in, honed a "gossipy" repertoire of jokes and style, and succeeded in a syndicated daytime talk show that won her an Emmy Award for excellence. Following that program, she joined the fledgling E! Entertainment network and has changed the way America watches awards shows. She and her daughter, Melissa (the baby who slept in Johnny's arms for two hours a lifetime ago), host the extremely popular live red-carpet broadcasts, where they interview the stars as they arrive and

gossip about what the stars are wearing.

On Phil Donahue's show in 1991, Rivers commented on the five-year-old Johnny Carson "feud." After her husband's death, she said, she was amazed that she had not heard "a syllable from Johnny Carson. Never."

Rivers added, "I put all this behind me. I had met Edgar through Johnny Carson. And no matter what had gone down between us, I think at certain points in people's lives, you pick up a pen and say this is terrible.

"When Johnny's son died so tragically, I picked up a piece of paper and I wrote to him and said, 'How terrible, how sad, these events happen in our lives.'

"No, I never heard a word," she responded to the host's question. "It was disgusting, and it was wrong, and it was his problem."

Regardless of their past, Rivers remained complimentary during all of the hype surrounding Carson's retirement in 1992. She still points to Johnny as the man who put her on the map. Carson seems indifferent and probably just prefers she not point at all.

Buddy Hackett, known for keeping Carson on his toes with provocative jokes, became one of the host's preferred guests. (April 1967)

Everyone in the studio—including Johnny—wanted him to rip one off during the break, absolutely killing the audience and the band. Then, when Johnny returned from the commercial, Hackett usually restarted the story, only to have Johnny to nervously cut him off. "Why don't you let me send you out into the world," Hackett pleaded, trying to spit out the blue joke any way he could.

Hackett described his edge with Johnny in 1991. "I walk along the edge so carefully, the audience is with bated breath thinkin' 'How is he gonna get out of this one?'" Hackett said, describing his usual *Tonight Show* visit. If you're not a Buddy Hackett fan, or you've never seen him in concert, his stories are usually hysterical and blue—maybe intense violet. But never is his act laced with random cursing to shock an audience like the tactic some stand-ups employ. Each word of Hackett's delivery is carefully planned, distinctly delivered, disciplined, and funny. That's what Johnny liked most about Hackett, his honed comedy and his confidence.

Over the years, Hackett got laughs like no one else on the show, and it was not beneath him to, say, impulsively start removing his clothes just out of the camera's range while Ed McMahon was busy doing an Alpo commercial. Any Hackett night was just great play, full of jokes and ad-libbing with Johnny. Hackett loved to plug his upcoming Vegas gigs and was grateful to Johnny for the forum to do so. "You can go on any part of episodic television and play a great part and get nominated and such," he said, "but that won't bring one person to see you in a nightclub. Every time I went on his show to plug an upcoming appearance, it was sold out. The same people who stay up to eleven-thirty to see John, these are the same people who go to nightclubs and theater."

For Hackett, or any comedian on the show, the object was to crack up Johnny. "I was only nervous ahead of time, trying to think of what stories to tell on the show," Hackett says. Spontaneity was the secret. Before the show there might have been a brief exchange or a "hello" between the host and guest in the makeup room or the hallway. Never anything more. Johnny preferred it that way, with most every guest. "One time I let him see me in the hall with a beautiful blue suit and a red tie," he says. "And Los Angeles had been going through such rain you couldn't believe it. As soon as he saw me, I went back to the dressing room, changed into a white suit with shoes and socks, and stood in the shower until I was soaked to the underwear.

"When he announced me, I walked out and said, 'It's still rainin', John!'"

Any other night, you might have caught Hackett skirting off-color jokes, performing a little Three Stooges slapstick with Johnny, talking about his family, or discussing a gig. The "weirdest" appearance he recalled was out of New York, the night of the Academy Awards telecast.

"We had just started discussing the Awards as though they had already been on—but this was five-thirty, late afternoon," Hackett says. "We talked about which movies and which people won; it was just something I started, and John played along like nothing was up. We guessed every one right.

"After that, Price Waterhouse wanted to know how we had the information. Earl Wilson, the columnist, came to my house and asked me how we got it. It was strange. We just guessed at it all and talked about it in the past tense, and it hadn't happened yet."

Carson called Hackett one of the "self-starters" who came on the show wired and ready to entertain, leaving the spot open for an effortlessly great time because the guest was prepared. And with Hackett, even when he was called to appear in a pinch because the show had a cancellation, whether he was prepared or not, he'd lay the audience out with laughs. Johnny counted on that. But Hackett turned that around and said the success was due to Johnny's interview technique: "He is so brilliant. If he feels me needing something, he knows exactly what to say to bring it out of me. John makes every performer a star on his show, and I can't say enough about him. He's so utterly human. The only regret I ever have with John is that I don't see enough of him."

Reflecting on their friendship, Hackett recalled a few instances that meant the most to him. "Of all the great times I've had," Hackett said, letting you in on his life, "one night Johnny and I were together and went and watched comedians. We had a couple of drinks. Maybe more. He's one of the great laughers in the world. We went to see the burlesque comedians in Las Vegas. John fell out of his seat on the floor. But we laughed and fell on the floor, rolling around in spit. I've never laughed so hard, and John too. Of all the nights I've spent in Las Vegas, that was the best night after work I ever had."

Another highlight in Hackett's years was a particular birthday celebrated at a nightclub called the Candy Store in Los Angeles. Carson was broadcasting from New York at the time, and this party fell on a show night; the Hacketts were positive that Johnny would not have time to swing a trip cross country, so an invitation was contemplated but not extended.

Johnny fondly reminisces with Liza Minnelli about her legendary mother, Judy Garland, who had appeared on *The Tonight Show* near the end of her life.

"It was maybe close to midnight, and the place was packed," Hackett remembers. "George Burns was there, Jack Benny was there, and everyone you could imagine. Johnny walks in. He walks right up to me and says, 'Who do you have to know to get invited to this party?' I was so thrilled he'd flown in, I couldn't even answer him. He said, 'Oh, you don't want me here?' I hugged him and kissed him.

"It was 1966 or '67, and about thirty people came to the house after the party. Jack Lemmon and his wife. Steve Allen. Nobody wanted to end the night. Johnny was sitting on the floor with a pot, banging on the pot doing rhythms, you know. It was a wonderful night. And of all the birthdays I've had, that's one of my favorites. He made that night for me.

"So if you get an idea from this conversation that I'm a great Johnny Carson fan—I am."

# PHYLLIS DILLER

*Carnac:* Eleven

**Question:** *Bo Derek and Phyllis Diller*

"There are some really funny things that Johnny's said about me that I adored," said the wacky comedienne with the fright wig from hell. "He was talking about a woman being raped. He said, 'Well, if it ever happened to Phyllis Diller, it would be Breaking and Entering.'"

Today, the Diller style that stung America in the early 1960s is passé. "I can't dress funny anymore," said Diller, who is now in her eighties and still doing stand-up. "They call it punk now. In vogue. Do you realize that spiked hairdo for five years was chic? Who do you think started that?"

In or out of sync with the trends, Diller admitted she and Carson never clicked much at the *Tonight Show* desk. On her last appearance with Carson, she performed a standup routine for the audience, a rarity for a performer as established (and old) as Diller. She emerged from the curtain in an elaborate gold-trimmed metallic-frilled dress, something out of *The Herculoids.*

"They finally let me do [stand-up] because I feel comfortable doing that," she said. "I felt I didn't always click with him. I didn't want to risk it. Some people, for instance Charles Nelson Reilly, I mean— I have been positively on the floor. I don't know whether it was the problem of whoever briefed me for him or what. There were times we were sensational, but then there were times it didn't work." Twice, while the show emanated from New York, she was beckoned to guest host. It was an important move, an honor, and a career opportunity of a lifetime, even for the most established talent. But that didn't work either time, she recalls: "The first time, a group of my agents came screaming into the

Phyllis Diller, in surprisingly graceful attire that she hurriedly borrowed just before the show, was present for the wedding of Tiny Tim in 1969. (Courtesy of Phyllis Diller)

Tennis champion Arthur Ashe brought along the 13-pound, 24-karat solid gold tennis ball that he was presented with after winning Wimbledon in 1975. "I've been offered fifty thousand dollars for it," he told Carson, "but I'm keeping it." (April 1978)

dressing room while they were calling me onstage! They had had cocktails, darling. In those days, I was young and nervous. It was a lot of responsibility. When I have to rush onstage after scraping off three drunk agents, I'm not in any condition to do a show. Unfortunately, they had chosen guests whom I didn't even know! Isn't that swell?"

Regardless of the chemistry, Diller can be proud of one show from 1969. It was an event. Somehow, she ended up there on the couch on a stellar night, a stand out if there was one. Diller was in attendance for Tiny Tim's highly-publicized wedding. For that alone, she knows it was all worth it, the good and the sour, and through it all she still loves Johnny Carson and watched him as much as possible.

"As he got older, he was extremely partial to male guests," she said with a wry cackle. "Unless they were young girls that he had screwed . . . and that's where my appearances started thinning out."

## CARL REINER

In the days of live television, Carl Reiner was busy writing comedy, performing on Sid Caesar's show, and starting his own collection of Emmy Awards—eleven in total, he says, which "sit quietly at home oxidizing." So adaptable was Reiner, his association with late-night television went way back to Steve Allen, then on to Jack Paar (whom he called an "open nerve"), and he then proceeded to appear regularly with Johnny Carson, never imagining he'd be doing it for thirty years. Reiner loved the late-night manifestations and his ad-libbing skills were never sharper than on these nights. Above all, he feels Carson was the best TV had to offer.

Reiner says he always liked the personae, physical image, and talents of Johnny Carson. In fact, casting the starring role on what became *The Dick Van Dyke Show* in 1961, Reiner, the sitcom's creator and producer, reduced his list to just two clean-cut actors: Johnny Carson and Dick Van Dyke. Carson probably wouldn't have chosen to leave the security of his game-show gig as host of *Who Do You Trust?*, but it's interesting to contemplate how differently things would have turned out if Johnny had brought Rob Petrie to life.

Carson and Reiner have remained friends for years, with regular *Tonight Show* fixes that seemed to include just about everything. Once, Reiner came on stage with a special present for Johnny: a tuna sandwich. Another time the topic was his handsome toupee, which he removed right there on camera to sample other rugs he had brought . . . all to seek audience approval. In the last several years of the show, Reiner made a habit of bursting from behind the curtain and performing a wild, eccentric little dance that only lacked foam around his mouth. Within thirty seconds he was out of breath, slouching down in the seat next to Johnny. Usually no explanation.

Reiner says he met Johnny during the host's *Who Do You Trust?* years, and sometimes the Carsons and the Reiners all went out to dinner in New York City. Always wonderful memories, he says. "We've considered ourselves friends even though we don't see each other a lot anymore," says Reiner, "except during poker games." Reiner doesn't want to divulge the other comedians on

Carl Reiner wanted to make certain his appearance would be included in the next anniversary show's clips, so he took out scissors and proceeded to cut up Johnny's new black suit. Stunned, Carson resumed the show with his suit in shreds. (December 1979)

the roster at these summits, but he insists that Johnny's a good player. "He doesn't cheat. You'd think he might because he's a magician. He probably could if he wanted to."

It was when they first met that Reiner predicted this Carson fellow would go far. "I knew he was good the first time I saw him. He had a boyish charm about him. He always surprised you that he was so smart as he was. He looked like just a cute guy.

"Nobody knew that anybody could stay on television for thirty years. How did he do that?"

## JIMMY STEWART

Expectations of James Stewart were always high—from his directors, from his costars, even from his fans. And he always delivered. On *The Tonight Show*, no one was ever disappointed when Ed McMahon read his name as the first guest. Over the decades, the aging actor made many appearances, but sparingly, so as not to wear out the welcome mat. He talked about his pal Ronald Reagan, director Frank Capra, talking rabbits, and one night, Stewart even brought his old accordion along and played. In the last ten years of his appearances, Stewart found the perfect forum for his latent talent: poetry. He favored America with some memorable readings.

Johnny usually asked if he'd brought anything and Stewart would hesitatingly grasp the crumpled piece of paper his poetry was scribbled on. Out of another suit pocket he'd pull his black horn-rimmed glasses and slowly put them on. The eyewear was stark next to his silver hair.

One of the best poems, and certainly one of the funniest, was about a hotel in Junïn de los Andes, a small area in western Argentina where the Stewarts were vacationing. The top step in the hotel was slightly offset, and everyone in the Stewart group tripped and stumbled when they reached that top step. So aggravated by the step, Stewart took to the pen to release his funny frustration, and composed a gem he called, "The Top Step in the Hotel Junïn (Is Mean)."

The May 3, 1983, *Tonight Show* audience roared as he stammered through his delivery that night, unveiling the clever piece on national television.

Other poems followed: "I'm a Movie Camera," about the little handheld movie camera he purchased for his daughters just prior to a family safari in Kenya. The camera was snatched away by a hyena and mangled in its jaws around the midnight hour. In first person, speaking for the poor camera, Jimmy created another narrative that flowed like Longfellow.

One of the most touching of the bunch was about his beloved dog, Beau. He was a feisty golden retriever, Stewart said. "Beau was a fine-looking pup, but we soon found out we had a problem. Beau was on the wild side. He tried to bite holes in furniture." Eventually Beau won his way into the hearts of Stewart and his wife, Gloria. The handsome dog even crept up in bed to slumber between them, while they patted his head. Years later, while filming a movie out of town, Stewart was summoned and told his dog was seriously ill; the actor rushed home. Beau had to be put to sleep. "I could hardly see to drive home because of the tears in my eyes," Stewart remembered. Suffering the loss, he was compelled to put it in rhyme as therapy to get through the pain. When Stewart read the poem, there were tears in the eyes of many in the studio audience, because it hit a chord with nearly every pet lover, maybe as a sweet reminder of the pets we lost.

One evening, Stewart had a cold, and his tolerance seemed low. Even his stammer seemed stuck in low gear. Slowly relating a story to Johnny Carson about a tedious eight-hour, flat-tire-ridden journey to Lake Beringo in the western part of Kenya, Stewart said he dabbled a bit with a poem about the experience and gave the audience a preview:

# The Matinee Lady: An Unsolved Mystery

*Carol Wayne's death is unsolved, certainly. But I don't think it was a drowning. A drowning, yes, of course, but there's more to it than that. . . .*

—William LaCoque, U.S. consular official,
Manzanillo, Mexico, June 1990

One of the most popular recurring comedy sketches on *The Tonight Show* was the "Tea-Time Movie" with the lecherous Art Fern, played by Carson wearing a jet-black wig and wielding a stick he loudly cracked on the table. His sidekick was the "Matinee Lady," a buxom blonde beauty named Carol Wayne, the master of the double entendre with a squeaky voice that invoked a dumb-blonde characterization.

Wayne made more than a hundred appearances with Carson and became the butt of on-air jokes about her bountiful breasts. Her eye-catching figure, smooth skin, and flashing eyes made her a perfect comic foil for Art Fern in these sketches. Writer John Austin commented, "Carol Wayne's forte was her ability to make innocent statements seem suggestive. If [Wayne] asked somebody if they would like a cup of coffee, it sounded as if she was asking them to go to bed with her."

One night on the show, Wayne announced to Carson during a sketch, "I had my first big affair . . . I had forty people." Of course, the audience went into hysterics, because her delivery was perfect. Another night, Wayne was talking to Carson about a beer commercial she had done when she told Johnny, "I never knew those beer people were so fussy. If your can isn't turned just the right way, they let you know." And as the kicker, she added, "Then they have special stuff they spray on your can to make it look wet and delicious."

Offscreen, Wayne reportedly became very friendly with Carson, and speculation about their relationship lingered. In a February 1984 *Playboy* photo layout and interview, Wayne noted of her employer's divorces and her own, "There was always bad timing—he loves me," she said. "I love him. It's an understanding, a given. He still sees me every day in his dreams. When he shuts his eyes, what does he see? Me!"

These quotes appear to have been part of a mystique Wayne attempted to create between herself and Carson. One writer speculated it was her personal fantasy. Carson never publicly voiced any feelings about his sidekick of many years, although reportedly he was "quite shaken" when he was informed of her death.

When Carson cut the length of *The Tonight Show* from ninety minutes to sixty, the Art Fern "Tea-Time Movies" began to diminish and eventually disappeared. Wayne's appearances on NBC were limited, and she found it difficult to get work. She finally declared bankruptcy in Los Angeles on December 13, 1984—mostly due to a heavy cocaine habit and an increased abuse of alcohol that hastily depleted any funds she had built up. She was divorced, lonely, and seeking work. Reportedly, around this time comedian Richard Pryor, a friend, offered her a role in his upcoming film with the stipulation that she check into a drug and alcohol rehabilitation unit—all funded by the comedian. Then the news hit.

"The fully clothed but horribly bloated body of Carol Wayne was found floating in

The death of actress Carol Wayne, a prominent member of the Mighty Carson Art Players, remains a mystery.

a sun-drenched Santiago Bay at Manzanillo on January 13, 1985," wrote John Austin in his book *More of Hollywood's Unsolved Mysteries.* Austin continued:

Fisherman Abel de Dios was casting a net from his wooden fishing boat about 300 yards out in the bay when he spotted the body floating no more than twenty feet away. When the body was brought ashore in a police launch and identified as that of Carol Wayne by employees of the Las Hadas resort, Edward Durston, with whom she had checked in earlier in the week, could not be located. A few hours later it was discovered he had left for Los Angeles two

days before Wayne's body was discovered. Strangely, he had deposited her luggage at the airport, saying she would "pick it up in the morning."

Attempting to dry out on her own, Wayne had accompanied Durston, a Los Angeles used-car salesman, down to Mexico for a stay in January 1985. Near the end of the trip, on January 10, the couple were separated because of a dispute about accomodations: they couldn't agree on which hotel to stay at on their last night in Mexico. After a heated argument, Wayne headed out to the beach for a walk. Durston checked into a hotel. That was the last time anyone saw the Matinee Lady alive.

According to authorities, Carol Wayne had been dead about thirty-six to forty-eight hours when she was discovered by the fisherman, and tests proved negative for traces of drugs or alcohol in her system. The waters of the Santiago Bay where she wandered were quite gentle and shallow. Austin noted: "Wayne would have had to wade out 250 to 300 feet just to reach water four feet deep." An accidental fall was ruled out by Deputy District Attorney Arturo Leal, who said that nearby were two outcroppings of rocks on the beach, but Wayne's body showed no signs of cuts or bruises. The case remains a mystery to all parties who investigated the death.

Austin also pointed out: "It was Durston who was with another aspiring actress the night of October 4, 1969, when she either jumped or fell from a sixth-floor apartment window near the Sunset Strip." That actress was Diane Linkletter, daughter of famed TV host and huckster Art Linkletter. Reported as a suicide related to LSD, Linkletter's case has also remained a mystery.

In his book, reporter Austin raises suspicious elements surrounding Carol Wayne's death:

- How could Carol Wayne, who could not swim and never liked to be near water, drown in a calm, shallow bay? This was a tragically ironic demise, especially considering the clichéd joke she inspired around *The Tonight Show,* "With that chest, this lady will never drown!"
- Could Carol Wayne have had her head held under water until her lungs were full and she drowned?
- Why did Durston take Miss Wayne's luggage to the airport before he left, rather than leave it at the hotel awaiting her return?
- Why did Durston leave Manzanillo while he knew Wayne was still missing? [No missing persons report was ever filed.]

Wayne was forty-two when she was found dead. In the late 1950s, she and her sister Nina were professional ice skaters with the Ice Capades until Carol suffered an accidental fall on a skate blade, ripping a five-inch gash in her left knee. The two eventually worked as Las Vegas showgirls at the Folies Bergère. The sisters crept into television, landing Nina a role on the sixties sitcom *Camp Runamuck*; Carol would later land her job at *The Tonight Show.*

Married three times, Carol had one son, Alex, with her second husband, Barry Feinstein. Her last, unsuccessful marriage was to producer Burt Sugarman. It ended in divorce in 1980. Sugarman later married *Entertainment Tonight* coanchor Mary Hart in 1989.

*Lake Beringo is a body of water*
*Its surface is smooth as glass.*
*But getting to Lake Beringo*
*Is a genuine pain in the ass.*

For several years, Johnny's staff at NBC was hounded with letters from viewers pleading for a copy of each poem; eventually Stewart was contacted by a publisher and the actor signed a contract to assemble these quaint ramblings in a small but mighty book. Besides, Stewart said, his personal office could hardly accommodate the requests for the poems either. Published in 1989, *Jimmy Stewart and His Poems* was released with a bang. The little hardcover gift book sold over 230,000 copies and became a best-seller. Stewart toured the country briefly, stopping in a few select states to autograph copies for the trailing lines of fans that usually wound around bookstores, sometimes down blocks. In Chicago, he signed more than a thousand copies in just a few hours. The lines to meet this living legend never ended.

"It's the first time I've gotten into this publishing thing," Stewart confided. "But for a book like this, my publisher said it did very well."

The poems' success story began with *The Tonight Show*, Stewart explained, although it's not mentioned in the book. "I enjoy doing *The Tonight Show*," he said in 1991, "and being with Johnny so much. He's a wonderful friend. When I'd go on it, I'd throw these poems in as a sort of surprise for Johnny for the fun of it."

Inevitably, Stewart was hounded for more, fans asking when the next book was due. He said, "I have sort of an established answer to that. I just say, for these four poems I have in this book, it took me twenty years to write these. Number one, I don't have twenty years left; and number two, they are all about special things that happened to me. It's been sort of quiet lately. So, I think this'll be my final attempt at writing poems."

In 1990, near Christmas, Johnny invited Jimmy Stewart on the show to finally talk about *It's a Wonderful Life*, the movie classic most associated with Stewart, and the actor's favorite film of all from his long career. He gently spoke about the movie that has become a yuletide favorite, and about respect for life.

Jimmy Stewart died July 2, 1997, at the age of eighty-nine.

# BETTY WHITE

She was Jane to Johnny's Tarzan. She portrayed the first lady reporter allowed in a men's locker room. She was Eve when Johnny was Adam.

"I always accuse him that whenever Johnny wants to take his clothes off, he calls me," laughs Betty White.

One classic skit from the 1970s that White remembers vividly was a spoof of the heavy rains pummeling Southern California at the time. "We were having terrible

*Above,* He's an acquired taste, yes, but in nearly one hundred obnoxious appearances on *The Tonight Show,* Don Rickles never failed to be an unpredictable, hilarious guest. (Also appearing: Cloris Leachman, April 28, 1976.) *Below,* Paul Lynde made only two appearances on *The Tonight Show,* both in 1976.

storms along the beach here," she says, prefacing the routine. "There was a romantic love story, a dinner for two at a beach-side café with a strolling violinist. The waves became a bit high, and they began to splash through the window a little bit." Then more than five hundred gallons of water pounded down on both White and Carson while they sat on the stage pretending to continue eating dinner.

"We couldn't rehearse that kind of thing," White says. "Fred de Cordova said, 'Now when the water hits you, pretend to fall off your chair.' When the water came down, it washed me clear across the room! Johnny thought I was dead."

Although she may not be most remembered for her stints as a Mighty Carson Art Player, this golden girl went way back with the *Tonight Show* host. The two chummed around when Johnny was hosting *Carson's Cellar*, in the 1950s. "Johnny and I had dinner one night at Trader Vics right before he started *The Tonight Show*," she remembers. "Jack Paar had retired, but they had signed Johnny and they had a few weeks of different hosts during the summer before he actually took over. Johnny was sitting there grousing, 'I wish they'd stop auditioning people for my job!'"

## Jonathan Winters

*A guy once said to me, "Wow, appearances on Carson are incredible exposure."
So one day I took that exposure and went over to Bullock's here in the valley and picked out an Italian sweater for $585.*

*And the woman said, "Mr. Winters? It is Mr. Winters, isn't it?"*

*No, it's Spanky McFarland, dear, and the Little Gang has turned racist.*

*"Is this gonna be cash or charge?"*

*And I held out the palm of my hand, which was empty. She said, "I don't understand."*

*I said, "That's exposure." I told her it was forty to fifty thousand dollars worth of exposure.*

Jonathan Winters has one observation when quizzed about Johnny Carson: "Wealthy. Very wealthy."

And for Winters, although he appeared with Johnny "mehnnnee, many, many times," he admits it wasn't a fantastic paying show. "Whatever I made on *The Tonight Show*, I still have on me."

"Over all the other hosts, I preferred Johnny," he says in a rare moment of seriousness. "I've always had a lot of fun with Johnny. Any time I'd go on, I'd come in a uniform or some crazy thing. We'd set up questions like, 'What was it like when you were a kid?' or 'What did you do in school?'—and we'd just go from there. We'd improvise. You can't do that with everybody. I don't think I could do it with Leno, to tell you the truth."

It's only matter of seconds later when the seriousness runs out and one of the Prince of Improv's personalities takes over. "Letterman," he says, "he looks like he's been running down the hall marking all the lockers at the University of Indiana sayin', 'Watch me Saturday, 'cause I'm gonna be at the Big Eye Club.' That's all I get from him. There's a guy that's Mr. Rudeness. He talks to Paul and throws cards through papier-mâché windows. That's his act. I'm still sayin' 'What the frig does he do?' Jesus, I don't get the man. You stand him up at Eddie Polino's in a little gig outside of Moline, Illinois—you now, for Joliet prisoners, and this son of a bitch will be torn to pieces.

"I don't deal in jokes. I deal with reality."

Some might wonder about the reality in which Winters exists. His humor is thrown at audiences with abandon, and it's rapid-fire. To appreciate Winters, one must listen closely, as with Robin Williams. When both Winters and Robin Williams appeared on *The Tonight Show* in 1991, Carson warned the audience, "Tonight we have two deeply disturbed gentlemen on the show. . . ."

On any given night, the wobbly-jowl comedian might show up in Confederate Army garb or in a general's uniform, armed for anything. When the curtain parted, Carson and the audience never knew what sort of outlandish character resembling Jonathan Winters might emerge.

"I've come out in different wardrobes. A look is important," Winters explains. "We're talking about a visual medium. Obviously, today people are coming out in sweatshirts and workout suits, and Bermuda shorts and sneakers, cowboy boots and God knows what. To come out in something you can play off of is good. I could come out as a cowboy and I'd say:

Jonathan Winters holds the original edition of this book. He reflects on those junctures with Johnny probably every day. Let it be known, Winters is a discriminating collector of autographs; he proudly displays an inscribed photo of himself with Johnny on *The Tonight Show* right alongside the signatures of other great figures like Orville Wright, Laurel and Hardy, and the Pope—all in his bathroom. True.

I wish I had time to change. I just came from the set. The last thing I did was a shoot-out. I can't even remember who it was with. God, it was fun. I jumped off a building. I remember it was the Flowers Hotel or something and jumped onto the horse and killed it. Terrible thing. 'Course, I'm a pretty heavy guy. I shouldn't have jumped four stories, and when I hit the horse, it just drove him into the ground. It was a Shetland pony. Poor thing couldn't get up. It was sad. God knows I didn't mean to do it. They shoulda had a fake horse. But apparently when they panned down, it was a fake and when they pulled away, it was on rollers. So it looks bad in the film. I hope they don't use it.

Winters adds, "And of course, in the audience, they're sayin', 'Did he really do this?'"

# CHARLES NELSON REILLY

I thought it would be difficult to track this guy down, but I got Charles Nelson Reilly on the phone rather easily. But he immediately stopped me: "Did you ever see the movie *The Great One*, with José Ferrer? Well, it was about the demise of this great comedian. José Ferrer went around trying to get some nice remarks from people, and he had a terrible time."

Reilly knows how to handle the conversation in any atmosphere; that's why he was the perfect guest on the talk-show circuit. He spread flamboyance like butter on all the shows and became famous for his silly, disarming humor, twisted and funny, always brilliantly witty, guided by an impeccable inner metronome. Because he mastered his skills in theatre, his timing in front of an audience was always perfect on the talk shows. He'd done all of the biggies in the '60s and '70s, including some sixty appearances with Johnny Carson. But when he jumped over for a visit on Joan Rivers's show, which was opposite Carson, he fell out of grace, he says.

"Joan asked me to be on her New Year's Eve show, and I knew full well that I'd never be on Carson again," says the irascible, theater-trained actor. "But I directed Joan in a student thing probably in 1963 or 1964. And when she had her first television show at WOR, which was with one camera and she had black hair, I was her first guest ever. I have a friendship and allegiance there."

Carson "never really liked" his vaulting from one talk show to another, Reilly explains. "And they would tell me that every time I went [on *The Tonight Show*]. Shirley Wood would say, 'Johnny's very upset that you do Merv.'"

*Tonight Show* producer Fred de Cordova humorously—if not strangely—described Reilly in his 1988 memoirs like this: "Charles Nelson Reilly can't be reached by phone. You have to leave a letter under his doormat; he'll call you back as soon as he looks under the mat. He's often out of town for a month or so, which means that your messages may turn out to be a bit dated."

Reilly responded: "The problem I have with de Cordova is that when I was in good graces, he told me he was writing this book. He said that I was born to be in talk shows and I was fabulous. Then, when I fell out of grace, I saw the book in Chicago while I was directing an opera there. I picked it up, and he said I was impossible to reach. No one could ever find me when they wanted me on the show. All of that's not true. Of course I've got a phone.

"I was never scheduled on that show. Any time I was on, they would call me between ten A.M. and four in the afternoon. 'Can you get right over here?' People would cancel, or be ill, or not be able to get a plane. I was on the show so much because I'm up the street. I could get there in eleven minutes. Sometimes they'd call and I'd cancel things to go on. I was very good to them. That was my little niche there."

For years Reilly would appear sporting a fitted suit or even a tuxedo. He killed audiences with his elaborate stories about adventures on Broadway or in Hollywood, and his delicate, sometimes catty, effervescence created a wonderful storytelling atmosphere. His laughter and his attitude remains completely infectious, whether on television, on the stage, or on the telephone.

Writer Glenn Esterly recalled one appearance in *TV Guide*: "Reilly portrays himself as the bewildered victim of various catastrophes, finally confessing: 'I don't know why I even came here to tell you this.' The audience laughs. Good-naturedly, Carson discloses: 'I'm not sure either,' which builds on Reilly's laugh."

"It was difficult," Reilly says of his appearance. "You realized it was the best and you had to be good or you wouldn't be back. With Merv Griffin, Mike Douglas, Jim Nabors, John Davidson, Dinah Shore . . . there was no 'Johnny-ism' about it. That's why it was the best show, I guess."

Despite a talent coordinator's warning minutes before entrance ("We want six minutes of hilarity"), Reilly always turned a slow show into a racing pace of laughs, even if he had temporary caps in his mouth that day. Carson laughed right along with the audience. Reilly's quick to point out: "A critic for the *Chicago Sun-Times* did a story. He was very lovely. He listed the guests, the history of the show, and said by far I was the best guest because I made them laugh every time and laugh aloud. He said a perfect night would be Carnac, a baboon from the San Diego Zoo, Angie Dickinson, and me."

Like Winters, Reilly certainly didn't appear on the *Tonight Show* for the paycheck. "I don't make any money in this business. I never work in things that pay money. I make my living from these game shows and talk shows. I direct theater. I don't go on to plug movies or TV shows. I don't make movies. I'm not on a sitcom. I just went there to help them out all the time. Joan Rivers was my friend longer than he was. What goes on between them has nothing to do with me.

"Johnny was always overly protective of his show . . . and I guess that's why it was the best."

# STAN KANN

Stan Kann is one of the few in an elite group of individuals—like Joan Embery—who began as a "civilian" guest and became a celebrity, mostly because of *The Tonight Show.*

You might recall Kann as the collector of crazy contraptions who frantically demonstrated the objects of wonder to Johnny and many guest hosts during his frequent appearances on *The Tonight Show* in the '60s and '70s. It was Phyllis Diller who suggested Kann, a former St. Louisan, to the producers. A talent coordinator said "show me," and Kann flew to New York for his first appearance with Johnny in 1968.

Kann's unusual hobby for years was collecting vintage vacuum cleaners and bizarre household devices. This passion began when he was a youngster and became fascinated with his neighbor's old Ohio vacuum cleaner, which became extinct in the home around 1930. Soon, he became so curiously enthralled with the machines, he would visit neighborhood homes and ask the housewives' permission to listen to their vacuum cleaners. He could surmise the make, model, condition, and whether the bag was full simply by listening to the whirr.

On his *Tonight Show* debut, Kann thought he'd bring on about a dozen different makes and kinds of vacuum cleaners. Some of the more unusual ones, which can only be discovered in antique stores, were boxed up for shipment to NBC Studios in preparation for the show.

At the studio, Kann became "terribly nervous and upset" when he realized only a portion of the shipment arrived and one box was missing. He sliced right through his tie in his nervousness opening a box, and he demonstrated to producers a model that had to be operated manually. "You had to run with it to get it started," Kann explains. "People in the offices peeked out to see what the whizzing motor was."

He was set to appear with Johnny in a few short hours. With only parts of the vacuums, they would have to wing it. Things got worse. Making a wrong turn in the building and walking down the emergency exit rather than taking the elevators, Kann ended up in the underground tunnel and eventually across the street from Rockefeller Center, completely lost and nervous, sweating, and trying to find his way back into NBC's studios. People were passing him everywhere. He made his way backstage again through the audience entrance, "and the makeup man could hardly put makeup on me I was so nervous," Kann remembers.

Johnny introduced Kann first. He demonstrated an old "pump" vacuum, which the stagehands had assembled "because of union rules," he says. Of course, the vacuum wouldn't pick up any dirt. "Then I threw down angel hair on the floor. It wouldn't pick that up either. I tried to step over it to get another vacuum and my pant cuff got caught on another vacuum and it tripped me and I fell." The audience went wild. "I was mortified," Kann says.

Next, Kann demonstrated the Regina "bubble machine" vacuum, which you push and run with to activate the motor. "It made a chugga-chugga sound when you pushed it," he says. "When I gave it a shove, the handle fell off, and it went past the desk, off the platform, and across the studio. The audience was in hysterics."

Kann's first of seventy-some appearances lasted over sixteen minutes. Other talk shows flew him in to demonstrate wacky gizmos on their programs and Kann was becoming a name in the circuit.

Audiences loved the fumbling character of Stan Kann almost as much as the devices he would bring along. He rattled around like a cross

Contraption collector Stan Kann frantically demonstrates an unusual orange-peeler to guest host David Brenner.

between Don Knotts and Sid Melton, sweating, tripping, and stammering. His voice would quiver and shake and then rise a few pitches. Sometimes he would have to yell over the audience's laughter. "It is a character," Kann agrees. "Because they never wanted to give you enough time. You had to go like a bat outta hell on those shows. Especially *The Tonight Show.*" While frantically showing guest host Bill Cosby a cheap kitchen contraption that sliced pineapples, Kann broke the prop and quipped, "Well, I like canned pineapple . . . nothing wrong with that."

Recalling his *Tonight Show* appearances, Kann says he preferred Carson over the others. One night that he says he'll never forget featured Don Rickles as guest host. One of the items displayed that evening was a little battery-operated toy train that ran around on a track on any surface, floor or desk. "I wanted to show you could even use it without the track," he says. "I put it on the floor and the camera followed it. Rickles said, 'All right Stan. Enough of the train, Stan! Let's do something else, Stan! Ya got some more toys, Stan?'

"I went to grab the train, and the cars came loose from the engine and it kept going," Kann laughs. "I went to go for the engine again, and it got away from me. It kept getting away from me. Finally, Rickles ran over to this little train and smashed it to pieces with one foot. He picked up the wreckage and said, 'Here, Stan. Take it and fix it. You'll have much more fun trying to put this damned thing back together.'"

"Spiderman" Danny Goodwin made headlines in 1981 when he successfully scaled Chicago's 110-story Sears Tower and was subsequently arrested for the stunt.

# 5

CIVILIANS

*[Johnny's] favorite kind of guest is the elderly lady, the very amusing—not necessarily precocious—child. Somebody who is not a performer in the arts. It's a piece of gold to him.*

—FRED DE CORDOVA

Johnny was unquestionably at speed when he interviewed the frail and feisty little old ladies. Sometimes it was the old geezer who said whatever was on his mind—and could get away with it. Or it was a clever little kid, like the little girl who invented "food tape" because her "brother's burritos kept falling apart."

They all kept Carson on his toes and usually, with a little luck, their segments ended up as some of the most charming and spontaneous moments in television since, well, since Art Linkletter was on television. Kids really did say the darndest things.

Around the offices of *The Tonight Show*, those guests were known as "civilians." There was no military reference, it was just a friendly term to mean "non-performers." There was a staff of two to three people who routinely scanned newspapers from across the country to find these unusual guests. The *Phoenix Gazette* may have had the perfect story about an eighty-three-year-old man who collects cowbells. Or *USA Today* may have run a piece about a woman who runs a nut museum. Or they'd discover a piece about John Twomey, who played songs by cupping his hands and releasing air, just like flatulence. Oh, it got better. This guy tooted his palms to the melody of "Stars and Stripes Forever."

The variety of civilians was great on *The Tonight Show*, although there were a few themes, like the children inventors, the cowboy poets, the national yelling competition, and the high school bird callers.

One of the more elaborately planned civilian appearances was that of a man named Specca, who spent nearly six hours in the studio painstakingly setting up seven thousand dominoes in a design that encompassed nearly the whole backstage area behind the colored curtain. The dominoes were individually laid in rows by the man, and they spelled out Johnny's full name, as captured by a wide-angle camera fixed above.

That evening, the band played softly, and everyone walked on tiptoe backstage while the domino king watched over his creation during Johnny's monologue. One wobbly domino or a slight California tremor could ruin everything. Finally, the moment came, and Carson was hesitant to "ruin" the massive undertaking by knocking over the first domino. With a little drum roll, he triggered the motion; the clicking of the tripping dominoes was heard through the silent studio as the camera followed the stream. It lasted two and a half minutes while the intricate domino highways and intersections rambled on. One section included an amazing eight rows of dominoes interweaving and falling simultaneously. The audience silently watched, everyone holding their breath. When the last domino fell, the audience erupted in applause and Carson was amazed.

Another evening, in April 1979, found the audience in stunned silence, however this time not from a stunt but from a fiery mishap. Karate expert Riche Barathy came on the show to demonstrate how he could smash blocks. He had just smashed thirteen granite blocks that were set afire with burning oil when his sleeve attracted some of the flame. Carson and others around the stage rushed to help smother his burning clothes. Barathy suffered second- and third-degree burns.

■ ■ ■

The coordinators for the civilians had vast resources, rooting out just the right people to meet face to face with Johnny and regale him with tales or demonstrate a talent. Some guests froze when they stared at Johnny for the first time in the hot seat with cameras on, red lights flickering, and an audience in mild expectation of something funny. More often than not, the civilians would steal the show, however, leaving even the most popular actor who was guesting that night sinking in the cracks of the couch.

Carson's secret at the game was his ability to become a chameleon and adjust to each guest. Johnny was informed ahead of time by the talent coordinator what each guest was like, based on a pre-interview: Were they talkative, funny, loud, obnoxious, or serious? Or maybe they would clue him in to what would set off the guest into a hilarious tirade. This would rattle around in his mind briefly before he met the civilian on the air. The guest was usually excited about the appearance and had been flown in all expenses paid, including limousines.

Johnny was keen to surmise just the

Johnny chats with the residents of Essex, California, a tiny town near the Arizona border, which was one of America's last outposts without television service in 1977. Television broadcast signals could not reach Essex because of the surrounding mountains. NBC brought almost the entire town of sixty-one residents to attend a taping of *The Tonight Show*.

proper approach with each guest. Rarely was his aim off. With kids, Johnny would slump in his chair, leaning in, like a pal ready to "play." His guard was down, so theirs

Louise Gaddis, 88, and Elsie Stahly, 87, explain to Johnny that they are the only remaining students of Danvers High School class of 1918, of Danvers, Illinois. (1988).

would fall too. And rarely did he criticize any guest, which created a comfortable aura from the start.

With the elderly, he had an ability to scan them immediately, assess their mood, figure their age and level of sarcasm, and then zoom! Carson had an uncanny ability to draw out the best in every guest. Until 1981, his oldest guest was 103-year-old Tillie Abrahamson of Van Nuys, California, who told him, "I'm three years younger than the telephone." A few years later, Mildred Holt, age 105, appeared on the show. Carson has a theory about the civilians, he told *Rolling Stone* in 1979: "I like to work with elderly people and children. I don't know why," he told reporter Timothy White, "Maybe it's the vulnerability of them. There's a charm about older people that sometimes is childlike, and I enjoy them because, first of all, they can say anything they want to, which is just great. Age gives you a leg up on what you can say, because you don't have to account to anybody. You've lived your life and earned the right to sound off. They'll say, 'Oh, well screw that,' and 'I don't like that,' and 'That's a lot of shit.' And they lay it right out."

There have been some doozies on with Johnny, like the elderly lady who played the piano and wouldn't stop long enough for him to jump into a commercial. Frank Hill was flown in from South Carolina to appear on the show. This old fella specialized in making jewelry out of quail droppings. Dressed in a hunting cap, untucked plaid shirt, and jeans, he spoke with a thick southern drawl and proudly presented Johnny with a large star-shaped pendant and told him, "I'm gonna break da mold—that's a first limited edition. It's a big droppin' for a big star."

"I don't think I've ever been so moved, if you'll excuse the expression," Johnny joked, examining the gift. "You're kind of the Cartier of caca, aren't you?"

■ ■ ■

Johnny welcomed civilian guests from every state, from every class of society. Here are a few folks you may remember.

**Fran Tate,** owner of Pepe's North of the Border, the only Mexican restaurant in Barrow, Alaska, appeared with Johnny on March 24, 1984. She was booked on the show based on an article that appeared in the *Wall Street Journal* about the hassles she encountered attempting to open a fast-food restaurant in the northern tip of Alaska, where the population at the time was three thousand and it's dark twenty-four hours a day from November through January. McDonald's turned her down.

Tate was feisty and funny, and she even brought Johnny a few Eskimo artifacts to examine. One of them, a walrus "usig," is the male sexual organ on the animal. Highly collected up there, she told Johnny. Tate presented the object, which resembled a bone, to a near-stymied Johnny, who blurted, "Someplace, there's one unhappy walrus!"

Tate spoke of the success of her independent eatery and life in northern Alaska, dealing with twenty-foot-high snowdrifts and all. Following her, actress Amy Irving was the guest. Carson reminded Irving that he heard she bathed nude in the French Riviera on a special, private platform. "What were you doing there?" he asked the actress.

"I was waiting for some walrus with a million dollars," Irving said.

Johnny gently assists his oldest guest, 105-year-old Mildred Holt, onto the stage.

One evening, the guest was potato chip collector **Myrtle Young,** who brought along some of the character-shaped munchies she preserved while working in a potato chip factory. She had one that was shaped like a dog and another that resembled a sleeping bird with its head nestled to its breast ("cute"), and she even had a chip

# The Grand Couple of *The Tonight Show*

I approached them for this interview in 1991 when I was sitting in the audience, waiting for the show that night to begin. I sent a scribbled note across the aisle and down a few rows: *Hello. My name is Steve Cox. I'm writing a book about The Tonight Show and I've heard you've been to MANY. I've heard a lot about you. May I speak with you after the show? Steve Cox. P.S. Look behind you.*

Betty and Bob stood up as if Studio One were their living room and waved with huge grins. "Sure!"

Betty and Bob Kelly were like the grand couple of *The Tonight Show.* In 1991 she was sixty-nine and he was seventy. They were both in their retirement and doing exactly what they wanted in sunny southern California. The couple attended hundreds of *Tonight Show* tapings; they were all smiles each and every time. And then they'd go home and watch the show that evening as well

Betty and Bob had seen close to eight hundred *Tonight Shows* live in Burbank. Without hesitation, they named Sammy Davis Jr. as their favorite singer on the show, "by far." They braved heat and rain and waited in line for hours like everyone else to get in. They were the first to clap during the warm-up. Carson saw them in the front row almost every night, but they never met "their Johnny."

"Some people think we're crazy, coming and standing in line," said Bob Kelly, a retired manager of a warehousing company, during an interview in 1991. He looks a bit like Bert Lahr, with a pleasant laugh to match. Betty sparks a familiar, gentle giddiness . . . sort of like Edith Bunker or Dody Goodman. "It's a different show every night. Different guests, different music," Bob professed. "If you've seen the show here, you know the music is good."

Betty's favorite segment at the time was Floyd Turbo. Bob said he couldn't decide. Some shows stand out, though. They remember one particular show from which a woman with a knife was carted away by NBC security. At the holidays NBC would lay out a buffet spread in the lobby for the audience, they said. Pictures prove they met Jay Leno tanking up one of his classic cars at the gas station across the street.

Though they never met Johnny, "One of the crew got his autograph on this picture," says Betty as she points to a color still signed to both of them. There's nothing special in the message, but it's definitely Carson's signature.

"We've always known he's a private person, so you don't go flag him down," Betty said. In a personal scrapbook, they'd assembled odds and ends from the shows: tickets, photos, autographs, articles, dates, notes, and mementos from NBC. One piece of paper is autographed by the entire *Tonight Show* band.

"There was another fellow who used to come here and we had figured out that he had seen something like twenty-five hundred shows," Bob said, "for fourteen years, he came every night! Dunno what happened to him."

Of their stops at NBC each morning to pick up tickets and their later wait in line that afternoon, they said that Michael Landon's last appearance was the most tense that they could recall. Barry Manilow and Julio Iglesias both had very vocal fan clubs that camped out in line overnight to catch appearances. And they had stumbled across some rude, impatient first-timers who jump the line; that was an occurrence they witnessed all too often. But believe it or not, they never volunteered to play "Stump the Band" because they can't sing.

"Those people are always picked ahead of time," Bob explained in 1991. "Johnny knows where they are sitting. We're a wealth of information," he laughed. Because they were routinely at the head of the line, most first-timers asked the Kellys questions. The NBC pages at the time almost counted on the couple's good-natured assistance in handling the crowds before the doors are officially opened. Once allowed in, it was "Hi Betty! Hi Bob! How's your day goin'? Oh, I brought some pictures to show you . . ." The pages were like grandchildren to them, and Betty occasionally baked cookies for them and brought them in.

When they turned on Carson following the news some evenings, they saw themselves once in a while, but they were not particularly

Californians Betty and Bob Kelly, regulars at NBC, attended nearly eight hundred show tapings, including Carson's last. They've seen Jay, but they remain loyal to Johnny, they say.

excited about that. Watching *The Tonight Show* taped was a life they found enjoyable and relaxing. They said they knew entertainment, "so why pay tickets to see concerts when it's free most every week?" Bob asked.

Although they never had a tête-a-tête with Johnny, the Kellys were lucky enough to get tickets for his final show, a hot pair of tickets in Hollywood that night.

Alaskan Fran Tate shows Johnny a walrus usig. "Let's just say every male walrus has one," she explained. (1984)

of Yogi Bear. Of course, Johnny noticed Yogi's head had been glued. "Yes, I broke his neck," Young said.

Young looked a lot like Edith Bunker from *All in the Family,* and she had Edith's laugh as well. (Wouldn't that have been the perfect plot for an episode—"Edith Goes on *The Tonight Show*"?) Young displayed her tray of fragile chips and gently held them up for the camera to get a close-up. When Ed McMahon diverted her attention for a moment, Johnny reached for a chip from a bowl behind his desk that had been hidden from view and loudly chomped it, scaring his guest. As Young looked at him with a horrified expression, Johnny said, "oh . . . no, no" and held up his fresh bowl of chips. Laughing almost uncontrollably, Carson nearly spit out the chip he had in his mouth. It was as if her reaction to his little trick was even better than he had hoped.

Johnny introduced four-year-old spelling champion **Rohan Varavadekar,** of Houston, Texas. The bespectacled little boy, dressed in a bright blue warm-up suit, was there as a kid—no little suit and tie for this guy. You could tell he was all boy, uninhibited, puckish, well mannered around adults. This captured Johnny's heart, especially when it became obvious the little guy had done his homework on Johnny.

"When . . . when I read a book about you and you were thirteen, you used to do magic tricks," he said to Johnny. "Can you show me some?"

Johnny smiled and obliged. He reached into his pocket for a coin and made it vanish in his hands, and then he pulled the quarter out of little Rohan's left ear. It was like an uncle and a nephew at a Sunday afternoon family get-together, and the audience cheered right along. Johnny even offered to show him how the magic was done, after the show.

"How do you really make it disappear?" the boy asked.

"You get married," Johnny answered.

Four-year-old spelling champion Rohan Varavadekar of Houston, Texas, captured Carson's heart in March 1987. Johnny asked the bespectacled little Rohan his favorite words and the youngster responded by spelling such words as "inextinguishable," "abbreviate," and "biochemistry." Rohan mentioned that he was celebrating his fifth birthday the next day and asked Johnny if he could come to his party at Disneyland.

A spirited **Minnie Black,** from Kentucky, was invited on the show to tell Johnny about her collection of gourds. Johnny noticed she brought along her own drink to quench her thirst on the show; he inquired innocently about the beverage.

"I had to bring a little something along to help me with my congestion," she said. "You want to see what that is?"

Johnny smelled the tip of the coffee mug and puckered, then looked away over toward the band. The audience was roaring.

"This is booze!" he said. "Do you brew that yourself in Kentucky?"

"Now listen . . . Kentucky is known for their good bourbon . . . but I take that for medical purposes."

"How often do you get that congestion?" Johnny asked.

In 1985, the self-appointed International Queen of the Polka, **Vlosta Kersik,** sent Johnny a color snapshot of herself playing the accordion atop a cow in the middle of a pasture. "Now this is my kind of guest," Carson laughed, holding up the snapshot for the camera.

Kersik had written polkas for Pope John Paul II and Ronald Reagan, she said. She wanted her chance to serenade Johnny on the show, so she was invited. When the talent coordinators booked Vlosta's flight, they probably had no idea how funny this segment was going to turn out.

Kersik, an outspoken, witty, buxom redhead, appeared on the show in an elaborate, homemade, wildly exotic dress. She spoke with an accent, possibly Polish, and told Johnny how she tests out her new tunes on her husband. "I wait when my husband takes a bath," she says. "Then I'll take my accordion, sit on the toilet seat, Johnny . . . Honest! Honest!" By that time, the audience, and Carson, were laughing so hard, the rest of her sentence was lost. Later, she took center stage with her electronic accordion and sang her ditty, "Johnny, Johnny, Come an' Dance wit' Me," which was really a pretty catchy tune. It had Johnny bouncing.

Johnny Carson returned from a commercial and said, "As I mentioned earlier, this lady performed one of the most famous classic roles in movie history. She was Walt Disney's Snow White—will you welcome **Adriana Caselotti**."

Caselotti, a trim and young-looking bubbly Italian woman in her seventies, was more animated than her Disney counterpart and a little bit daffy. She made the perfect guest. It was the occasion of Disney's sixth reissue of the classic animated film to theaters, and Caselotti was more than thrilled to appear on *The Tonight Show.*

During the interview, Johnny naturally asked Caselotti if she ever found her real Prince Charming. Caselotti answered by telling what seemed like her life story, all about dating a foot doctor, Dana Costigen, when she was very young. She left Costigen, married another man, and divorced. Then she married Norville Mitchell, remained married for twenty years "and he died, unfortunately." The she called the foot doctor, married him soon after, "then he died."

"You don't think that after hearing this on national television anybody else is gonna marry you, do you?" Johnny asked. "That's like saying, 'Good-bye Charlie!'"

It was all in fun and Caselotti knew it. She wanted to sing for Johnny, so she sang a bit of Snow White's voice, a bit of the movie's famous lyrics, and then segued into an impromptu version of "Oh Johnny" which had the band joining in and the audience clapping.

After the song was over, Johnny asked, "Is that what killed the last two husbands?"

**Bertie McKay,** 103 years old, stepped out slowly from the curtain and automatically lifted her elbow to give Johnny the signal that she needed assistance. Incredibly agile at her age, she walked past Johnny's desk and made a beeline to kiss Ed McMahon and compliment him as the host of television's *Star Search*, one of her favorite shows. She gawked and fawned over Ed. "I look at ya every Sunday," McKay professed to Ed, nearly ignoring Johnny. "Ever' Sunday . . . I just love your program." Of course, by now, Johnny was sullen and the audience was laughing.

Into the interview, Johnny said, "You have a sister, I'm told."

"Yes," McKay replied, "she's dead. I'm sure she's dead. I had her cremated."

On the eve of Valentine's Day in 1991, Johnny welcomed an old gentleman named **CF Corzine,** from Illinois, to talk about his unusual annual ritual. Corzine was seventy-

Enjoy true-to-life Color from RCA Victor with
Solid Copper Circuit dependability

Most true-to-life color . . . so natural and sharp you'll compare it to color motion pictures. And the High Fidelity tube gives you the brightest pictures ever from RCA Victor.

Dependable RCA Solid Copper Circuits replace old-fashioned "hand wiring"—eliminate over 200 possible trouble spots. This means fewer service headaches, greater reliability.

Specially designed circuitry of this kind is used in space satellites. More TV servicemen own RCA Victor Color TV than all other leading makes combined.

RCA pioneered and perfected Color TV . . . is the world's most experienced maker of color sets. More people own RCA Victor Color TV than all other brands combined. See why—at your dealer's now!

RCA SOLID COPPER CIRCUITS REPLACE OLD-FASHIONED "HAND WIRING" FOR GREATER DEPENDABILITY, BETTER TV PERFORMANCE.

"Brought to You in Living Color": Johnny Carson's burst into nighttime television paralleled the gradual bloom of color broadcasting throughout the decade. By 1968, color had replaced black and white television in the United States.

In a rare motion picture appearance he'd probably rather forget, Johnny played himself opposite star Connie Francis in the light comedy *Looking for Love* (1964). *Below,* With guests Harry Belafonte, daughter Shari Belafonte, and Charles Nelson Reilly. Frenetic and sardonic, Reilly was a popular guest who relayed hilarious stories that usually concerned him getting into various catastrophes.

*Left,* The flashy, multi-colored curtain draped open on a larger, more impressive stage on May 1, 1972, from the new home base in Burbank, California, and became a trademark for Carson's *Tonight Show. Below,* These are among the earliest "More to Come" artwork bumpers shown before and after commercial breaks, circa 1960s. (Courtesy of Art Trugman/ NBC).

WE'RE JUST GETTING WARMED UP

MORE TO COME

Johnny Carson was the cutting edge in wardrobe for middle-aged American males. His sporty attire reflected the best in changing fashions, a trend he parlayed into a successful, upscale apparel line. This vintage ad, plucked from the mid-1970s, featured suits made of dacron polyester, complete with the giant wing lapels. *Below,* Johnny interacts with members of the audience during a "Stump the Band" segment.

Carson was attuned to comedian David Letterman's style because it had a midwestern feel, akin to his own, and the young protégé became a favored guest and substitute host on *The Tonight Show. Opposite Page,* NBC celebrated its sixtieth anniversary with a nostalgic special in 1986, described as a "panorama of radio and television heritage." For the first time, four of the network's late-night living legends gathered: (front) Jerry Lester, Jack Paar, (back) Steve Allen, Johnny Carson.

A "More to Come" Exhibit: Carson's *Tonight Show* became a nightly art exhibit featuring distinctive images as "bumpers" before and after commercial breaks. Viewers were treated to a bevy of creations from many artists who worked at NBC over the decades, including: Art Trugman, Dave Rose, Rick Andreoli, Joe Meserly, Carolyn Collins-Hughes, Bill Davis, Susan Cuscuna, Leo Duranona, and Don Locke (shown here at his drawing desk in 1992).

The decades flew by and so did the endless parade of visitors. Nights with the old classics, like Jimmy Stewart (shown below), usually made for charming moments. *Opposite page, Doc Severinsen, Johnny Carson, and Ed McMahon make history with knowing grins.*

Like a Virgin: Madonna's first talk show appearance with Johnny in June of 1987. *Below,* Johnny and Bob Newhart—pals outside the studio—always found something to stammer about during Newhart's fifty appearances between 1970 and 1992.

*Left,* Kids usually opened up around Johnny, like young actress Drew Barrymore. *Below,* Veteran radio comedy team Bob & Ray (Bob Elliott, in the chair, and Ray Goulding) made many appearances over the years with their sublimely witty interview routines.

*Above,* Carson carefully cuddles a baby kangaroo, well aware of the marsupial's powerful hind legs. *Right,* Johnny makes a rare appearance on the other side of the desk when he is interviewed on *Late Night with David Letterman.*

*Above,* Singer Grace Jones appeared four times in the mid-1980s. *Left,* Joey Bishop dusted off the mandolin on the show in 1985. *Below,* Boxing champ James "Buster" Douglas sat with Johnny just days after grabbing the heavyweight title in 1990.

At an NBC affiliates convention in 1991, Johnny Carson surprised everyone by announcing his retirement in the next year. What immediately followed was an unrelenting onslaught of media coverage the likes of which no television performer had seen before. *Right,* Two tickets to paradise: Carson's final two shows, Thursday, May 21, and Friday, May 22, 1992, will remain some of television's finest moments.

seven at the time and resembled a thinner Santa Claus (he'd played Santa for many years during the holidays). He was brought to the attention of Carson by a St. Louis television reporter, John Pertzborn.

For forty years, Corzine had sent the exact same 25-cent Valentine card to his wife, retrieving it and resending it every February. Naturally, Johnny asked the obvious question: Why?

"I wanted to get my money's worth," Corzine said.

He brought along the simple card, which had no special meaning attached, he said. It had been canceled and tattered by the post office for so long, the address wasn't readable. Corzine admitted his wife had been so sick of the card that she attempted to trash it a few times, but he kept hiding it and presenting it to her again and again.

Maybe the funniest part of the show involved his name. When Johnny tried to guess what CF was short for, Corzine explained that CF stood for nothing. When CF was a teenager and attempted to enlist in the army, the officers said they had to put something on the forms, so it was officially registered: "C-only F-only." For years he was called "Cone-ly Fone-ly," and he said he still, to that day, received mail addressed like that.

The segment went very well and ran overtime, bumping another scheduled guest. "Being on the show didn't make me nervous until after it was over with," Corzine said. "After we got back to our hotel suite, Mr. Carson had sent to me an enormous bouquet of roses, and the card said, 'For a gold performance.' Wasn't that sweet?"

St. Louis barber **Bill Black** was scheduled to show Johnny items from his unusual hobby—objects made from human hair—however, time ran out and Black became one of the

Johnny sent this inscribed picture to CF Corzine following the old-timer's endearing visit to *The Tonight Show* in February 1991. Corzine, a gentle midwesterner who had just initials for a first name, explained to Johnny why he resent the same Valentine's Day card to his wife every year for forty years. A year after the show, Corzine died, and according to his family, his *Tonight Show* experience was a treasured moment in his life.

# The Best of Floyd R. Turbo ("Mr. Silent Majority")

He's been described as "the liberals' foe whose effectiveness as a conservative spokesman is impaired only by his inability to read the TelePrompTer faster than an IRS form." The heavily opinionated Turbo, always decked in plaid hunting garb, stands nervously delivering his mouthful of editorial message, all the while shifting his weight like a little boy who can't find the rest room. He's mangled all the topics: gun control, war, women's lib, hunting ("If God didn't want us to hunt, He wouldn't have given us plaid shirts; I only kill in self-defense—what would you do if a rabbit pulled a knife on you?") He's the Emily Litella of weeknight television ("Never mind!") crossed with pseudo-newscaster Ted Baxter delivering a home-made editorial. His sentences are riddled with syntax errors. He's Mr. Malaprop himself.

Turbo has been compared to Archie Bunker on many occasions. Johnny Carson, a professed fan of Norman Lear's TV classic *All in the Family,* might possibly have fashioned the blowhard Turbo after witnessing Bunker's televised opposition to gun-control.

One 1972 *All in the Family* episode ("Archie and the Editorial") had Archie delivering an editorial comment on local television, provoked by a gun-control editorial he saw on television. According to Bunker, guns don't kill—people do. A popular thought. And in Bunker's wisdom, how do you stop people from killing people? "Bring back the death penalty!"

In his twisted rationale, Archie Bunker nervously offers his opinions, which actually reinforce the gun-control issue: "Now I wanna talk about another thing that's on everybody's mind . . . and that's the stickups and your skyjackers here . . . which if it was up to me, I could end the skyjackers tomorrow. All ya gotta do is arm all your passengers. . . ." Later in the day, Archie and family adjourn to Kelsey's Bar, where a man who had seen him on television asks to shake his hand—and then holds him up at gunpoint.

Ten years later, Carson told *TV Guide*: "Turbo . . . takes the redneck view of something. What you're doing is showing the stupidity of that particular view so that you can make your point comedically. If he's for handguns and wants everybody to arm themselves, it's obvious to anybody who's watching, the point we're trying to make," he says.

Of Turbo, Carson told *Rolling Stone* reporter Timothy White: ". . . he's the epitome of the redneck ignoramus. I find things each week when I go out to do it that I throw in: his gestures at the wrong time, his not knowing where he's supposed to be, his feeble attempts at humor, his talks about things he doesn't quite understand."

And now . . . a taste of Turbo.

## Turbo on Nuclear Reactors

Put me down as one American who favors building nuclear plants. I say nuclear plants are safe. Each and every one of us must get into the fight to have DDT. It worked so well that now we don't have to use it anymore because it's working everywhere, in the rivers, in our food, and in our lungs. And what's all this fuss about plutonium: How can something named after a Disney character be dangerous? So what if an atomic plant blows up? The people who say that, they are afraid to die. I'm not afraid to die because all my life I have lived by the good book, the American Legion magazine. They say if there is a leak in a nuclear power plant the radiation can kill you. Nix! Radiation cannot kill you because it contains absolutely no cholesterol. They say atomic radiation can hurt your reproductive organs. My answer is, so can a hockey stick . . . but we don't stop building them. I told my wife that there was a chance that radiation might hurt my reproductive organs, but she said in her opinion it is a small price to pay. Let us assume for the sake of argument that there is an atomic explosion, just for the fun of it. It would have very little bad effect, especially here in Los Angeles where we are shielded by a protective layer of smog.

Sure, nuclear leaks will affect the forest animals. So what if a deer grows up with two rear ends? They're easier to shoot, and that's what America is all about. What do they expect us to use for fuel—buffalo chips? Now, these jerks want to use solar energy for electricity. Doesn't that take the cake? How do they expect me to plug my drill into the sun? I'd need a very big stepladder. . . . Some people are even talking about wind power. Phooey! Who wants windmills on their house? Next thing you know we'll be wearing wooden Dutch shoes and sucking cheese all day. So in my simple way, I'm asking that you support nuclear energy. Remember, being an American means being powerful, proud, and pushy, and in conclusion let me finish by ending. . . . Thank you.

## Turbo on the Draft

Recently this effeminate station gave off with an editorial against the draft. But as usual, they showed you only the front of the question. I am here to give you a good look at the behind.

They say drafting people into the army is undemocratic, un-American, and unproductive. My answer to that is, "Oh yeah?" But that is not my only reason. I believe that everybody should have the opportunity to serve this country and be ready to kill at the drop of a hat. I happen to be proud of my war injury. I have some shrapnel in my brain. Luckily, it landed in the part I do not use.

The draft is good for the country. It will not only help the unemployment situation, but it'll take crime off the streets and put it in the army where it belongs. Being drafted by the service is educational. It'll give you a great opportunity to learn all the words to the national anthem. If it wasn't for the draft, who'd fight the wars? I can't do it alone. Answer me that.

War promotes brotherhood. You learn to aim an M-1 rifle at those of a different race, creed, or color. Some people say the army is too strict. To that I say, "What do you put on a shingle?"

This station wants no draft. They want to deprive a boy of the army. The army is educational. The army teaches you how to do dental work—with the butt of a rifle. Also the army teaches you how to learn killing as a trade—which many people say is the coming thing. The army provides you with medical care, and even gives you free checkups to make sure you have not caught a romantic disease. You get to see army training films, all about bad ladies. These films are in glorious orange. And for protection, they put stuff in your food so that you will not get sexually excited and attack your duffel bag. The army makes a man out of you and prepares you for later life. They teach you how to crawl on your belly, which comes in handy when you're looking for a job in the private sector. The army is a good career. Our army has produced fine men such as General George C. Scott. I, Floyd R. Turbo, learned a lot in the army. It was a great experience, except for the bed wetter who slept in the top bunk.

The army taught me survival. I was in the Pacific. I learned how to survive in the jungle. I learned, for example, how to tell what time it is by making a sundial out of a dead person. I learned how to make beer out of bird droppings and also how to make a rubber girl out of an inner tube.

In conclusion, to sum it all up in a nutshell, I say we should not end the draft. We should increase it. We have a moral obligation to give Bob Hope soldiers to entertain. Fellow Americans, it is an honor to be drafted and to serve your country. Thank you, bye-bye, and buy bonds.

"bumped" guests in 1991. He stayed over to appear the next night, but Jay Leno was mysteriously called in to guest host.

"I was told there had been some death threats to Carson," Black said in 1991. "They had special agents and a lot of security backstage, I noticed. I took a picture of my name on my dressing room door, and Security came running over to me when they saw the flash. They wanted to take my camera away."

Black appeared that second night and showed Leno his items, although he was disappointed that he didn't get to meet Carson. Black wore his necktie made of human hair, the tassels on his shoes were of hair, and he brought a vest that could be worn. Black even wore his hairpiece.

"You don't make underwear, do you?" Leno asked.

Quadruplets **Allison, Brooke, Claire, and Darcy Hansen**—all sixteen years old—filed out from behind the curtain and sat on the couch one night in 1991. The beautiful girls, all very similar in appearance and wearing flowery sundresses of matching material, were flown in from San Antonio, Texas. Of course there were the typical "Do-you-fool-your-friends?" questions, and then came the payoff.

"Somebody told me you have sort of a strange relationship with *The Tonight Show,*" Johnny said.

Answering in unison, they finally deferred to one sister. "We understand that we were conceived while our parents were watching *The Tonight Show,*" she said as the audience laughed. "During the monologue."

Charles Galioto, of New York, illustrates how he topped the Guinness World Record for coin-catching. He carefully placed seventy coins on his forearm and snatched them in mid-air with Johnny and the cameras watching closely. (1976)

"That bad, huh?" Johnny said. "Did your parents remember anything about the show?"

Another sister answered, "Tommy Newsom was leading the orchestra that night."

"Yeah, Tom has that problem," Johnny said. "When he's on, people often leave and go into another room."

"I think this is the first time we've had a toilet trespasser on the show," Johnny said, introducing **Denise Welles** in 1991.

Welles had attended a George Strait concert at a Texas arena when she noticed the women's rest room had a thirty-foot-long line at the entrance; Welles couldn't wait and entered the nearly vacant men's room. "So I just went in," she said. "There were probably six or eight gentlemen in there."

"What was their reaction when you walked in?" Carson asked.

"They all had their backs to me . . . I don't know," she said, as the audience erupted in laughter.

A police officer in the men's room caught her and reminded her of the city ordinance forbidding any entrance "in a manner to cause a disturbance." She was arrested. Her plea was necessity, she claimed. "I wasn't window-shopping."

"I think the correct term is comparison shopping," Johnny said.

Welles's turmoil did not stop at the arena. After she was kicked out of the concert, her picture and an accompanying story were run on the front page of the *Houston Post*. Morning radio shows poked fun at the story on the air. At work the next day, she says, her coworkers put a sign on the men's room: *Men and Denise Only.*

# A Few More Civilians . . .

On the show one evening were Helen and Frank Beardsley, parents of twenty children. Johnny asked, "How do you manage, having twenty children?" Mrs. Beardsley replied, "I'm doing what I enjoy most . . . I guess I was just made for it."

The audience, and Carson, broke up. After they left, Johnny said, "I only have three children, I don't know how they do it."

Someone in the audience yelled, "Oh yes you do!"

■ ■ ■

A female pretzel baker was on *The Tonight Show* demonstrating to the host the precise method of looping the strands of dough into the common pretzel shape. Carson attempted to twist the dough, but it didn't work. The lady gave him another strip of dough, saying, "Here, try this piece. I don't think yours is long enough." The audience roared at the unintentional double entendre.

He quipped, "Yes, I think I've heard that before."

■ ■ ■

A butterfly collector was a guest on the show one night. The fellow showed some frames to Johnny that displayed the colorful butterflies under glass. Johnny asked, "How do you mount a butterfly? It must be very difficult."

■ ■ ■

It was Beauty and the Beast one evening when Johnny had five Miss America contestants, among other guests, on the show. After the monologue, he said: ". . . and on our show tonight, we have five Miss America contestants, and also some dogs [audience roared] . . . I mean real dogs [more laughs] . . . come on now, you know I mean dogs that bark!"

Stand-up comic Louie Anderson blew Carson away during his *Tonight Show* debut in 1984.

# 6

# A COMIC'S DREAM

## BY JOE RHODES

Louie Anderson heard his name and knew it was time to move toward the light. There was no more time to worry, no more time to dream. There was only time to straighten his tie and swallow hard, to catch a glimpse of the stagehand who was holding the gray curtain open, who was gesturing for him to go ahead.

He walked through the curtain, looked briefly to his right, and smiled at the scene that was just as he'd always hoped it would be. There was Johnny Carson, behind his famous desk, in front of his famous Hollywood backdrop, smiling and clapping his hands. Robert Blake, dressed in black and fingering an unlit cigarette, was in the guest's chair. And yes, on the sofa, there was Ed McMahon, clapping along.

Louie Anderson found his mark, two pieces of green tape stuck to the floor in the shape of a *T*, and positioned himself in front of the camera. To his left, Doc Severinsen was giving the signal to end the music, the generic brassy music they use for every new comedian. This time, though, the music sounded different to Louie Anderson. This time the music was for him.

"I could work the rest of my life touring in clubs, and tomorrow night more people will see me than in all those clubs put together," Louie had said the day before. "This is what every comic dreams of. It changes everything because for the rest of your life, wherever you go, they say 'As seen on *The Tonight Show*.'

"Not many people get a chance like this—one night that can change their whole life."

■ ■ ■

The amateurs were everywhere, tables full of people who thought they were funny, waiting for their shot at making strangers laugh.

It was another take-your-chances Monday night at the Comedy Store, the legendary comedians' proving ground on Hollywood's Sunset Boulevard. Monday is open-microphone night, which means anyone who wants to make a fool of himself in public need only take a number and wait in line.

Most of the applicants were crowded in a back corner, a huddled mass of wretched comedy refuse, laughing at one another's jokes, the only ones laughing in the room. Some of it was painful to watch, the feeble attempts at being funny.

They would go to the stage, one after another, always moving too fast, always fumbling with the mike, trying to get one laugh before their three minutes expired. One guy showed up with a two-by-four and said things like "I found this at a board meeting." One was doing Mary Jo Kopechne jokes. Another simply froze and uttered not a single intelligible word. He just stood there muttering, waiting for the light to shine on Eddie Cantor's portrait, the sign that his time was up.

It was an endless parade of half-wits and loudmouths, guys who thought they could get laughs just by saying dirty words and making faces. If, by some incredible accident, one of them uttered a line that was even remotely humorous, the crowd would go crazy. Mercy laughs.

But mixed among the pitiful amateurs, there are always a few people who know what they're doing, young comics who have come from other places, ready to take their shot at the big time. If you're going to make it as a comedian, this is where you have to start, taking a number and standing in line on Monday night at the Comedy Store.

That's what Louie Anderson did. He came to L.A. in September 1982, four years after he had taken a dare and gone onstage at a comedy club in Minneapolis, a cramped working-class bar called Mickey Finn's. He was a social worker at the time, a kid who'd grown up dirt-poor in a St. Paul housing project.

Louie was funny and he knew it, a 350-pound guy who could make fun of himself and everything around him. He was a hit the first time he took the microphone, and it wasn't long before he left social work behind. Deep down, he says, a comedian is what he'd always wanted to be.

After accomplishing all he could in Minneapolis, he took off for California. He planned to stay a year, and then, if he hadn't gotten on *The Tonight Show,* he'd go back to Minnesota. A year passed. He didn't get on. He stayed anyway.

He'd become a paid regular at the Comedy Store in February 1983, only six months after his arrival. He'd even gotten an early audition for Jim McCawley, the *Tonight Show*'s talent coordinator. But McCawley turned him down, said he wasn't ready. Louie swore he'd never audition for the show again.

"I was devastated," he said. "I'd been rejected, and I took it very personally. I'm immature. I think comics are immature people."

A few months later, abandoning his promise, Louie auditioned again. And he was turned down again. By then, though, he was getting plenty of work in comedy clubs on the West Coast and working as an opening act in Las Vegas for artists such as Neil Sedaka and Connie Stevens. So he stuck it out.

Finally, McCawley came through. He called Louie back for one more audition in mid-November and decided he was good enough.

"You're gonna get your show," he told him. "We'll do it in the next three or four weeks unless someone cancels."

The Friday after the conversation, Louie's phone rang. It was McCawley.

"You're doing it Tuesday," he said. "This Tuesday."

Louie calmly went over the specifics. He'd have seven minutes and would go on after Robert Blake. Fine, he said to McCawley, thank you very much. He then proceeded to call every human being he could think of.

"I don't care if I haven't talked to you in three years," he said to one long-distance friend. "Watch the show."

# Little to None

If you had to name just three of Johnny Carson's mannerisms, you could do it. Over the years, his little idiosyncrasies, quirks, and trademarks became so intimately familiar to the viewing audience that anyone could be identified silently mocking Johnny by a mere hand gesture. This characteristic shtick mounted over the years. Merv Griffin, guesting with Carson once, said that impressionist Rich Little counted twenty-eight Carson "tics."

"He came out once and did a whole bunch of things, and I watched it and went crazy," Carson responded. It was somewhat unsettling when someone "did" Johnny in his presence. Jimmy Stewart felt odd about the same experience. But with the amount of television exposure Carson had built up over the decades, imitations were inevitable.

Rich Little confirms the number. And as Johnny said, he did perform his Carson shtick right in front of him, on The *Tonight Show,* and it broke up the host. "He has an awful lot of mannerisms, and I use them when I imitate him," Little says of his night-club act, which includes Carnacs and come-backs. "It gets a great reaction. I did my impression of him on his show all the time. He used to laugh. He seemed to like it. We had a great rapport there, and then suddenly it stopped."

Carson may feel that imitation is not a form of flattery, but rather mockery. Many comics and actors have "done" competent impressions of Johnny: John Byner, John Roarke, Dana Carvey, Kevin Spacey. Even Howard Stern's *Tonight Show* parodies on his television show in the early 1990s were funny. Whether Carson has expressed displeasure with these portrayals is not known; Carson's no stranger to the impression game, either. Johnny has imitated Jackie Gleason, Jimmy Cagney, and many others during his conversations with guests. His own highly accurate and amusing spoof of Ronald Reagan was actually praised by the former president. Demonstrating his famous

Rich Little's impression of Carson was dead on, so much so that it actually made Johnny a little uneasy. Despite that, Little appeared on *The Tonight Show* more than twenty times. Years later, the master impressionist actually portrayed Johnny in a riveting TV movie, *The Late Shift,* which dramatized the behind-the-scenes battle between David Letterman and Jay Leno to become Carson's successor.

"You are correct, sir!" Phil Hartman and Dana Carvey spoofed Ed and Johnny in a popular recurring *Saturday Night Live* sketch. (Courtesy of NBC)

sense of humor, Reagan inscribed a picture of Carson as the president and presented it to Johnny as a gag.

Rich Little, one of the first to get a near-perfect handle on the Carson mannerisms and distill them into an act, has run into Carson socially ("and he's always friendly, and smiley and polite," Little says), but the impressionist remains mystified over his status as a "no book," which he feels was stamped on him years ago. Little said in 1991: "People think I still do the Carson show, but it's been a long time. We had a falling out, and I really don't know the reason. It just stopped. They say they don't book impersonators on the show anymore."

Little guest-hosted the show for Carson about a dozen times and says the exposure was terrific for his career. Little invited some of his favorites on the show, like Jimmy Stewart and Jack Benny, and, of course, matched voices and wits.

Little didn't mince words when interviewed a year before Carson's retirement: "I think as soon as Johnny leaves, hopefully, I will get back on the show," he says. "Until that group, you know, Freddie de Cordova and all, [goes] I don't think I'll get on at all. I *know* I won't. I'll be glad when he's gone."

Reminded that there's a rumor about a "little blacklist" looming over the talent coordinators, Little confirmed its existence and added, "Oh it's quite a big list."

Perhaps Rich Little took his perceived ban from the show personally, which is understandable. But the era of the impressionists came and went. Who knows if there will be a renaissance? During the '60s and '70s, Rich Little edged out much of his competition and became the most versatile impressionist around. Although extremely talented impressionists like Frank Gorshin, Jack Carter, and Larry Storch were working, they never quite grabbed as much exposure as Little. But then a whole new crowd of standup comics converged on America, funneling through the comedy clubs; it seemed that half of the performers did impressions in their set. It was the extremely versatile

Comedian John Byner performed a parody of "Carnac" on his syndicated comedy show, *Bizarre.*

ones who stood out, Martin Short, Dana Carvey, Phil Hartman, and many others from the various casts of *Saturday Night Live.* As the decades passed, the use for a performer who was solely an "impressionist" nearly vanished, or at least, was redirected, and the comedy club circuit changed also. As on *Saturday Night Live* itself, it was no longer enough to merely impersonate a famous face or voice. The joke was in what the performer *did* with his impression. Today, very few comics base their act solely on imitations, and there are fewer who are talented enough to have that option. It attests to just how much of a unique commodity Rich Little actually became.

He had spent the weekend honing his act, working on the lines McCawley had liked, taping his club performances and playing them back against a stopwatch.

And now it was Monday night, the night before the big show, and he was in the midst of all the amateurs so he could try out his *Tonight Show* set for one last audience. A final dry run.

While he was waiting to go on, every comic in the back hallway was asking questions and giving advice. "Is Johnny gonna be there?" they wanted to know. "Do you get to sit down?" "What are you gonna wear?"

He was loving every second of it, basking in the glory, hamming it up, trying to pretend he wasn't nervous and doing an awful job.

"Do you think I need a haircut?" he asked. It was 11:00 PM. "If you don't feel good about your hair, it makes a difference. I better get one tonight. If I can find the woman who cuts it for me, will you drive me over there? Great."

He did his set twice that night, the same jokes in the same order that he would do them for Carson and 18 million viewers in less than twenty-four hours.

"Sorry, I can't stay long," he said as he walked onstage "but I'm in between meals."

Small laughs. Very small. He was hurrying too much, rushing the punch lines, forgetting jokes. The lines were good, but his delivery wasn't. What should have been a seven-minute routine clocked in at under five.

"I went shopping today," he said. "What's this one-size-fits-all stuff?"

"Terrible crowd," he said, walking backstage.

He decided it was too late for the haircut and instead ending up going to Cantor's Delicatessen, a comedian's hangout.

"What time is it?" he asked after he'd ordered a Reuben sandwich.

"Twelve-fifteen," he was told.

"I'm gonna be on *The Tonight Show* tonight."

■ ■ ■

Louie lived in a one-bedroom apartment in North Hollywood, a town that is separated from the real Hollywood by hills, canyons, and money. There is no glamour in North Hollywood. It is an ugly sprawling mass of prefab apartment buildings, construction-supply warehouses, and fast-food restaurants.

But it's cheap and it's convenient. A working comic's dream.

Louie's apartment—the walls covered in greenish drywall, the bathroom cabinets stuffed with hotel towels—was crowded with comedy paraphernalia. There were old movie posters, ventriloquist dummies, a shelf full of props. The desk in the living room was covered with eight-by-ten promo shots of Louie, the paneling above the kitchen decorated with pictures of him arm in arm with assorted celebrities—Henny Youngman, Robin Williams, Mr. T, and Ray Charles.

"That's a good one," Louie says. "He thought it was Gleason."

# A Comedy Tonight!

It's a depressing thought, but most of Johnny's 1960s *Tonight Show* tapes were wiped clean or reused, never to be viewed again. All of those hours are gone, the comedy, the music, the banter, banished from existence. What a vast and wonderful collection of vintage entertainment that could have been, and to taste some of those classic moments on television now would make them even sweeter. Gone is all that footage of the late greats who made their debuts or appeared in their masterful prime.

Granted, things are spicier these days; tastes have changed drastically in recent decades. Dick Cavett, who began as a writer on *The Tonight Show* during the Jack Paar years, went on to write for, appear with, and later guest host for Johnny Carson. The days and nights were so different then. While substituting for Johnny, he kidded the audience one night and mentioned a rumor that Carson was out with "Portnoy's complaint," and not the flu. He was bleeped. Later in the show, the more blatant reference—the actual word, *diarrhea*—was mentioned, and it too was bleeped.

Johnny knew how to maneuver with his comedy. Verbal guffaws and innuendos were his specialty, intentional or not. One night, during the monologue, an audience member asked if his wife was in attendance. "No, she only comes on anniversaries," he replied with utter innocence. The audience convulsed, while the host blushed. How about when Carnac the Magnificent accidentally knocked the cup of water all over his crotch? "My God, I've been cold-cocked," Johnny joked. That last word was bleeped. That wouldn't happen today.

Cable television not only introduced variety, it deeply widened the scope of what society considers "acceptable" on television much farther than anticipated. Carson witnessed an evolution in American comedy, right there in front of his eyes, and he may even have molded some of the changes.

During his years on *Tonight,* Johnny saw the styles and trends in stand-up comedy expand immeasurably. But one thing remained a constant: *The Tonight Show Starring Johnny Carson* was by far the best launching pad for a career in comedy. Even today, nothing compares.

"He was my major break in show business," says comedienne Roseanne. "Oh absolutely. I did the show, and there were all these managers waiting backstage to talk to me. I thought this was par for the course, but I found out later that it was pretty unusual. It had all been set up by *The Tonight Show.* I guess someone there knew that I might make a big splash, which I did. The next day, I had enough work that I could move out of Denver and my [then] husband could quit his postal service job."

Drew Carey, a virtual unknown at the time, hit a homer when he made his debut with Johnny and "within weeks," said the Cleveland-born stand-up comic, "I was turning down offers I would have crawled across broken glass to get before that appearance.

"Friends who were there told me Carson was laughing so hard that he had to hold onto his desk so he wouldn't fall out of his chair," Carey told writer Rick Sherwood in the *Hollywood Reporter.* "He called me over at the end of the set and sat me down and kept me there the whole show. You just can't imagine how that felt. It was like having the Pope bless you."

After Carey's appearance, the star-making machine took over and now, ten years later, he's in his fifth season starring in his own situation comedy, with a contract for several more seasons. The list of names whose careers have been pushed or even launched by appearances on *The Tonight Show* is impressive: Bill Cosby, David Letterman, Alan King, Steve Martin, Jim Carrey, Roseanne, Phyllis Diller, Robert Klein, Steven Wright, Jerry Seinfeld, Eddie Murphy, Richard Lewis, Bill Maher, Bob Newhart, Richard Pryor, Woody Allen, Jay Leno, Tim Allen, Gabe Kaplan.

Johnny, a keen student of comedy, knew what American audiences would enjoy as the climate changed over the years. As for the comedy minds who got their shot, he changed the lives of many of them, and with the velocity of a seasoned magician he made their dreams come true. Take David Brenner. The comedian insists he had to borrow cash to buy a three-piece suit (with the wide-open collars, remember?) for his *Tonight Show* debut in the 1970s. By the next day, his agent had him locked into $10,000 in bookings. Things just went well when you were with Johnny. On Roseanne's debut, Johnny predicted she'd be a big star. Bang! Zoom!

Recalls Whoopi Goldberg: "The first time I was scheduled to go on, I was nervous as a tick. Before we went on the air, I met Johnny, which made me more nervous. But he was so smart, he sensed something was up. Looking at me, he said, 'Whoopi, are you nervous?' I could barely get the words out. 'Yes . . . I am,' I told him. He answered, 'Don't be, because you'll be just fine.' The way he said that did calm me down. Everything turned out, as he said, just fine."

*Top,* Flip Wilson on *The Tonight Show* in 1976. *Center,* Accountant turned comedian Bob Newhart, performing one of his famous telephone routines on *The Tonight Show* in 1965. *Bottom,* Before hosting his own talk show, Dick Cavett wrote comedy for Jack Paar. He later wrote for Johnny Carson, and he eventually performed his own material on *The Tonight Show* (1966).

But Louie did most of his work from his bed. He had surrounded himself with everything he needed: telephone, answering machines, tape recorders, bookshelves. He stayed in there for hours at a time. The day of his *Tonight Show* appearance, he stayed in there until nearly 2:00 P.M.

Friends called, telegrams arrived. Louie wandered into the shower and stayed there for almost an hour, listening to Prince's *Purple Rain* soundtrack over and over.

"Last night before I went to sleep, I went through the set in my head," he said, finally emerging from the bathroom only an hour before he was supposed to be at the studio. "I also had this dream that every bad thing I ever did in my life, Johnny had a list of it."

He seemed jumpy, a little disoriented. He couldn't find his socks. He said he was fine.

"I'm not nervous," he said. "I'm excited."

The taping didn't start until 5:30 P.M., but Louie wanted to get to NBC's Burbank Studios, a half hour away, by 4:00.

"I want to get there early," he said, "so I can see where I'm supposed to stand."

"After the show, Louie would have to go directly to the Burbank airport and catch a flight to Las Vegas, where he and some other Comedy Store regulars were appearing at the Dunes Hotel. So now, there was a mad rush to pack his bags, to get everybody in the cars and caravan over to NBC.

The back-entrance security guards found his name on the list and waved the whole gang through, pointing out the proper parking area, very near Johnny's sparkling white Corvette. Everybody was piling out when Louie made a sickening sound.

"Oh God," he said. "I've left my suit at the apartment. The one I was going to wear on the show."

He wasn't nervous. Just excited.

One carload of comedians went back to retrieve the suit and Louie found his dressing room, a small paneled cubicle with a dressing table, a plaid sofa, a TV monitor, a coffee table, and a bathroom.

"Who was in here for the last show?" someone asked the security guard.

"Lee Meriwether, I think."

"Louie's name was printed on a card that was fastened to the door and decorated with the *Tonight Show* logo. "I'm gonna save that," he said.

He asked the guard if he could walk onto the set. "You're the boss tonight," he was told, and wandered past the curtains into the empty studio.

"This is it," he said, looking up at the five hundred blue seats, turning to take in Johnny's desk, the couch, the cameras, the bandstand. "This is history."

He walked to Carson's star, the place where he stands to deliver his monologues, and stood there for a while, not saying anything.

HERE'S JOHNNY!

By 4:45 the guys were back with the suit, and the tiny dressing room was filling up with friends, most of them nervously chewing on vending-machine pretzels.

"Nice place," one of them said. "Think we ought to knock on the door and see if Blake's in there?"

"No," Louie blurted. "Don't do that. Don't start acting like jerks."

Then he went to the bathroom.

Comedians kept showing up, Comedy Store regulars who'd done *The Tonight Show* themselves and were there to help Louie through his first time, sort of like a comedy support group.

"Louie, it's an easy room," said Bill Maher, a young comic who'd done the Carson show a dozen times and who had just signed to star in his own sitcom. "It's the easiest room you'll ever play."

"You won't sit down unless you go long," Maher told him. "If you go long, they can't bring out the third guest, and you get a freebie sit."

It happened so rarely—when a comedian debuted on *The Tonight Show* and was beckoned by Johnny to have a seat. Nineteen-year-old Freddie Prinze was a standout when he was introduced to late-night viewers in December 1973. Fame quickly enveloped Prinze, who was soon starring in his own NBC sitcom, *Chico and the Man*. He made seventeen guest appearances on *Tonight* within three years and subbed for Johnny as well, but Prinze ultimately found life and success hard to handle and committed suicide in 1977.

Louie was looking into the mirror. "I'm glad I didn't cut my hair," he said. "It looks just right."

At five-thirty, as the show started, they tried to turn on the monitor but couldn't figure out how to get it to work. The monologue was over before the picture came on. Johnny and Ed were on the couch by then, doing a bit about McDonald's selling its fifty-billionth hamburger.

"Ohh," Louie said. "That should be my opening joke."

"Just wait," Maher told him. "Listen to this. You don't want to step on his routine."

Carson was rattling off statistics about McDonald's using 435 cows worth of beef a day and 32,000 pounds of pickles.

"I should walk out there and say I was just in McDonald's," Louie said, "and all those statistics have changed."

"Don't do it," Maher warned. "Stick to the script your first time."

"You're right," Louie said. And then he went to the bathroom.

"It was 6:00 P.M. when the knock came. It was McCawley, the talent coordinator, ready to escort Louie to the backstage area. After the next commercial, Louie was on. They went down the back hallway together, turned right, and disappeared behind the curtains.

The pack of comedians made a mad dash through the green room, which isn't green at all, almost trampling Selma Diamond, who was to be the show's third guest. They were headed for the tunnel, the area behind the main camera, a place where they could watch Louie live, without a monitor, without having to peek through a curtain.

The commercial ended. Carson put out the cigarette he had been smoking while he was talking to Robert Blake off-camera. The spotlights were trained on the gray curtain, the stagehand standing behind it, out of sight.

"And now," Johnny Carson said, "will you welcome, please, Louie Anderson." This time the music was for him.

■ ■ ■

"I can't stay long," Louie said, coolly scanning the crowd as the music faded. "I'm in between meals."

It was like an explosion. The laughter rolled down like a wave. And it was his opening joke. Maher had been right. The easiest room he would ever work. Louie took the chance.

"I just got back from McDonald's," he said. Maher winced. The whole tribe of comedians, by then nearly a dozen, held their breath. "And all those statistics have changed."

Another roar. And Carson was bent over. Laughing.

"I've been trying to get into this California lifestyle," Louie was saying, as calm as he could be. "I went to the beach the other day, but every time I'd lay down, people would push me back into the water."

Every joke was perfectly timed, every punch line smoothly delivered. Louie did double takes. He waited for the applause, which came often. They were in the palm of his hand. He had a series of jokes about trying out for the Olympics, about how he drove the pole vault into the ground and straightened out the uneven parallel bars, and here it comes, the big one.

"Broad jump?" He waited for the beat. *One. Two. Three.* "Killed her."

Another roar. Carson, the master himself, was pounding on his desk he was laughing so hard. Louie had scored beyond his wildest expectations. It was a fairy tale.

The last joke was followed by a thunderous ovation Louie acknowledged, like a heavyweight fighter who'd just delivered a knockout punch. He turned, finally, and went back through the gray curtain. But the applause didn't stop.

# Second String

By the end of the 1970s, Johnny Carson's work week began to get shorter and more guest hosts filled in. It had been commonplace to have a guest host pinch-hit while Johnny was on vacation, only now, Johnny was pioneering the four-day work week, then down to three days a week, and the other nights were guest hosts and reruns.

In the 1960s, Jerry Lewis and Joey Bishop were deputized, hosting frequently. Singer Jimmy Dean—yes, the country sausage king—was the first guest host for Johnny in 1963. Rat packer Joey Bishop hosted a record 117 times before landing his own late-night talk show on ABC-TV in an attempt to lure some of that evening audience away from Johnny. Bishop's show, with Regis Philbin as second banana, ran from 1967 to 1969. It was a good program and won some ratings, but it didn't make much of a dent—a common fate suffered by similar shows that were put up against Carson.

Several times while hosting *The Tonight Show,* Joey Bishop was graced with the appearance of his fellow rat pack buddies. "Dean Martin came on one time with a bottle in his hand," says Bishop. "I said, 'Dean!' and he just kept walking. He said, 'I didn't come on here to be a guest, just tell me, where's the bathroom?' and he left. He never came back.

"I had some terrific guests on," Bishop says. "Edward G. Robinson would not do a talk show. I asked him to be on the show, but he would not, simply because he could not hear.

"I had Shelley Winters on one time. She was scheduled second, but the first guest was late coming. I asked if Shelley was here and they told me 'yes' and without thinking, I said, 'Ladies and gentleman, let's welcome Shelley Winters.'

"She was in her dressing room naked," Bishop says, "so she threw on a fur coat and came running out. I said, 'Shelley, it's a beautiful coat, but you're not going to wear that for the whole interview. . . .'"

Winters nodded her head yes. "If I take this off, this place will be a garage. I'm naked underneath."

Bishop couldn't believe it, so the actress walked Bishop upstage and opened her

Frank Sinatra sang and chatted on *The Tonight Show* in 1976. He seemed to dig the scene, so no one refused when he returned the next year as guest host.

Della Reese chats with Ed while guest hosting in 1975.

"You look maah-velous." Fernando Lamas guest hosted and actress Jean Marsh was his guest. (1976)

coat with her back to the audience. The audience cheered her on.

"I got a good look and I turned to the audience and said, 'Yes, she's naked.' With the heat of the lights, I may have gotten turned on for a moment. But I doubt it."

Guest hosting for Johnny became a prestigious gig, and the list of those subbing for Johnny grew into an eclectic, if not elite, club: Barbara Walters, Burt Reynolds, Joe Garagiola, Dick Cavett, Diana Ross, Robert Goulet, Chevy Chase, Roger Moore, Frank Sinatra, George Carlin, Rich Little, Rob Reiner, Michael Landon, Richard Dawson, Orson Welles, Vincent Price, Kenny Rogers, Burt Bacharach, John Denver, Barbara Mandrell, Wayne Newton, Don Rickles, Robert Blake, Dom DeLouise, Kermit the Frog, Freddie Prinze, Billy Crystal, Tony Danza, among them. As time went by, several recurring names floated to the surface,

such as David Brenner, David Steinberg, Bill Cosby, McLean Stevenson, and Jay Leno.

For executive producer Fred de Cordova, none were as memorable as singer John Davidson, who became almost a staple with the show. "John Davidson was so upset with himself when he forgot the lyrics of his song . . . he kicked an audio monitor and shorted all the electrical equipment in the studio. I couldn't even go to a commercial," he said. "We telecast a 'Best of Carson' rerun that night."

During Carson's era, the most frequent guest hosts (aside from Jay Leno) were: Joey Bishop (117 times), Joan Rivers (93 times), Bob Newhart (87 times), John Davidson (87 times), David Brenner (70 times), McLean Stevenson (58 times), Jerry Lewis (52 times), and David Letterman (51 times).

John Davidson served as guest host more than forty times between 1971 and 1987.

And then, something that never happens. Carson called him back for another ovation and came over to shake Louie's hand.

"Did you see that?" one of the comics gasped. "Johnny never comes over like that. That's as good as it gets."

Louie took the extended hand and leaned forward, whispering into his idol's ear.

"Thank you," he told him, "for making a dream come true."

After the show, the dressing area was like a World Series locker room, all back-slaps and war whoops. It all went too fast. There was Peter Lassally, the show's director, coming back to tell Louie that Johnny wanted him to do some concert dates with him, and then, the man himself.

"Helluva good spot," Carson said. "You were funny as hell. I'll have you back whenever you want."

Louie went to the bathroom.

There was not much time for parking-lot euphoria. There was that plane to catch for Vegas, but Louie's life had changed. All in seven minutes. He was thirty-one years old, and he knew nothing would ever be the same again.

Carson left in his white Corvette, McMahon took a limo. And finally, Doc Severinsen wandered out into the parking lot.

"Hot stuff, Louie," he said. "A beautiful set."

Louie Anderson said something about his dad, how he was a trumpet player, too. He blurted it out, just something to say, anything. The night suddenly felt so unreal, too much like the dream he'd had for so long.

"See you soon," Severinsen said, climbing into his car. "Undoubtedly, see you soon."

■ ■ ■

*JOE RHODES and comic Louie Anderson, both from Minnesota, have been pals for years. Formerly on staff with the* Dallas Times Herald, *Rhodes has contributed extensively to* Entertainment Weekly *and* TV Guide.

# 7

# PAGING JOHNNY CARSON

*Johnny: It was so hot in Los Angeles today . . .*

Ever wonder what happened to the brash members of the audience who shouted at Johnny, interrupting him—especially during the monologue?

*"How hot was it?!"*

They were promptly and quietly escorted out of the studio with no chance of seeing the remainder of the show. Cruel and unusual punishment, wouldn't you say? It was the responsibility of the NBC pages in their dark sportcoats, happy, with a smile, to scan the audience for the loudmouth with his hands cupped and respectfully—but adamantly—yank the individual from his spot.

Sure, everybody wanted to be heard on the air. Lots of people yelled out, "We Love You!" or something obnoxious, later alerting friends to watch the show in anticipation of the brief howl or scream. NBC was clear: try it on the Carson show, and on the tube is the only way you'll see the action.

NBC pages Tamara Anne Fowler and Ken Crosby secretly posed at Johnny's desk for this personal snapshot after the show one evening. Who wouldn't?

Playing bouncer for Johnny was one of the negative duties of an otherwise desirable position. The ultimate, however, was the actual appointment to work the show among the pages' other chores.

"Five pages were in-house, instructed not to watch Johnny, don't watch the monologue, don't enjoy yourself," explained Ken Crosby, a former NBC page who is now producing television. "Just watch the audience. For any 'How hot was it?' or 'Whoop!' the culprit was ushered out. It happened at least two to three times a week."

On his first day paging a *Tonight Show* with the Man, Crosby could hardly repress himself in expectation of catching his first glimpse of Johnny in person. "I'm a celebrity freak and excited about seeing him," said Crosby in 1991. It was his second week at work and the rewards were about to kick in. "Fred de Cordova came out and reminded the audience that Johnny had been away for two weeks and that he was back. Five, four, three, two . . . then the theme. Carson comes out from behind the curtain, and it was like a rock-concert-type thing. Everyone rose to their feet in a roar, yelling out. For a new page having anxiety about seeing Carson, it was frightening."

With the popularity of Arsenio Hall, audiences had become louder, more rambunctious, and bold enough to scream, bark, and hoot. Sometimes the hooting became chants by the entire audience, waving their fists in a circular motion, like only Arsenio fans know so well. Audiences became ruder during tapings.

"People get rowdy," Crosby explains. "They're in town on vacation and some overtly run across the street to the liquor store to get beer to drink while they wait in line. I'm five-feet-seven and I'm not an imposing page, but asking these frat buddies to leave the studio in silence was a bit unnerving."

One audience in 1991 was so rude . . .

*How rude was it?*

So rude, it had Carson completely tongue-tied. Openly aggravated by one heckler in particular, Carson looked up in exasperation and said, "Oh, shut up!" delivering an "up yours" arm gesture to the person. Pages could not zero in on the guy during the desk piece, which seemed to bomb that night. He once again loudly announced from the audience his opinion of the bit: "Stop, you're killing me!"

"It's a thought!" Johnny countered.

The audience roared. That night, even guest Bill Cosby, like a sassy schoolmarm scolding the class clown, playfully instructed the audience to apologize to Johnny for its collective rudeness. Indeed, it was a rare night for the fairly unflappable host.

Evenings such as this were jittery ones for pages like Crosby, who guarded his job with pride and competitiveness. Crosby arrived in Hollywood in 1984 from his home in Hawaii where he left a "prestigious position as cashier for Toys R Us." His passion for Johnny Carson and *The Tonight Show* ushered him to the job, which paid a meager $5.20 an hour and had a maximum service of eighteen months. If you were good, you received an extra month or two extension, he explains, but much of the glitter wore off after a year.

More than one hundred people applied each month for the coveted entry-level position at NBC in the mid to late 1980s. In 1991, the page system was thrown out, a victim of network cutbacks, but prior to that nearly fifty pages might be employed at once. The waiting list was extensive. Paging was a hybrid position, the responsibilities of which included conducting the studio tour, ushering the show, serving as guest-relations personnel, prompting the audience ("APPLAUSE!"), doing clerical work, and generally being a gofer. Sometimes you were sent on a "limo run," escorting a celebrity to the studio. Sixty percent of the training was geared toward *The Tonight Show*, maintaining security and order and handling the nightly mass of ticket holders who may have stood for hours in less than pleasant weather to see the King.

The *L.A. Times* reported, "Pagedom began the climb to stardom for celebrities

# Johnny's Mug

One evening as he got settled at his desk, Johnny was visibly upset. His coffee mug was missing. Usually, it sat right there next to the two-headed pencils he tapped on the desk and the wooden cigarette box next to the lighter and the microphone. His desk set was rarely disturbed, but this night his coffee mug was distinctly absent.

Someone asked him where they come from. He shook his head and said, "I don't know."

"We have our name on the bottom," said Alma Olney, owner of the Burbank Mug Shop, in 1991. "He's not very observant."

When her husband, Robert, died, Olney took over the mug-making business he had begun in 1972. It still operates from the same building, converted from an old lawnmower shop in Burbank. Olney ran her business with excitement and a sense of adventure. Her most famous product, although it was rarely advertised, was the mug that bore the face of Johnny Carson . . . seen nightly by millions of viewers for almost twenty years.

In 1974, Jack Grant, the propmaster for *The Tonight Show,* wandered into the shop and asked if a picture could be applied to a mug. The Johnny mug was thus designed, and the same shop kept their most famous customer in tan-and-brown ironstone beverage containers for the rest of his run. Until 1991 when a more recent shot of Carson was applied to the mug, the photograph was a 1970s close-up of Carson leering to one side. It's possibly the most famous coffee mug ever made, although for most of Johnny's audience, herbal tea might be more appropriate at that time of the night.

"Johnny's mug is the worst," said Olney of its construction. "Just a horrible thing to work with because of the concave surface." To illustrate, she pulled out a little paper decal reminiscent of the water-soaked tattoos children used to buy in bubble-gum packs. The decal was soaked in warm water, applied to the mug with a small squeegee, and finally fired in a kiln for permanence.

She estimated there might have been five hundred of the tan-and-brown-colored mugs produced since 1974. The mugs regularly disappeared from the set. They were given away; Johnny autographed a few for charity auctions; and a few were simply broken along the way. Remember when Dolly Parton knocked one off the desk? How, you ask? Don't ask. On countless occasions, animals have jolted the mugs off the desk with their hind legs.

These little treasured mementos of *The Tonight Show* were not easily obtained during the show, and are even more rare today. Every once in a while one of the Carson mugs pops up on Ebay and fetches a nice sum. NBC never marketed the mugs in the gift shops next to *Late Night with David Letterman* sweatshirts or *Cheers* beer mugs. No Johnny Carson T-shirts or posters. His mug has remained a sacred item, a little ceramic container that was produced exclusively for Carson Productions.

Olney designed and produced mugs for other television shows over the years, including *Goodnight, Beantown; Our House; Falcon Crest; The Munsters Today; Matlock;* and *Sweethearts,* to name a few. Her client list over the years included some big boys as well, like Lockheed Aeronautical and MCA Corporation.

Pictures framed on the shop's walls and atop some shelves attest to the celebrities who have commissioned her work: Sammy Davis Jr., Don Rickles, Carson. In the eighteen years her company produced the mug for Carson, she and her husband attempted to reach the star twice. Both times they met with no success.

"My husband served as the mayor of Burbank from 1981 to 1982, and he attempted to contact Johnny Carson by telephone," Olney said. "He just wanted to say hello as mayor, introduce himself, and also remind Johnny that he made his mugs. He could never get through.

"Years later I wrote him after my husband passed away, but he never responded. He never acknowledged that Robert Olney made his coffee mugs. Robert was a big fan, though. We teased him once, when he was working in the back; we told him Johnny had just walked into the store. He went out there all excited, and no one was there."

Olney continued filling NBC's orders for Johnny's mug right up to the end. The last order was for several dozen—the largest order to that date. She applied the name decals on the guest mugs, which read GUEST 1 and GUEST 2. Ed McMahon's had ED on the reverse, and Johnny's name in Gothic type is on the reverse of his mug as well. Jay Leno had a special request on his: no photo, just the word "Manimal."

During Carson's era, hundreds of letters per year were marked "Mug Request" and delivered from NBC to Olney's shop. She has sold a few in the past to persistent fans, but Carson Productions has warned her not to mass-market the item. "I'm not making a living on Johnny's mug, that's for sure," she said in 1991. "People write from all over for these, and it's been delivered to me for years. What do they expect me to do with them?"

Alma Olney exclusively produced Johnny's coffee mugs for the show, and to this day she still receives inquiries about the famous prop.

like Kate Jackson, Richard Benjamin, Steve Allen, and Eva Marie Saint, as well as several top executives who have served as pages during the fifty-one years since the studio began the program in New York." Comedian Chris Elliot, the late game-show host Bert Convy, and even Regis Philbin started their careers as pages. Daily exposure to the goings on at a major television studio was not only thrilling to the pages, they hoped it would prove a successful entrée into the network. Competitiveness among the pages could be described as "fierce."

Peter Lassally, a former page who worked his way up to the position of producer for Johnny Carson, said he felt a special warmth for pages who approached him for advice. "I'm happy to talk to them and give expertise," Lasally told the *L.A. Times* in 1984. "It's a lot harder than when I was a page back in the 1950s. There was more opportunity to get into television because radio was still the big deal."

Being an NBC page in the 1980s could've meant bumping into Johnny, Ed, or maybe Vanna White in the hallways or around the studio. Carson was labeled "strictly hands off." You might cross the path of producer Fred de Cordova steering his personal golf cart (with a drink in one hand and a lovely female page in the passenger seat), zipping through the studio, or maybe you'd schmooze with a few celebrities visiting the studio that day.

"The job as a whole certainly had its pitfalls, too," admitted Crosby. "The tour was basically walking backward for an hour showing people from the Midwest empty studios and trying to create some sort of magic that just isn't there in most cases. Foremost for me was doing *The Tonight Show*."

On a good day, experiencing the famed NBC tour meant you'd be taken to see studios such as Studio Four, where Elvis taped his 1968 comeback special, and where Fred Astaire danced on his NBC specials. During the 1980s, *Wheel of Fortune* was taped at NBC and the set was a flashy extravagance to see. For the sake of pure climax, most tours were led into an empty, chilly Studio One, to stare at *The Tonight Show* set with just a few dim lights shining above the desk and the orchestra area. The NBC page would say, "If you can imagine, ladies and gentleman, in no more than three hours from now, through these doors that you are about to pass, Mr. Carson will arrive. . . . He will have along with him Mr. de Cordova, or an assistant, going over the show's events, and he will go through here and right around to the curtain." The page would explain the history of *The Tonight Show* and its New York roots. The story of Shelley Winters falling asleep while on the couch during a show would familiarize tourists with the boom mike that detected her snores from above. And if you were lucky enough to have tickets for that evening's taping, you stayed around the area and secured a place in line.

The tour was usually a blast, especially for out-of-towners, unless—unaware that it was the final voyage of the day—you purchased a ticket for the 3:30 P.M. "Death Tour." News studios had closed their doors and Studio One was strictly off-limits that late in the day. "People just didn't get their money's worth and [the pages] complained to NBC to cross off that tour, but they wouldn't."

Crosby added that one treat you did get on the Death Tour was a chance to see, up close, Johnny's car in parking spot Number 1. "I'd tell 'em, 'I know *The Tonight Show* doors are closed, but I've got a treat for you folks . . . I really shouldn't be doing this, but come on out here. . . .'"

"By God, there would be Johnny's white Corvette, and the women would swoon," Crosby laughed. "The car was the saver on those tours. But anyone approaching the car to test the locks or touch it would quickly

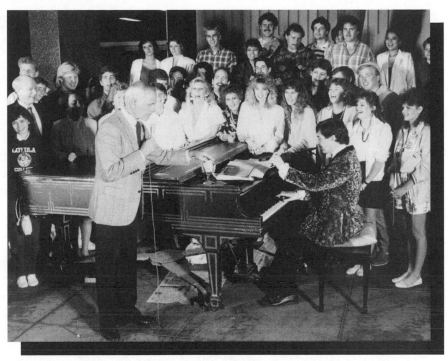

Johnny serenades the fans outside Burbank's NBC studios who were unable to attend his twenty-fifth anniversary show taping because there weren't enough seats. (Courtesy of Betty and Bob Kelly)

find us obedient pages throwing ourselves between the gawker and the car. It was much more important for you to lose a limb than let one of the people hurt Johnny's car."

It became a military operation of sorts, ushering in the audience for *The Tonight Show*. Usually it ran so smooth, like machinery, due to the pages and their routine. Some of the pages were confident and proud, like the peacock on their blue blazers. Other pages were proud, but a little too cocky, ready to ruffle the feathers of anyone who got out of line. Following the Persian Gulf War, a walk-through metal detector was installed, and a guard who peeked inside purses with a flashlight and observed bulging pockets was stationed right inside the entry door. Cameras were strictly forbidden, and audience members were instructed to take them back to their vehicles before entering the studio.

Audience misbehavior always makes for a good story, like the urban legend about the woman who handcuffed herself to the studio's railing and the show had to be stopped until she could be carted off.

"I missed that one," laughs *Tonight Show* band member Tommy Newsom. "I don't think that ever happened. But there's always a fruitcake in the audience. Some lady came down from the audience hollering 'Johnny! Johnny!' All she wanted was to give him a hug. So, he gave her a hug. That's how they handled that."

One night, things became a little more tense. It was a night, Newsom recalls,

Johnny's old friend, legendary comedian Red Skelton, was just as spirited as ever appearing on the show at age seventy (December 1983).

when he was subbing for Doc Severinsen as the bandleader. "I was standing in front of the band and I had my headset on," he remembers. "I was getting the countdown from the booth and a guy walked past me in front of the band and I thought it was a stagehand. He came from somewhere in the audience and he was walking quickly into the curtain.

"All of a sudden, the producers are waving at me to start and this guy was heading right toward the curtain where Carson would come out. The stage manager came flying around and actually went and tackled this guy and we saw the curtain flop open. I don't know what he was up to, but they apprehended him. Who knows what he was gonna do?"

If you were the OIC (Outside in Charge) page, it was your job to keep the VIPs placated. Friends of staff or those with the show would be instructed to pick up their

# By the Numbers

*("That's wild stuff.")*

His statistics were almost incomprehensible, his career historic. The records he set will never be matched in late-night television. Just how remarkable was Carson's tenure, you ask? Think of it this way: When Johnny came in, there were only three or four choices on television in almost every city, and when he left three decades later, there were more than thirty or forty choices on television. And out of all the numbers listed below, one number stands out: When Johnny left, he was Number 1 in the ratings.

- Number of human guests appearing on *The Tonight Show Starring Johnny Carson*: **more than 22,000**
- Number of animal guests: **more than 212**
- Average nightly audience in 1962: **7.5 million**
- Average nightly audience in 1972: **11 million**
- Average nightly audience in 1978: **17.3 million**
- Average nightly audience in 1991: **12 million** (This decline is due to the fractionalization of the TV universe.)
- Number of NBC affiliates airing Johnny Carson nightly in 1992: **212**
- Number of times Johnny's set was redesigned: **7**
- Number of questions Johnny has asked from behind the desk: **more than 200,000**
- Number of seats at NBC's Studio One in Burbank (in 1992): **465**
- Number of ticket requests that arrived daily in 1991: **between 200 and 300**
- Number of members in Doc's band most nights: **16**
- Number of guest hosts: **more than 120**
- Number of Emmy Awards won by *The Tonight Show Starring Johnny Carson*: **6**
- Number of competing talk/variety shows Johnny clobbered over the years: **14**
- Number of people who attended a *Tonight Show* taping during Johnny's reign: **nearly 3 million**
- Approximate number of sponsors: **850**
- Number of commercials aired: **more than 250,000**
- Number of people watching the wedding of Tiny Tim and Miss Vicki in 1969 (according to A. C. Nielsen Co. data): **21.4 million**
- Amount a minute of advertising cost on the show in 1968: **$17,200**
- Amount a minute of advertising cost on the show in 1973: **$20,000**
- Amount thirty seconds of advertising cost on the show in 1991: **$35,900**
- Amount thirty seconds of advertising cost on Johnny's final show: **$200,000**
- Number of minutes Johnny broadcast on NBC: **over 486,180**
- Number of hours: **just over 8,103**
- Number of broadcasts of *The Tonight Show Starring Johnny Carson* between 1962 and 1992: **8,564** (6,583 were original, Johnny hosted 4,531 of these; the rest were reruns)
- Salary that Johnny Carson earned at his first job in 1949 at a Nebraska radio station: **$47.50 a week**

- Salary that Johnny Carson earned as host of *The Tonight Show* in 1962: **$100,000 a year**
- Salary that Johnny Carson earned in 1991: approximately **$20 million a year**
- Amount per minute on the air that Carson earned in 1991: **about $2,380**
- Number of hour-long shows Johnny was to host per his last contract: **111**
- Number of weeks paid vacation afforded to Johnny in that same contract: **15**
- Number of times Johnny Carson has been married: **4**
- Number of pounds lost by Ed McMahon in 1990: **42**
- Percentage of NBC's total annual revenue accounted for by *The Tonight Show* in 1991: **15 percent ($60 million)**
- Estimated number of viewers who have watched Johnny host *The Tonight Show* over the years: **83 billion**
- Number of letters Johnny received each week during the last several years of the show: **500 to 700**
- Estimated number of viewers who joined Johnny for his final show on May 22, 1992: **23 million** (according to the Associated Press)

Johnny marks his fourteenth anniversary and the 3,641st first-run telecast with a two-hour *Tonight Show* special in 1976.

tickets at the air-conditioned guest-relations bungalow where "tape and hold" seats in their name were on a list. Those lucky enough to obtain these preferred arrangements were placed in highly desirable seating, and there were no lines to deal with outside.

Just as scary as being in charge of audience removal was the position of handling the master clipboard and having to advise someone that, for some reason, their name was not on the list.

Few complications halted any facet of *The Tonight Show* tapings, explained former page Tamara Anne Fowler in 1991. "I was there once when a little old lady had a heart attack during the taping. The show went on. It stops for almost nothing."

Fowler abandoned her berth at a Los Angeles ad agency, suffered a massive cut in pay, and moved back in with her parents at age twenty-five to fulfill her dream of paging *The Tonight Show*. Her goal was the highly visible position of passing the prize envelopes to Johnny during a segment of "Stump the Band." Alas, she never got the chance before her time was up. Her favorite memory from the NBC experience was meeting Marlon Brando while she was on "screening room duty." The larger-than-life star was running some Super 8 footage about his private island hideaway, pitching a documentary concept to network executives. "It was one of those days where nothing went right," Fowler recalled. "The film wouldn't stop flickering. Then no sound. Then the film broke and we had to tape it.

"At the end, another page and I were rewinding it and I waited by the door to see Marlon Brando go by. He rounded the corner and came right in. He shook my hand and said thank you, but not sarcastically. He was huge and very imposing."

Celebrity sightings were one of the perks for a page at NBC. Ken Crosby vividly recalls working an NBC tribute to Lucille Ball and opening the door for an approaching Dean Martin, Frank Sinatra, and Sean Connery, bidding them "Have a nice evening, gentlemen."

"We shall," Connery answered. It wasn't often Matt Helm, Tony Rome, and James Bond exited the building at once, Crosby mused.

# 8

# CARSON'S WILD KINGDOM

*When he has an animal on, he hopes it craps.*

—TONY RANDALL

It's a wonder none of the animals that Johnny ever held up for the camera leaped from his grasp and went for his jugular. Naturally, he has been nipped on the hands a few times by rodents and squirrelly creatures the proper names of which no one can pronounce, let alone remember.

"I've never had anyone injured on *The Tonight Show*," said Joan Embery, an ambassador for the San Diego Zoo who appeared nearly eighty times with Johnny. "There have been other animal people on the show, and I've heard stories about accidents, but not with me." Every imaginable critter has slithered around Johnny's desk; from aardvark to zebra, with everything in between—except a panda.

Embery, now in her fifties, began her job with the San Diego Zoo as an aspiring veterinarian in the 1960s. At the time, the zoo needed someone to give lectures and travel with the animals, so she filled that position. Eventually, she set aside her yearning to become a vet and became the famous zoo's goodwill ambassador. Her expertise in the animal world has taken her to almost every zoo in the United States, and onto many television shows with hosts such as Steve Allen, Art Linkletter, Dinah Shore, Virginia Graham, and Jay Leno. She's brought animals on *Good Morning America*, *Hollywood Squares*, and *Truth or Consequences*, and she even appeared on the situation comedies *ALF* and *Newhart*.

Embery most enjoyed bringing animals on with Johnny, and she confirmed that it was Carson's nature and professionalism that helped him ward off attack by beasts visiting the show. He never prepared for the animals appearing on the program, not even a look or a pat before airtime. Still, he maintained control of otherwise unpredictable situations.

"It may not look like Johnny is in control, but he is," said Embery in 1991. "He's a master at what he does. All you have to do is work with everybody else in the business to know and appreciate that."

During the transfer of animals from her arms to Johnny's, Embery would keep close watch as the animal moved around. If she instinctively felt the animal was restless and situation might become "dicey," she didn't hesitate to proceed abruptly to the next animal. It was a transition the audience rarely detected. Carson trusted Embery completely. He had to.

It was during the handoffs backstage that the trickiest part of the appearance occurred. One lion cub couldn't handle the band behind the curtain, so his appearance was nixed. A monkey ran amok backstage once, so that chimp lost its chance. "Johnny's a very willing participant, but he also had the sense to know when to back off and give them a little space," said Embery. Many hosts she's worked with throw themselves at the rare creatures she introduces before they have time to settle; as a result, the animals have become defensive and sometimes hostile.

Embery pointed out that Joan Rivers had, on occasion, ridiculed or degraded animals, attempting to be funny. "The audience takes that to a point, but when you go overboard with it, the audience rises to the defense of the animal, and it backfires on the host or the comedian," she said. "Some hosts on *The Tonight Show*, or on other shows, just don't know the line."

Most of the time, viewers put themselves in Johnny's place, cuddling the little baby orangutans. Carson had to practice great restraint with some of the guests, such as the hairy tarantula that crawled up his arm and got a little close to his face. "I find them fascinating creatures, but I don't like handling them," Embery says.

Talent coordinator Craig Tennis recalled the arachnid incident. "Of all the animals Joan eventually brought, the one that undoubtedly caused the most revulsion and fear—even in Joan—was the tarantula," he said. "Now, one of the things that Johnny always does best is to appear terrified and shocked by animals, which, in fact, he is not at all. In this case, I think he was somewhat repulsed."

Embery gingerly picked up the giant spider and put it on Johnny's hand as she squirmed inside but attempted to keep her cool for the camera. Embery told Carson it would not bite unless alerted or maddened by something, and even then it would be like a wasp sting—but still painful. It moved around, then climbed at a quick pace up to his bare neck beneath the television lights as the audience held its collective breath.

"Exactly what kind of thing might I do that would annoy it?" Carson quipped on cue.

■ ■ ■

The real star of the November 4, 1971, *Tonight Show* was Carol, the four-year-old Asian elephant that Embery escorted to the studio with the help of two assistants; Carol rode in a horse trailer for three hours to get there. Craig Tennis had heard about the peculiar talents of this elephant from a story on the Associated Press wire service. The elephant was trained to paint with a brush, creating a mural of colors on the floor.

*The Tonight Show* that evening was taping in Burbank on a trip west; New York was still home. Tennis noted that Carson enjoyed the elephant's appearance, "because he learned very early on that if he put a handful of peanuts in his pants pockets, the elephant would smell them and keep going for Johnny's crotch with his trunk."

Carol was one of Embery's favorite animals ever. She had helped raise her, and the young elephant was her buddy. "Interestingly," Embery laughs, "in the first few years, people used to call me Carol, and I'd say, 'No, Carol is the elephant.'"

The night before Carol's appearance, Embery was worried that the studio audience might frighten the elephant. Carol had appeared in public before, but not quite

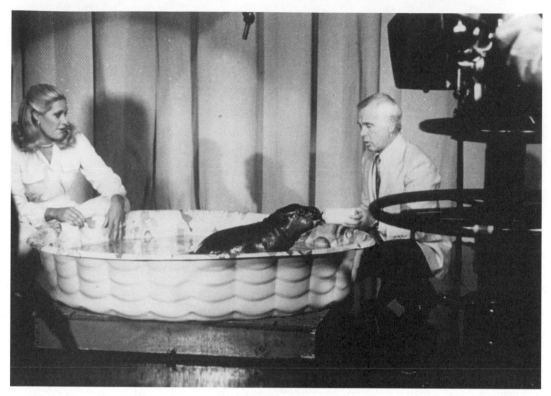

*Above,* Feeding a baby hippo, Johnny tries to keep his suit clean. (Courtesy of Joan Embery and the Zoological Society of San Diego) *Below,* On her first *Tonight Show* appearance, Joan Embery introduced young "Boom Orang" to Johnny and the audience in 1971.

in this atmosphere. Would she react adversely? Would she go nuts and run around crazed? And of course the *Tonight Show* staff wondered: "Would she paint?"

Embery recalled: "I started getting really jittery the day before the show, and I was up all night getting my clothes ready and studying the notes I'd made on each animal. I've spent the night before almost every *Tonight Show* that same way. I'm especially nervous if there's little time to prepare, but even if I have everything ready, I lie awake for hours thinking about what I'm going to say."

She was also thinking of the time, just four months prior, when she rode Carol's back in a Fourth of July parade; the five-foot elephant, weighing in at a ton and a half, took off at a trot and nearly plunged into the side of a house.

Backstage, the pachyderm's giant ears were perked. Although clearly nervous from the mirrors that surrounded her onstage, Carol, soothed by Embery, held the brush in her trunk and painted with enthusiasm on cue. The audience loved her. She splattered colors on the floor everywhere, including over Johnny's shoes.

Also on the show that evening were a baby orangutan named Ken and a hairy-nosed wombat. A wombat looks like a rodent, "but it is a marsupial, a member of that group of mammals, including the kangaroo and opossum, that raise their young in abdominal pouches," Embery explained. Ken, the innocent, baby-faced orangutan, nicknamed "Boom Orang," was a hit. Carson loved cuddling this bowlegged little baby with big, expressive eyes.

Another guest on the show that evening was Dudley Duplex, a two-headed California king snake that was about eighteen inches long with black bands running crosswise around his body. Indeed, this snake had two functional heads, the result of an "incomplete twinning process," Embery explained on the show. She handed Johnny the snake, and he lost his grip. It started to slither up his sleeve. It was with this reptile, Embery explained in her book, *My Wild World*, that she first witnessed the expertise of Johnny Carson:

> Johnny widened his eyes and rolled them back; then his expression froze and he went rigid all over. I thought of the keeper in the reptile house who had warned me, when I arranged to take Dudley to the show, that he was quite rare and I had to make sure nothing happened to him; in my mind's eye, I could see the keeper watching the show. What if, in his fright, Johnny somehow hurt the snake? Immediately, I reached over to grab Dudley, but very subtly, Johnny put his hand on mine to stop me, and I realized that he'd let the snake crawl up his sleeve. I sat back and watched with some astonishment—that moment probably marks the beginning of my appreciation of Carson's professional genius—and when Johnny had had his fun, he stood up and shook his arm and the snake slid out. It turned out to be an incredible spot—one that people remember to this day.

The funniest bits with animals are the spontaneous ones, which was most of them. "When you force something or try to make something happen with animals, it never works," Embery stresses. The key booking for one evening was a koala bear—cute, furry, and funny. The audience cooed over the bear. But the real screams came when the next guest, a little tropical American monkey called a marmoset, crawled from Johnny's arms to the top of his head and stayed there. Embery had just finished saying that it loved to climb. It was perfect timing, as the cameraman secured a close-up of Johnny sitting still with this little monkey perched atop his head. As Embery attempted to remove it, the little monkey started to dig at Johnny's scalp and pull his hair out. There was more. Johnny felt something funny and patted the top of his head. The monkey had dribbled, marking its territory with its scent on Johnny's noggin. The audience was in hysterics, while Johnny's deadpan "Why me?" face was captured dead-center in the camera's eye.

■ ■ ■

Birds of a feather have mostly flocked together when appearing with Johnny. A few have actually sung, like the big green parrot that warbled "I Left My Heart in San Francisco," or the parakeet that was trained to do impressions of a cat or a dog. There it was, for all to see: a bird actually meowing and barking. Then it called out, "Here kitty, kitty, kitty!!" Those bird spots were rarities on the show, and the footage became priceless gems that made it onto countless anniversary shows. Some of the birds weren't as cooperative with Johnny, who always saved the situation with a joke. After witnessing a silent bird one evening, he joked in his following night's monologue: "We had a nice lady on last night from British Columbia with her pet parakeet—supposed to squeak a hundred and fifty words. The bird didn't do nuthin'! After the show, it was too bad, I finally got the bird to talk . . . just as I was sealing him up in a Shake 'N' Bake bag."

One night, a scheduled guest had flown in to Burbank for an appearance with his pet

Johnny got to see a California condor up close in 1984. (Courtesy of Joan Embery and the Zoological Society of San Diego)

parakeet. The guest had invited a companion to accompany him to California. At the Sheraton Universal, where the guest, the companion, and the bird all stayed the night; the bird freed itself from its cage during the night and flew over near the pillow of the owner's companion. The fellow rolled over, flattening the little bird, and it wasn't discovered until morning. Nonetheless, Carson had the guest on the show to explain, and as a gift Johnny had purchased a beautiful new

Joan Embery and a visiting koala bear. (Courtesy of Joan Embery and the Zoological Society of San Diego)

parakeet for him to train with an invitation to return. A year later, the guest appeared again, this time without a companion.

Transporting the nonhuman guests can sometimes lead to problems, like the time Joan Embery and seven guys loaded a giant Galapagos tortoise into the back of a van for the three-hour trip to NBC. The giant turtle began crawling over the driver's seat on the highway, Embery said, "It wasn't fast, but it was very powerful, so we had to stop him, pull over each time and move him."

■ ■ ■

Jim Fowler, usually clad in his African safari khakis, also appeared with Johnny numerous times to feature an exotic animal that he had procured from a private collection or "borrowed" from an animal institution. Appearing on behalf of *Mutual of Omaha's Wild Kingdom* program, Fowler's animals were more of the exotic selections, such as large bats.

A flurry of hundreds of animals have popped into the *Tonight Show* living room to nestle in Johnny's arms or relieve themselves on his desk. Of course, the latter would prompt Johnny's perfect ogle of embarrassment—usually funnier than anything the animal might do. Johnny has welcomed pygmy hippos (which excrete a slimy substance that becomes quite messy during appearances), rhinos, a hundred-foot snake, and even opossums. Johnny's favorite? The apes.

Once, Embery strolled out two five-month-old baby orangutans in a twin baby carriage. They were fitted in diapers, with little bows affixed in their hair, and they couldn't have looked or acted more sweet. Johnny embraced them in his arms and hugged them. One orangutan kissed him in return and wrapped its long arms around Johnny's neck and hugged him back. Then, as Johnny laughed at the baby orang's innocent expression, it delivered the perfect stare of wonderment into Johnny's face.

Another appearance featured a sloppy kinkajou (akin to an organ-grinder monkey) that climbed atop of Johnny's shoulder and chewed a banana, leaving a mess on Johnny's maroon sports coat. Then the kinkajou climbed up on Ed's head and ate a banana, making another mess. Ed just seemed thrilled that one of the animals, outside of an Alpo pup, finally noticed him sitting on the couch.

■ ■ ■

Precautions and timing were everything, said Embery of her appearances on the show. "We're not talking about trained Hollywood animals here. These come from the wild, and may have been born in captivity. Some in their adult stage might not be safe to handle in a live studio situation."

It's a good thing Ed McMahon exercised caution one night when an animal trainer, who McMahon preferred to leave nameless, brought a calm-looking jaguar on the show, held back only by a chain leash. "He came in quietly enough . . . but there seemed to be no way the trainer could hold him," said McMahon, fearful the jaguar might leap. Johnny was supposed to scoop fresh vanilla ice cream—the feline's favorite—from a gallon drum, put it in a bowl, and place it in front of the powerful cat. "At the same time, I happened to glance at the trainer and said, 'Johnny, I don't think he's hungry.' This surprised Johnny, who looked at me," McMahon recalled. "I pointed to the trainer's hand. There was blood pouring from three long, deep scratches. The cat had already clawed him."

Johnny glanced at the blood and said, "Yeah, you may be right. He's probably not hungry. Anyway, it's too late for ice cream." He quickly topped the ice cream drum with the lid and the jaguar was not asked to return as a guest.

# "The Following Is a Public-Service Announcement . . ."

This is Johnny Carson here. If you've been following the news, you'll know that Humphrey the Humpback Whale went the wrong way and was trapped in the San Fernando River for three long weeks. Because of this, the unlucky mammal will be too late for the mating season off the coast of Mexico.

This is an urgent plea. If you manage an aquatic theme park such as Sea World or Marineland, or if you just own a female whale in heat, you can help Humphrey. Contact:

*Tail for the Whale*
*Baja, CA*

■ ■ ■

Hi. This is Johnny Carson reminding you that the days that it was a good idea to donate your body to medical science are long past. Nowadays, every medical school in the country is filled to the rafters with more cadavers than it can possibly use.

But you can still donate your body to a worthy cause . . . to your local fast-food restaurant, where it will be used as a speed bump in their parking lot. In this way, you'll be remembered by your loved ones every time they come in for some burgers, drive through too fast over you, and wreck their front-wheel alignment. For a donor card you can keep with you at all times in your wallet, send to:

*Jack-in-the-Asphalt*
*Studio City, CA 91604*

■ ■ ■

Hi, this is Johnny Carson making a plea directly to you women in Beverly Hills. Do you realize that there are women in rural communities of your country less fortunate than you? Ladies who live hundreds of miles from a plastic surgeon? Yes, I'm talking about flat-chested farm wives. Won't you help out? Send your extra silicone to:

*Boobs for Rubes*
*Twiggy, KS 80725*

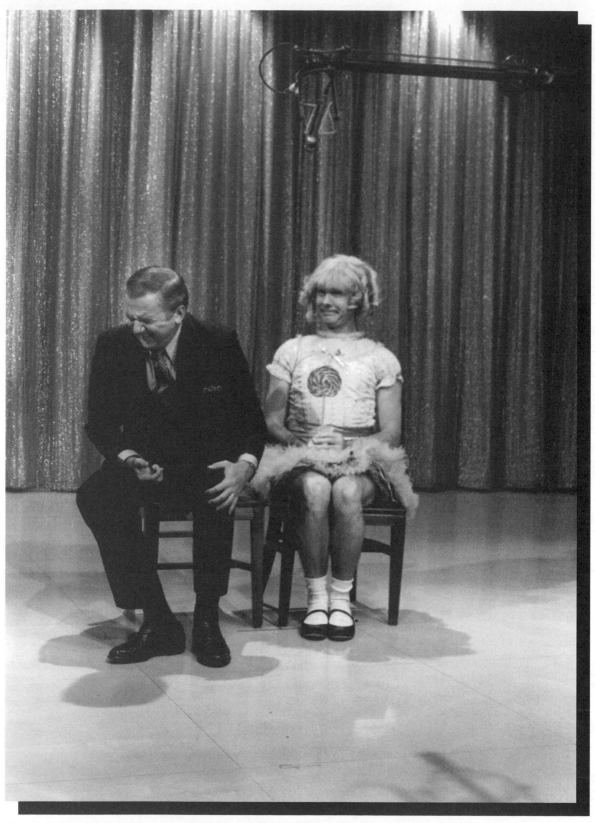

Good Ship Lollipop: Johnny's reaction to Shirley Temple Black's announcement that she was running for Congress in 1966.

# 9

# TELEVISION'S PARADE OF HUMANITY: GRAND MARSHALL, JOHNNY CARSON

## BY JOHN LOFFLIN

Communications theorist Neil Postman, in a cranky but provocative argument against television and its effect on society throughout the century, asserted that television is "our culture's principal mode of knowing about itself." He offered that insight without apparent reference to *The Tonight Show Starring Johnny Carson*, although he could not have failed to recognize that for thirty years *The Tonight Show* had, in fact, told us more about our culture than any theoretical tract (except perhaps the rantings of that wild Frenchman Alexis de Tocqueville, who visited our shores in the early 1800s). In fact, *The Tonight Show* has often told us more about our culture than we wanted to know.

Through it all, Johnny Carson has been the narrator of our story. If you tuned in most any weeknight between 1962 and 1992, you'd find him presiding over a parade of cultural clues fairly begging to be noticed: actors and actresses with bits of film to sell; writers as diverse as wry Calvin Trillin and mischievous Henry Miller, sometimes with books fresh off the press to promote, less often armed with nothing more than their public personae; musicians with music to perform and sell who were, coincidentally, awful interviewees; athletes and jugglers; zookeepers; health nuts; starlets at one end of the fame spectrum and the great washed-up at the other; comedians and psychologists—psychologists were often unwittingly funnier; politicians (one must guess they have always been the easiest guests to obtain); heroes; and fools. Each spoke to us with his dress and manner as much as with words that were often muttered away into the darkness of the rooms in which we watched. Some were newly in love and it showed in their eyes, others so bored with life that even the prospect of being seen by 6.4 percent of the nation was not enough to shake them awake.

When hemlines slid up, *Tonight Show* viewers were the first to notice. When dress shirts were worn open instead of buttoned and tied, *Tonight Show* viewers were there. When dress shirts disappeared altogether in favor of T-shirts worn under twelve-hundred-dollar sport coats, *Tonight Show* viewers were there too. And when it became permissible to speak certain words in public, *Tonight Show* viewers were the first to hear. When it became fashionable to speak of a live-in lover as one would a husband or wife, *Tonight Show* viewers heard, as they heard when it became possible to speak of gay friends in less than a whisper, to criticize matter-of-factly all elites of government, to point matter-of-factly to waste and pollution, to laugh easily at the silliness of all tradition and ritual. It is hard from this vantage point in history to remember a time when private conversation, let alone public conversation, did not permit such discussion, but rest assured that time does not predate *The Tonight Show Starring Johnny Carson.*

It wasn't the Brooklyn Dodgers moving to Los Angeles that told us the cultural center of the nation had gone west. It was 1972 and Carson moving *The Tonight Show*

*Left,* As a surprise, Johnny addressed an NBC affiliates convention in Los Angeles in character as Ronald Reagan. (1982). *Below,* In November 1969, then–Governor Reagan and his wife, Nancy, appeared with Johnny when *The Tonight Show* migrated west for some shows taped in southern California.

Author Gore Vidal's appearances usually gave the audience something to think about. Producer Fred de Cordova described the noted conversationalist's spots as, "Bright, bitter, perceptive, and articulate. When he's with us, TV isn't quite so much of a wasteland."

permanently to the City of Angels did that. Carson has said it was easier to do his show there, closer to guests, better equipment. It was also warmer and friendlier there, leisure suits were just being fitted, and New York was about to go broke. New York was home to the dark humor of Woody Allen; California to the joys of Steve Martin. New York was *Looking for Mr. Goodbar*. California was *American Graffiti*.

What we have seen, even from the city that would make a good student union for Clown College, has not always been good. It was on *The Tonight Show* that we first saw with our own eyes how detached and greedy our entertainment idols had become. Perhaps they had always been such scoundrels; it was *The Tonight Show* that brought them into our living rooms. We often felt the urge to ask them to leave. It was also on *The Tonight Show* that we saw those entertainment icons come to grips finally, though perhaps superficially, with most of the fears we shared. We heard them admit addictions, we heard the baby boomers' angst over having put off childbearing too long, we heard badly disguised jokes about divorce and emotional impermanence.

And yet, we never had the feeling Carson intended such. Unlike the slimy schools of pseudorighteous afternoon and morning talk shows that swim through the decades in Carson's wake, we never tuned in to *The Tonight Show* expecting to learn, expecting to be shocked, expecting to be outraged, expecting to be mystified. Imagine the poor working stiff who tunes in to Jerry Springer for a moment's respite while he ties his shoes in the morning, only to see a panel consisting of four obese women dressed like belly dancers and four obese men dressed only in boxer shorts—well, not only in boxer shorts, one wearing a bow tie, another wearing a black cowboy hat and carrying a rope—discussing God knows what with a studio audience that seems to be keeping its raging emotions only barely under control. *The Tonight Show Starring Johnny Carson* was never, even at its most tasteless, so rotten.

In fact, it has always been Johnny Carson's flappability that most assured us. While humanity paraded past his desk through thirty years of cultural upheaval, the same Johnny Carson tapped his pencil, straightened his tie, winked. Researchers will long debate what he represented to his audience, but let them begin with these notions: He was, first, Nebraska to the core. Middle American. Decent. Caring. Befuddled. Romantic. Sensual. Capable of temper and sulk. Capable both of understatement and, like most of us, of dancing beneath a lampshade at a party of friends. Contrast that to almost any image you hold of entertainers, of Hollywood or New York, of the culturally hip or conservatively dour. So strong is this persona that we have often cringed when Johnny was embarrassed by a woozy guest or a starlet bent on displaying her entire charms. His has been the role of the permanent aside, of the narrator who simply told the story, without rancor, without accent or polemic, but not without passion or taste.

That is, perhaps, a particularly appropriate role for a narrator of American culture. American society is, after all, a society in which the distinctions between highbrow and lowbrow are constantly tested, in which change moves so rapidly that good manners must be chronicled daily lest they be obsolete by the time they are published. A certain lightness of step and balance are needed in this always unfinished society. Carson had that step.

Is it too much to say that

Johnny is given a team helmet by Miami Dolphins fullback Larry Csonka (left) and running back Jim Kiick. (September 1973)

across all those difficult years, he was a great balm to the queasy stomach this society has so often produced? Political scientist Murray Edelman has pointed insightfully to the many ways our entertainment and news industries reassure us about our world. If we have watched the nightly news, we are now reassured that we know all a citizen needs to know about the day's activities. Election night coverage reassures us the battle was a fair one, the best man won, and we will not wake in the morning to tanks in the streets. Television comedies, even the reruns, reassure us that couples of the opposite sex can live together without sin (*Three's Company, Friends*); that single women can function properly in bastions of maleness like broadcast newsrooms (*Mary Tyler Moore*); that blacks can move into the middle class without losing their blackness (*The Jeffersons, Family Matters*); that violence in the pursuit of good is always justified and

*Time* magazine: "Johnny Carson is a master of the cozy pace and mood that he believes are appropriate for the muzzy midnight hours."

fun (*The A-Team, Nash Bridges,* and others too numerous to list); that a sense of neighborhood is still possible in America (*Cheers*); that our roots are deep, our old values better, the common sense of the common man, whether he hails from the hills or the ghetto, is always superior (*The Fresh Prince of Bel Air, The Beverly Hillbillies*).

Most reassuring of all for three decades was *The Tonight Show Starring Johnny Carson.* When the Vietnam War was raging in the jungles, and protestors were raging in the streets, Carson still walked through the curtain to cheers and laughter. It is often said that former president Lyndon B. Johnson worried that if he lost (Walter) Cronkite, he had lost the war. However astute, Johnson probably missed the point. When Carson's monologues finally found humor in the war's follies, Johnson had unmistakably lost the war. Not that Carson was ever political. He simply made it safe to disagree.

In a 1979 interview with *Rolling Stone,* Carson seemed to see both sides. First, he said, ". . . I always look at myself as an entertainer. So it has bothered me for a while that we would get a little flak from the critics saying we're not doing anything 'deep.' That's not the idea." Then he added: "I think some of the material we've done on political things is some of the best material on the air. And it does get a strong reaction—especially in the political arena. We sense the mood of the country very quickly."

Again, Carson was best at staying within himself, playing to his strength. And, as he said, he knew his audience, and his audience was free with its opinion of him. He walked a fine line when his humor was political, but it was a line few other comics could even see, let alone respect. In the same interview, he illustrated the line with the problems of House Ways and Means Committee chairman Wilbur Mills.

"When Wilbur Mills was in trouble with the infamous Fanne Foxe and the Tidal Basin thing, it was funny until people found out he was an alcoholic. And then you knew immediately to stay away from it, because you were taking advantage. . . ." That is a sensibility few others with power in American television seem to grasp.

Never, however, did Carson give us the sick feeling in the pit of our stomach that some news stories gave us, that the world would never be the same in the trough of crisis. Edelman says that when the news gets most frightening, we say to ourselves about television programming (Carson is the most obvious example) that "if it really as bad as it seems, they would cancel these shows." A viewer of the Johnny Carson show may well have said to himself a half-dozen times during Johnny's tenure, "If things were as bad as they seem to be, would Johnny be smiling? Would his tie be straight, his collar crisp? Would he be making jokes, teasing with Ed and Doc, interviewing the empty-headed? Nooooo."

■ ■ ■

The idea could be pushed too far, but certainly there is some instruction in the notion that the earliest antecedent to *The Tonight Show* in this century is the Chautauqua circuit that flourished before radio and vaudeville took away the nation's attention.

The Chautauqua circuit had both religious and social roots in the late 1800s. At Chautauqua Lake in northwestern New York, Methodist faithful gathered on summer weekends for music, Scripture, and Christian education. As political scientist James David Barber puts it: "Before long, in that Victorian age, the founders of the program worried that the Devil might be lurking among the young people who were strolling at their leisure along the twilight shore. To fill their time, lecturers—not all of them ordained—were brought in. As night follows day, the founders progressed from modesty to ambition: they sought a star speaker. . . ."

Their stars were not unlike a Carson lineup, at least in occupation. Barber says the first star was none other than President U. S. Grant, and although sitting presidents were outside Carson's reach, the list of entertainers, like Edwin Booth and Jenny Lind, would have been well within Carson's grasp; as would Barnum's midget "General Tom Thumb," writers like Charles Dickens (who, Barber reports, made a quarter of a million dollars on the Chautauqua circuit in just two years), and Mark Twain.

In essence, the Chautauqua circuit was designed to lift the soul. It began as a religious experience and joined vaudeville and radio as general escape. When the Chautauqua circuit spread out from New York to the other shore, it often involved a full night's entertainment. After the parade from the railroad platform, Barber says, onto the stage would march the "'World Famous Bohemian Orchestra' in their colorful costumes, led by Mr. Giuseppi Bartolotta, sporting a large dark mustache, to sing 'Silver Threads Among the Gold.' Then perhaps a rousing xylophone rendition of 'Funiculi, Funicula,' then came the lecture, the educational centerpiece."

The centerpiece shared several important elements with the Carson formula. First as Barber points out, the speaker sought "a strategy of least objectionable programming: nothing risqué, nothing vulgar, nothing too disturbing." That meant no preaching, no Bible-thumping, no fire and brimstone. Political speakers came out in favor of democracy; reformers, Barber says, were generally against sins committed on other continents or, at least, in other cities. Speeches were short, sweet, happy and inspirational. Speakers knew well they would be followed by a girl who played piano and trombone simultaneously, "or the 'Anvil Chorus' perform[ed] on real anvils in the dark, as electric sparks showered around."

It was Carson's genius, like the genius of those who once managed Chautauqua shows, to understand his audience so thoroughly, so innately, as to rarely produce an unhappy guest. More precisely, it was his genius to understand the setting in which his audience partook of *The Tonight Show*. It was, he once said, a show people watched between their toes.

*The Tonight Show* occupied a special setting in our lives. It was seen in the shank of the evening in most places. Those who must be at their posts by 8:00 A.M. watch it almost certainly as the final act of the day (well, almost certainly). In Nebraska, for

HERE'S JOHNNY!

*Above left,* Carson as King Tut during mummy fever in the '70s, when an exhibit of the Egyptian pharaoh's unearthed treasures toured America. *Above right,* Was Aunt Blabby a takeoff on Jonathan Winters's character Maude Frickert? "Well, I wondered that years ago," says Winters, "but I just left that alone." According to Johnny, the sassy gray-haired granny was a character he had performed on local television years before. *Below,* Johnny does a sketch with the great Orson Welles. (1976)

instance, the evening's drama and comedy were finished, the local news was over, the weather and sports recorded, modest plans for the morrow made. Then, at no later than 10:36 P.M. came the familiar music, and invariably the next thought would be who will guest. (*To guest,* in fact probably entered the language as a verb in the wake of the Carson show.) In most traditional households, children below the age of fifteen were doubtless in bed; the house was probably still and quiet for the first time since alarms went off sixteen and half hours earlier.

A certain demeanor is demanded of a visitor at that hour. The core audience of *The Tonight Show* was not watching it on a television perched on shelves above a long oak bar. They were much more interested in a hot toddy of entertainment than a fuzzy navel.

A visitor at that hour ought not to be bombastic or loud. He ought not to raise great issues or great fears, even if he offers great solutions. He ought not to preach or gloat, or wring his hands, however righteously. If he offers a joke, and well he should, it might offer a mild laugh, it must be enlightening instead of disturbing, simple not complex. This is not time for rancor and angst, for the weird and disturbing tales that drive the daytime talk shows. This is a time for Charles Nelson Reilly and Tony Randall; for vulnerable moments with Burt Reynolds; for Tony Bennett, not Jimi Hendrix; for Dr. Carl Sagan, not Dr. Hunter S. Thompson.

In the *Rolling Stone* interview, Carson was clear about his vision of the audience: ". . . television is an intimate medium," he said. "I'm not conscious when I use the camera. I know it's there. I use it like another person and do a reaction at it— lift an eyebrow or shrug or whatever."

Later in the interview, sounding more like Dr. Marshall McLuhan than a talk-show host, he elaborated on his the-ory of television and television humor. "When NBC put on *NBC Follies* years ago, they spent a lot of money building a prosce-nium stage, and they had these girls coming down in Ziegfeld-like costumes, and it didn't

Another brilliant on-the-money caricature by Al Hirschfeld for *TV Guide* in 1977. (Reprinted with permission from *TV Guide,* News America Publications)

HERE'S JOHNNY!

work because that essentially is Broadway and Hollywood—and TV is still an intimate type of thing, basically. Take the obligatory dance numbers they have in Broadway. . . . You see twenty dancers come out with a huge production number. It's really a filler to get ready for the next sketch or whatever. TV doesn't need that. Ed Wynn told me years ago about girls on television: he said, 'What's sexy about a three-inch girl?' The point he was making was that when you see them on Broadway and they come down onstage and they're bigger than life, that's one thing. Then you see them on television, it's often pointless and unimaginative. . . .

"To me, it's still the performance on TV that is most important. The personality is more important than all of the dance numbers and the big production things. I've always thought those things have been kind of lost on television, because they ignore the automatic focus that TV provides."

That focus is a two-way street. For viewers, the focus of television is always sharp. In television there are few long shots of bicycles a mile away on dirt roads, few characters dissolved from focus or dissolved into focus. There are no stage wings to which a viewer might be distracted. And from the performer's view, the focus of the audience ought also to be sharp. Little ambiguity is tolerated in television performances. The audience is out there, in its home, staring in, and nothing less than precisely drawn characters and inevitable plots will do.

Because, this, for God's sake, is our bedroom of our home in the last minutes of our day. It is no wonder so many others, who did not understand the setting, have come and gone from competing time slots. Whom would you invite to your bedroom door for the last conversation of the evening as the cicadas sang—Johnny Carson or Howard Stern?

While Johnny was always the perfect guest, his guests did not always share his mission. Many seemed all too eager to shock, allowing black lace dresses to ride up nearly to their chin—or so it seemed—or holding forth with a series of words that would almost certainly be bleeped on broadcast. More often than not, the on-the-air Johnny Carson was not pleased, and he showed it, in gentle, subtle ways. Rarely was he offensive in our homes, rarely did he insult his guests, push them to reveal more than they wanted, milk their misfortunes for sensation.

In every mode of entertainment, there has been a man or woman for the season.

*Above,* Vice President Spiro Agnew talked to Johnny on April 21, 1969. *Right,* The stunning Raquel Welch in a rare visit in 1984. *Below,* Burt Reynolds was a frequent guest; during one appearance he proudly displayed his mother's scrapbook of clippings from his career highlights (1985).

HERE'S JOHNNY!

Mark Twain seemed to understand perfectly what Chautauqua-goers wanted, the same way he understood what joy a frog could bring to the floor of a country church on Sunday morning. Franklin Delano Roosevelt seemed to know perfectly what radio listeners wanted to hear as they waited for him to announce the end of the Depression, and later, that the Germans had been routed. Orson Welles and John Huston, as well as Steven Spielberg, seemed to understand perfectly how the movie screen ought to tell its story in their eras, what behavior would be most appropriate when the curtains parted. And, of course, Johnny Carson was the perfect narrator for the glass screen that adorned our living rooms, the electronic window on our world.

## ■ Johnny: The Poor Man's Analyst?

> But there is proof enough that, if greatly conceived, the popular
> arts can derive strength from a massive popular base and can
> reach the many by reducing themselves to simplest elements—
> that is, to their broadest humanity.

> —Max Lerner, social anthropologist

Johnny Carson always helped obscure the difference in modern society between high culture and low culture. Not only did he do it by mixing the performances of Garth Brooks with those of Luciano Pavarotti, but also by producing a nightly television show that bordered on art, at least by the standards established for the medium.

That he reached a massive audience is not the point. That he reached it with consistently polished and often excellent fare is. The popular culture has produced tons of schlock across the busy last century, but Carson, even at his Mighty Carson Art Players worst, was not part of it. He may have reached a little lower than the Smithsonian, but he did manage to harvest the fruits of the popular culture with style.

If Carson was indeed following in the footsteps of the Chautauquans, he went them, and virtually every other entertainer, one better. Often overlooked in criticism of *The Tonight Show* was the fact that it was done nearly every weeknight, fifty-two weeks of the year. There are, of course, others in radio and television who are as regular as the sunset, but most, until recently, were in the news. Today (no pun intended), mornings and afternoons are peppered with shows structured like *The Tonight Show,* or structured like a loose combination of *The Tonight Show* and an informal newscast. But few of those endeavor to bring viewers such a demanding array of humor and entertaining conversation every single day.

The demand, in fact, for something special every night—and supplying that seemed to be *The Tonight Show*'s aim to the end—is daunting. Name one other comedian who has faced a television audience, monologue in cheek, more often

# "Johnny's Theme"

Paul Anka was already an international teen idol with hits like "Diana" and "Put Your Head on My Shoulder" topping the charts when he met Johnny Carson in England in 1961. Anka was filming a television special, *An Evening with Paul Anka,* for Granada Television in London when producers decided they needed a comedic element for the show. Young, thin, brash television comic Johnny Carson was summoned and quickly flew to England to participate in the special; neither an unsuspecting Anka nor Carson realized then that they would eventually collaborate on an effort that would make millionaires of them both.

"I ran into him again in New York after that," Anka says. "Coincidentally, his managers had an office in the same building as my accountant. We started discussing things and he told me that he was contemplating taking over *The Tonight Show* and changing this and changing that.

"We discussed the music and sat down, and I said, 'Let me write a theme for you.'"

Anka did. Soon after their meeting, he sat down at a piano and plunked out a melody "that I thought would be fitting," Anka says confidently. "I think I knocked it off in one day." Then he sent, by messenger, a demo tape along with a lead sheet to Skitch Henderson at *The Tonight Show*; Henderson passed out the music to the members of the band for a trial run and further orchestration.

Johnny Carson listened intently to Anka's music. He smiled and enjoyed the theme. When the host eventually debuted in the fall of 1962, so did "Johnny's Theme," which bore the names of both Anka and Carson on its sheet music as cowriters. At that time, Carson was understandably nervous about following Jack Paar, and he felt a responsibility to oversee as many elements of his new show that he could, hoping to ensure its success.

"Actually, I wrote it," Anka admits, "but when we talked about it, I got certain attitudes . . . or suggestions from him along with his input, so I put him on as a cowriter."

Fate was good to Anka then, as it had been many times in his prolific career as a songwriter and singer. "Johnny's Theme" is not unlike his Academy Award–nominated score for the film *The Longest Day*; both musical milestones evolved from a simple inquiry.

"Johnny's Theme" is the only song written by Anka that lacks lyrics. It's been a consistent money-maker for Anka, who has cumulatively garnered "in excess of a million dollars" from it, he reports. Who knew he'd be receiving regular performance pay for three decades? Based on BMI's formula for payment, which has fluctuated over the years, he estimated in the early 1990s that the song had produced an annual income of "between fifty and seventy-five thousand a year." In a rare interview with Bob Costas on NBC's *Later,* Anka laughingly said the television theme "put a few kids through college."

Anka was quick to call himself "a big Johnny Carson fan," and he said that he watched the show as often as he could. He only appeared a half-dozen times, but that was the way he wanted it. After hearing his song night after night, week after week, for three decades, it would be no wonder if he was less than enthusiastic about hearing it once again live. But, he says, he never grew tired of it at all. "Are you kidding?" he asked twice.

Wisely, successor Jay Leno had in mind

from the beginning to revamp his *Tonight Show*, which meant introducing a new theme song. For Carson, it's his signature song and he will always be instantly associated with Anka's recognizable tune—as much as Bob Hope is with "Thanks for the Memory," or Jackie Gleason with his "Honeymooners Theme" or even George Burns and "Ain't Misbehavin'."

"It's so recognizable to the public despite the fact that they hear it each night for such a short time," Anka pondered in 1992. "What—maybe ten, fifteen, thirty seconds at the most each night? But everybody knows it. Simplicity is indeed royal."

Over the years, "Johnny's Theme" has remained just that: Johnny's. Used almost exclusively by Carson, except in live appearances by Doc Severinsen and a few members of *The Tonight Show* orchestra who have strayed for an out-of-town gig, the theme has not been altered through the decades. Its fame is not derived from any personal plugs by its creator, nor is it featured during Paul Anka concerts.

"I make light of it during concerts," he says, "but I don't really address it at any other time. Its usage comes up more orally from people. I've never recorded it or promoted it or changed it. That may be a paradox—something as important as that, I think."

Anka has plenty of other tunes to play with in his sellout appearances. He gave us "My Way," most popularly recorded by Frank Sinatra. He also wrote "Puppy Love" for Mouseketeer Annette Funicello, although most would probably recall Donny Osmond's version. He wrote songs such as "Having My Baby," "You Are My Destiny," and "Lonely Boy," among nearly six hundred others. His work has been recorded by the best: Sinatra, Barbra Streisand, Buddy Holly, Tom Jones, Connie Francis, Elvis

Presley. Sid Vicious is in there somewhere, too.

Anka has built an empire with some forty hit singles, eighteen gold records, and sales that have reached 100 million. And of all the tunes he's penned, possibly the most recognized one is his simple melody for the thirty-year king of late night.

Paul Anka, the singer and songwriter who gave us "My Way" and "Puppy Love," wrote "Johnny's Theme."

than Carson. It seems perfectly logical to believe that he has told more jokes to more people than any other laughsmith ever. Yet he never seemed to tire of the job. When he stood in front of the curtain and looked into the camera, his look was fresh and young, always, and he actually seemed excited to have been invited into our homes. In an era when shortstops who can't hit their weight are paid a million dollars a year to look altogether bored by the seventh inning, Carson's enthusiasm was a wonder.

His sense of wonder was also important to the sense of the world we collectively share as a society. Who, over the age of thirty, has not experienced some awful trauma—the death of a parent, a divorce, a lost job—and not turned ultimately to Carson for healing? He was, in an odd sense, the poor man's analyst. He didn't listen and didn't offer advice, but he was solace, and seemingly always there. The world will go on, he said with his presence, with his natty suit and his Nebraskan smile. The heart might be breaking, but Carson's warm glow persisted until 1992, promising a night of unchallenged entertainment.

Forgive us if he meant more than logic argues. Forgive Douglas Ward Kelley for suggesting in a 1978 article in *Argosy*—setting down in print what many of us had said to ourselves in jest—that Johnny Carson "would make a fine president." Kelley's logic went like this: ". . . Johnny Carson is one of the best men in America. His quick wit and positive demeanor have kept him at the very top of his profession longer than anyone could have predicted. . . . There is something solid about him, a unique vigor. . . . He is the greatest entertainer in America. . . ." Floyd Turbo for president? Not really so farfetched if you recall that the Republican party nominated a former actor the following year.

British writer Kenneth Tynan curiously saw Johnny as "a magnified leprechaun" in his famous *New Yorker* profile.

Carson could, then, be forgiven if nothing very important happened during his minutes. Who wanted the promise of a glimpse of Al Capone's treasure when he turned on *The Tonight Show*? Not its faithful. They settled for an increasingly rare "Stump the Band." Norman Mailer once said that the best of television rode the edge of a sinister meanness, like the 1950s Mike Wallace interview show *Night Beat*, on local television in New York, or perhaps Joe Pine in the 1960s, or Geraldo Rivera in the late 1980s. But that just illustrated how young both television and Mailer were when he made that statement. (All Mailer did was suggest to Wallace and the television audience that President Dwight D. Eisenhower was "a bit of a woman.") We can see today that the real charm of television, what keeps us coming back to it and its most successful performers and shows, is the gentleness of its ritual. At the beginning of this new century, perhaps that has changed. Now we have a whole slew of mean-spirited

A rare early shot of Johnny, comfortable at his first desk. Besides the microphone, he decorated his desktop with the same reachable items: a beverage, cigarette box, ashtray, lighter, and pencils. For years, smoking cigarettes during interviews was trivial and commonplace for Carson as well as the guest, but eventually the host himself eliminated smoking on-camera and only grabbed a few quick puffs of his unfiltered Pall Malls during commercial breaks until he quit altogether. The ashtray disappeared, but not the lighter and little box.

televised nonfiction. But will those shows last? Will they last the three decades Carson lasted?

Like that of many of the comedians he revered, Carson's own humor was anything but cutting-edge. Its dominant quality was gentleness. Even in satire, the Nebraska boy was both gentle and mannerly. In that, his humor was Middle America, perhaps an almost artistic display of everything that Middle America had produced in the way of human character.

Take, for instance, his satiric impersonations of former president Ronald Reagan. Here lie both the wit and charm of his style. Allow Abbott and Costello doing "Who's on First?" to rattle around in your brain a bit. Then see Carson made up to look more like President Reagan than President Reagan. Remember that Reagan's embattled secretary of the interior at the time was James Watt. We see Reagan sitting in the Oval Office. His secretary of state comes through the door and takes the chair next to the desk.

"Morning, Mr. President . . . Mr. President, your press conference is scheduled to begin in an hour, so there's not much time for me to brief you on the kind of subjects that the press may throw at you."

"I know the environment is on their minds, and I'm sure they'll ask me about my secretary of the interior."

"Watt?"

"Jim, I told you. I think they'll ask about my secretary of the interior."

"His name is Watt. You're scheduled to go swimming with him tomorrow morning at the Y."

"Where?"

"Y."

"Why?"

"That's right. With Watt."

"With what? I don't even know with who?"

"Not 'who.' Watt."

"Where?"

"Y."

"Let's go on to the Middle East now. I'll need the first name of the head of the PLO. That . . . ah . . . Arafat guy."

"Yasir."

"I said, I'll need the first name of the head of the PLO."

"Yasir."

"Jim, it's nice of you to be polite, but . . ."

The routine was, of course, just another way of doing "Who's on First?" Don't feel sorry for Abbott and Costello; they borrowed it from a vaudeville routine called "The Baker's Dozen." Both uses were consistent with an older view of comedy, that the timeless routines of vaudeville belong to a common stock, that the quality of the material is determined by its delivery, by that all-important element—timing. It was not a humor that ever promised to make its audience uncomfortable, to make its audience squirm. We left that for Eddie Murphy or George Carlin. It wasn't Carson's style.

*Mr. Rambo's Neighborhood?* Now that was Carson's style. *Mr. Reagan's Neighborhood?* (There were more than a few similarities in the way Carson conducted his late evening Chautauqua and the way Fred Rogers conducted his early afternoon Chautauqua, come to think of it.) Carson as a post office employee. ("We make sure your letter sees as much of the United States as possible.") Carson as Tarzan in a sketch absolutely brimming with innuendo (or repressed sexuality, however you wanted to look at it). His precisely delivered one-liners. ("Over the years I've seen 'em come and go, and that's just in my house." "Through the years I've learned to lean on Ed and Ed's learned to lean on everything.") Ed absentmindedly (in front of 20 million viewers) picking a piece of lint off Carson's collar.

Then, of course, there was the night in 1965 when Carson was visited by Groucho Marx. A nurse named Carol Ann had been interviewed first and was sitting to Groucho's right. Carson had the comic sense to stay out of their banter until precisely the right moment, looking almost sheepishly into the camera all the while pretending to read a piece of paper in his hand.

*New York Times*: "Probably no performer in the modern era has had as much impact on style trends as Johnny Carson."

A little polo practice in 1967.

*Groucho* (to the young lady on his right): How are you? In addition to that, who are you? That's even more important.

*Carol Ann:* Carol Ann.

*Groucho:* What are you, two girls?

*Carson:* Say the secret word and Groucho will come to your house.

*Groucho:* I see, my dressing room isn't good enough for her!

*Carol Ann:* My patients are in the hospital. I don't make house calls.

*Groucho:* Are you a physician?

*Carol Ann:* No. Registered nurse.

*Groucho:* Oh really? Where are you registered? Any place where I can see you?

■ ■ ■

We were able to see Mr. Carson nearly every weeknight for three decades. There was never any question where he was registered. *The Tonight Show* without him, no matter how greatly conceived, will never be *The Tonight Show* we have known. Distilled from nearly a century of show business, *The Tonight Show Starring Johnny Carson* exhibited ourselves in a manner that will not likely be replicated. Don't grieve. That, too, befits a society that has always placed its greatest value in the new, even while longing for the old.

One fears for the new—not necessarily the *Tonight Show,* for it seems to have been left in good hands; but the new mirror television will hold up to our face may be harsher and perhaps a good deal more exotic. Home videos of the most excruciating sort have been turned into prime-time entertainment. Perhaps such ugliness will fade, and others of the Carson sort will emerge from the plains of Nebraska. Perhaps.

But there will not be another ritual like *The Tonight Show,* the ritual of Carson the insomniac, the ever-evolving every-night touchstone of American popular culture.

## ■ The Tonight Show (sadly) revisited

In the decade since Johnny Carson left the American airwaves, one fact has become clear. We will not see his like again. The world has changed dramatically, and not for the better, and the world of television and other entertainment has changed even more dramatically and for even worse. The body of work produced from 1961 to 1992 by Carson is singular and, unfortunately, time-bound. Neither Johnny nor anyone like him will ever be here again.

The first reason we will not see another Johnny Carson is technological. In 1961, television was fuzzy, snowy, small, colorless, and new. Folks in big cities received three channels of it through the antenna on top of their big mahogany sets or, if they were cutting edge, on top of their chimneys. Folks in smaller cities or in the country were lucky to get two stations in those days. Perhaps a third station could be tugged into the living room with a large sheet of aluminum foil wrapped around the rabbit ears, the rabbit ears adjusted just right and the weather bright and clear. *The Tonight Show* had no competition for the American attention in those days. If you watched television after 10 P.M., you had three choices and, on many nights, two of those choices were pre-war movies. Johnny's reach into the American heart was enormous. A particularly wonderful joke, a bit of biting sarcasm, an inebriated guest, was grist for conversation everywhere in America the next day. More likely than not, the fellow you met across the water cooler had also been tuned to the show; the conversation tended to begin mid-sentence.

Consider the situation today. Many Americans choose from hundreds of channels each night, from the circus of wrestling to serious conversation, writers talking to tiny groups in Iowa about their novels to war-torn Afghanistan, baseball to dogs chasing Frisbees, Martha Stewart to the Playboy Channel. Who would have dreamed in 1961 that Johnny Carson would be competing with live film of police chases or *The Real World* on a channel supposedly devoted exclusively to music videos? That daringly dressed actresses fidgeting on the couch next to Carson's desk would compete with undressed women writhing in the most intimate human activity on the hoods of automobiles? The choices themselves are comic. Ab Rollers. Nads. Spelling Bees. The House of Representatives. Greta, Bill, Geraldo, Charlie. The human menagerie that is Howard Stern.

No late-night host will ever have such a captive audience as the audience in 1961. What that means is no late-night host (or other performer) will ever be the star Johnny Carson was. No late-night host will ever be as powerful. No late-night host will ever reach icon status, ever become such an integral part of American culture, ever embody so completely the American spirit. Imagine Lyndon Johnson watching Johnny Carson in 1968, listening to his razor-wire jokes about Vietnam and shuddering at the result on the American psyche he was trying so desperately to woo. Could an American president be sent trembling today by Jay Leno, David Letterman, Conan O'Brien? Only Oprah holds such power in 2002, and she chooses not to use it on the political stage very often.

The second reason we will not see another Johnny Carson is that our appetites have changed. Some thinkers have suggested television is a sort of collective American dream—a dream Americans experience together that is like the dreams you and I have alone, where we work out our problems, our fears, our fantasies. If that's so, heaven help us. If, as Neil Postman says, television is the cultural conversation we have about who we are, what does Jerry Springer tell us? What does *Cops* tell us? What does *The Real World* tell us? What do *Survivor* and the like tell us? Is Howard Stern who we are? Are we the characters in Dr. Dre's latest video? Are we Eminem? Are we the people who televise our dates, our weddings, our childbirths, our surgeries? Are we the drugged-out rock star biographies of the music channels? Are we, (think seriously about this), the Osbournes?

Once upon a time, we were happy to be Johnny Carson. Johnny represented what was good about us. He was our Midwestern roots, the Nebraska in all of us. Simply put, that's not who we are today. Nor is it likely to be who we are tomorrow. We will never produce another Johnny Carson to tuck us into bed at night. We'd rather sleep with our nightmares.

■ ■ ■

*JOHN LOFFLIN is the chair of the department of communication arts and associate professor of journalism at Park University in Kansas City, Missouri. He has written for* Money *magazine, the* New York Times, *and many midwest newspapers. He co-authored the book* The Abbott & Costello Story *and is currently working on a book about baseball fiction titled* Reading Baseball: The Slugger and the Fall from Grace.

# "More to Come"

More than just the bright feathers of the NBC peacock have fluttered out the doors of the network's graphic arts department.

Some of that department's most talked-about artwork during Johnny's reign were the objets d'art sandwiched before and after commercial breaks of *The Tonight Show.* Sometimes called "bumpers" or "art cards" and commonly known as "More to Comes" around the office, these elite examples of artistic expression, shown nightly on network television, could generate about as much success for and excitement in the artist as a shot on the air would provide a comic.

The pieces were memorable, but, naturally, they weren't identifiable as the *Mona Lisa.* Then again, the *Mona Lisa* is on diplay only in Paris's Louvre and has never enjoyed nightly exposure to millions. For graphic artists, the bumpers on *The Tonight Show were* the Louvre or the Metropolitan Museum of Art. Just because the medium exposed their work to the masses in numbers beyond the expectations of most artists, the appreciation and value of their artwork should not be diminished.

Originally, said Art Trugman, a thirty-nine-year NBC employee in 1991, the "More to Comes" developed in themes. When Carson took over *The Tonight Show* in New York, Trugman was a young artist in the graphics department who made the move to Los Angeles with the show. His real claim to fame had been body painting. Remember the bikini-clad beauties on TV's *Laugh-In*? It was Trugman, brush in hand, who happily painted words, shapes, faces,

Andrew Hoyos, Art Trugman, and Michael Bayouth display their artwork from *The Tonight Show* in the 1970s.

and golf balls around the navels of Goldie Hawn, Judy Carne, and other shapely beauties who shimmied to the groovy music on Rowan & Martin's hit variety show.

Trugman headed the NBC graphic arts department at the time of Carson's retirement, still encouraging and developing the talents of his young staff. Besides creating artwork for *The Tonight Show,* the staff artists conceptualize logos for television shows and create signs, cereal boxes, props, and posters—you name it—for every use in television. Their work is even seen on other major networks.

"When I first came here, it was myself and Dave Rose," Trugman remembered. "We drew little sight gags for the 'More to

Comes,' like the two Eskimos rubbing noses." Another early slide had Tarzan hanging on a vine over an alligator with the words "Hang in There" printed alongside. Eventually, the themes within the show illustrated animals, performers, musicians, comedians, signs of the Zodiac, and an array of unusual artistic expressions. Each artist called on to contribute a set—consisting of ten different pieces when the show ran an hour and a half, and later usually six slides—put his or her heart and soul into their "babies," said Trugman. With nearly ten artists employed in the department at any given time, these creations were the network's most prized pieces. They were the pièce de résistance of the television art world. They even sometimes provided a stepping stone for young artists. "A lot of kids have busted away and done very well," said Trugman.

Accolades are rare in the art department; however, staff artisans Rick Andreoli and Susan Cuscuna picked up Emmy Award nominations for their "More to Come" artwork in the 1974–75 race. The category was listed as "Outstanding Achievement in Graphic Design and Title Sequences for a Single Episode of a Series or for a Special Program."

These famous visuals, usually about 16" x 20" or 18" x 24", were created in whatever medium the artist preferred. They couldn't be too involved or too intricate lest they not "read" on television when flashed for the viewer. After completion by the artist, they were shot flat using a camera mount and made into slides. Then they were handed off to the technical personnel who incorporated them into the show by shooting them on tape. In the '60s and '70s, the bumpers were shown on screen for approximately 30 seconds, with music from the *Tonight Show* band heard simultaneously. This was ample time to allow the viewer to absorb the artwork and really get a nice look at it. Exposure time diminished over the years and by the early 90s, the "More to Comes" might have gotten six or seven seconds tops.

"This is the best part of the job for me," said NBC artist and designer Don Locke in 1991. "It's given me the opportunity to experiment with all kinds of styles. I work in markers, acrylics, airbrush, pencils."

His favorite set of bumpers is the jazz performers he created in markers on a chemically treated photographic paper, which appear like bleeding watercolors. His first set, which was seen occasionally even toward the end of Johnny's run, featured comedy stars like Harold Lloyd (hanging from the hands of an oversized clock face), W. C. Fields, and the Marx Brothers. He produced a series of sports figures, dancers, and anniversary images featuring Johnny, Ed, and Doc among others over the years.

Only once did the graphics department stray from its own stable of artisans for a "More to Come" image. "We hired a lady who was very unique in making little clay figures about three inches tall," Trugman said. "She did a whole set of an old couple watching television in bed, in a sauna, from their couch. It was real cute." Rarely did Trugman accept submissions in the mail from novices or freelancers, but he did consider suggestions contributed by viewers and fans of the show. Artists across the country aspired to create a *Tonight Show* set, "but we have to stick with the artists on staff and give them a chance," Trugman explained with a hint of regret.

Johnny Carson, who had always remained proud of the art, enjoyed peeking at the new pieces on the monitor when they were premiered during the show.

He had never requested one to hang in his office, or suppressed the staff's creative expressions, but he was known to compli-

ment certain styles that caught his eye.

Each artist was professional in his or her own way; they weren't starving artists peddling their wares on the street corner where a gas station has been boarded up. Some of the *Tonight Show* gems are worthy of placement in museums, many artists attest, and they range from abstract visuals to realism that provided a wonderful exposure to different artistic styles for audiences.

Not all the bumpers were successful, however. Former staff artist Rick Andreoli produced a set on women. They were anything but normal. "He was a bachelor, you know, and the women were in different positions," recalled Trugman, with a laugh. "One woman was on all fours, behind bars, like a lion in a cage. She had long hair like a mane. We had to take it off because there were complaints, but there was nothing vulgar about it. Some pieces we have to watch because they might be too complicated and they won't 'read' quick enough on the air."

The NBC legal department was summoned twice regarding the "More to Comes." A realistic conception based on an actual photograph of Albert Einstein prompted a remuneration request from the estate of the late photographer who had taken the picture of the wiry-haired genius in the 1940s. Another instance was a cartoon carousel horse painted by Don Locke that utilized an image Locke found in a photograph as a model. Although Locke's rendition was clearly not a direct copy, NBC paid twenty-five hundred dollars as a nuisance fee to the photographer; if it had pro-gressed to litigation, however, NBC would probably have prevailed, Locke added.

There is no limit to the themes displayed on *Tonight* via these canvas crafts. Cowboys, child stars, lions, cartoon clocks, boiling teakettles, ringing telephones, classic actors, horror monsters, and singers all flashed by while Doc's orchestra blasted through the screen. Two per night featured the wording *The Tonight Show Starring Johnny Carson,* and the rest were labeled "More to Come." And when a show was repeated, those programs featuring dated zodiac artwork were left on the shelf. (They had learned their lesson once when the stars were not in line: one night when an inappropriate Zodiac sign was presented on the repeat, the network was deluged with letters from viewers as well as astrologers).

Many collectors have inquired about obtaining the original pieces, and NBC has released a few for public auction, while a few have been given out by the artists.

"Two to three publishers have approached us about doing a 'More to Come' art coffee-table book," said Trugman. "A private company that called itself the More to Come Company made a deal with Carson Productions some years ago to produce a massive merchandising line based on the art. Planned were T-shirts, posters, books, placemats, and limited edition prints; even collector's plates were proposed. For a year, they were collecting items and organizing, but ultimately it fell through."

# 10

FAREWELL

*He is ingrained, burnished, lodged deep. Like no one else in a lifetime, his was the last face flickering onto the brain before so many billions of slumbers. Like sun and moon and oxygen, he was always there, reliable and dependable, for thirty years. Then he wasn't anymore. And he didn't just simply leave: He vanished completely; he evaporated into cathode snow; he took the powder of all powders. He did not even wean himself away.*

—BILL ZEHME, *Esquire*, JUNE 2002

Even Ed McMahon didn't know. It probably hit him like a sucker punch in the gut.

When Johnny Carson stepped out onto the stage at Carnegie Hall and delivered the news at the 1991 NBC affiliates meeting, no one was prepared. It was clandestine news: Johnny was saying farewell, calling it a night. The king was handing the scepter off to someone else and closing the chapter for the history books. *The Tonight Show* would never be the same. "The only person who knew he was leaving was Brandon Tartikoff," says Ed McMahon. "He and Johnny were great friends. Nobody on the staff knew. He didn't tell me. It was a surprise to everyone, all the executives, everyone on the show. It was a well-kept secret."

The countdown began and the clock was ticking. They'd had a fantastic run, almost thirty full years on NBC, a record probably never to be bested. Contemplating a world without Johnny was a painful thing, noted *Washington Post* critic Tom Shales. "Already some of us are having chills, shivers and angst attacks. For nearly thirty years he has been tucking us in at night. At a delicate and intimate hour, his is sometimes the last face we see. Now we are to get a new video nanny. It's natural to panic."

Johnny was not only leaving one of the best-paying gigs in television history, he was taking his audience with him. Most of the country's late-night viewers—generations of accumulated fans who felt a great allegiance to the king—could not fathom a replacement. Their habit of watching Johnny was too well established, too deeply rooted in our television viewing patterns. For the next year, trying to snare tickets for a taping of *The Tonight Show* was next to impossible and as the months and weeks drew close to the end, tickets were not to be found. Fans from across the country made a pilgrimage to Burbank in hopes of sitting in the audience for a personal audience with the man. They camped out, they brought gifts, they prayed for a miracle to get squeezed into the audience somehow. Sleeping bags lined the outside of NBC like never before.

Guests no longer stopped in to simply chat and plug their media wares. They asked, they begged, they gasped. The mawkish farewell wishes and tributes poured in from everyone who sat in during the last months. "Why are you leaving?" they all asked. Robin Williams presented him with a rocking chair. Even stone-faced Charles

Grodin admitted that he'd miss sparring on camera with Carson. Johnny was retiring from the show, and not because he was feeble. It was time for him to move on and do other things with his life. After, we may have felt like he was our Johnny, but we didn't own him.

In the waning days before his departure, Carson was drawing the best guests ever and the best ratings he'd had in years. Elizabeth Taylor made her first appearance on the show in February specifically because Johnny was leaving. "I'm not plugging anything," said the actress, clad in a leather jacket. "I'm not here to sell anything. I'm here to thank you for thirty years of brilliant entertainment."

The mood around NBC and the *Tonight Show* staff was tense and giddy and emotional for all of them as they realized the end was near. The country felt their impending pressure, and the media was relentless with an onslaught of tributes in every magazine and newspaper in the country—literally. The numbers poured in as writers and reporters attempted to capture the sadness and remind all of us just how long he had been a fixture in our lives. He hosted more than 4,500 shows, traveled with us through three decades, and made his way into the hearts of generations.

Nostalgia was oozing from every pore of *The Tonight Show*, giving way for some of the best television we'd seen in a long time, aided of course by the anticipation of his profoundly hyped final night. Johnny asked his staff to make sure invitations went out to his original guests, Mel Brooks and Tony Bennett, both of whom stopped by near the end, and all the biggies were booked during the last weeks: Jerry Seinfeld, Buddy Hackett, George Carlin, Steve Martin, David Letterman, Clint Eastwood, James Stewart, Robin Williams . . . and the final guest, "the last fool Mr. Carson will have to suffer gladly," as she said, Bette Midler.

When Johnny emerged from the curtain for his penultimate show, he was embarrassed, maybe stunned, by two minutes of solid, unrelenting applause from the audience, befitting a king. He shrugged his shoulders while the whistles and cheers loudly overcame the studio. He scratched the back of his hand, looked around at Ed and Doc, scratched the back of his ear. He ran out of tics. He couldn't even get a word in, but once it finally quieted, he thanked everyone. "I don't know what to say. Sure, you're in a good mood, you've been outside for twelve hours with a thermos of margaritas." Robin Williams proved a perfect guest to break Johnny up and keep the show moving at a clip, but it was the Divine Miss M's homemade lyrics to the song "You Made Me Love You," a tribute from a true diva belted out while sitting atop Johnny's desk, that brought the audience to their feet for another ovation. It was an electric night that triggered tears even from Johnny. He and Bette sang an impromptu duet of an old standard, "Here's That Rainy Day," that was touching and sweet. And Bette never sounded better as she serenaded the host with one of his favorites, "One for My Baby (And One More for the Road)". After her loving rendition of the Johnny Mercer saloon song, she ran over and kissed Johnny, then left the stage in tears.

The next night, Friday, May 22, 1992, was a national event. It was the night Johnny said farewell. He wanted to finish as he started . . . quietly. He started in 1962 looking dapper in a dark blazer, and he left in 1992 looking dapper in a dark blazer. This was a somber and atypical *Tonight Show*, however, with Johnny perched atop a tall stool in front of the curtain, right where he usually stood to deliver the monologue. Johnny was careful not to actually say "goodbye" as he thanked his cohorts, his staff, his family, and his devoted audience everywhere. He didn't want anything too heavy, but there was no way around the gush.

The studio audience was made up of invited guests, *Tonight Show* staff, and some of Johnny's family members, including his wife, his two surviving sons, his sister and brother, "and a sprinkling of nieces and nephews," he said. He addressed his sons: "I realize that being an offspring of someone who is constantly in the public eye is not easy. So, guys, I want you to know that I love you. I hope that your old man has not caused you too much discomfort." He visibly mustered his courage and maintained composure as he mentioned his late son, Rick, who had died in an automobile accident in the months prior. "It would have been a perfect evening if their brother Rick would have been here with us, but I guess life does what it is supposed to do."

He choked back tears as he told America, in a carefully worded sentiment, "I bid you a very heartfelt good night."

And with that, he blew a sweet kiss to the audience as tears welled up in his eyes and the closing music played. He walked over to his wife, who was waiting in the wings, and took her hand and they walked out the door. Just outside the NBC studios, a helicopter was waiting to whisk them off into the sunset over Malibu.

"He made that great speech," says Ed McMahon, "and he walked right off. I was standing in my usual spot and he didn't even look at me. It was emotional for all of us."

# The Last Show

*Date: Friday May 22, 1992, 11:30 P.M.–12:30 A.M.*
*Broadcast from NBC Studios in Burbank, California (Studio One)*
*Announcer: Ed McMahon*
*Music: Doc Severinsen and the NBC Orchestra*
*Appearing: no guests*
*Final theme music: "I'll Be Seeing You"*

Making his exit a graceful and classy one, Johnny introduced no guests on this farewell show, only vintage clips from the past three decades. The show began with an opening narrative from Johnny and a few audio excerpts (with photos) from his *Tonight Show* debut. As Johnny finally emerged from the curtain for the last time, he took center stage in his smart double-breasted jacket and tried to calm more than a solid minute of applause. After the monologue, clips and highlights were presented, a behind-the-scenes tour about the production of an average show, a few tender exchanges between Ed, Doc, and Johnny, and then a quiet goodnight. (The "More to Come" scenic photography as well as the exquisite panoramic sunset shown during the credit roll were images made by Carson's late son, Rick.)

**Highlights from the Monologue:** One of the questions that people have asked me, especially last month is, 'What's it like doing *The Tonight Show*,' and what has it meant to me? Well, let me try to explain it. If I could magically, somehow—that tape that you just saw—make it run backwards, I'd like to do the whole thing all over again.

. . . Now we don't want this to be mawkish. It's a farewell show. There's a certain sadness among the staff, but look on the bright side: You won't have to read or see one more story about my leaving the show.

. . . The greatest accolade though I received today. GE named me employee of the month. And god knows that was a dream come true.

I don't like saying goodbye. Farewell shows are a little awkward. I really thought about this, no joke, I thought . . . wouldn't it be funny, instead of showing up tonight put on a rerun.

**Johnny's Closing Words as Host:** And so, it has come to this. I am one of the lucky people in the world. I've found something I always wanted to do and I have enjoyed every single minute of it. I want to thank the gentlemen who've shared the stage with me for thirty years, Mr. Ed McMahon, Mr. Doc Severinsen. For you people watching, I can only tell you that it has been an honor and a privilege to come into your homes all these years and entertain you. I hope when I find something that I want to do and that I think you'll like, and come back, that you'll be as gracious inviting me into your homes as you have been. I bid you a very heartfelt goodnight.

In 1957, Carson became the host of a new game show, *Do You Trust Your Wife?* which was renamed—mercifully—*Who Do You Trust?*

# 11

# A KING AND HIS COURT

# JOHNNY

## ■ THE KING'S CASTLE

The most demystifying part of attending a *Tonight Show* taping at NBC's Studio One in Burbank and actually exploring the set with one's own eyes was the actual size of it all—an astonishment every newcomer experienced. While the stage seemed so marvelously ostentatious on television, it was really rather small. How long it seemed to take Johnny to stroll over to Doc at the bandstand. The stage where Johnny's desk sat with prominence seemed to be a fair-sized step up from the floor and the proscenium behind Johnny's couch was so deep, distant, and dreamy.

None of it was true. The distance between Johnny and Doc was a mere ten yards. Johnny took about nine steps from the curtain to his center spot for the monologue. The midnight skyline of the San Fernando Valley behind him was a mere few feet from his perch. The stage was scarcely six inches off the floor. The whole aura of grand-scale television had fooled viewers all those years. Almost universally, audience members took their seats and said to one another, "Oh, it looks so big on television."

The desk, the couch, the small set is the "home" that Johnny built and spent countless hours entertaining guests in. Almost everything about Johnny's "house" remained a constant; its surroundings were friendly, warm, and inviting for that hour of the night. (Eventually, a little motorized footstool was installed and with the push

One of Johnny's passions was playing the drums. It helped him relieve hostility, he said.

of a button would slide out from beneath the hot seat just for the diminutive guests who entered the domain. How quaint.) So comfortable behind his famous desk, Johnny once dragged along a collapsible brown replica that he unfolded and sat behind when being interviewed by David Letterman on *Late Night*. That desk became his security, although a few guests, such as George Peppard and Robert Blake, have convinced him to momentarily switch places during the interview just to see what it was like.

Johnny's broadcasts for the first ten years (outside of occasional visits to Southern California) emanated from New York's Studio 6-B at Rockefeller Center. It was a tiny set, dull in detail comparatively,

Johnny reads a bedtime story to his three kids, Chris, Cory, and Ricky, in 1955. (Photo by Gabi Rona)

and decorated modestly for the most part. The lighting was not elaborate and the studio possessed a hollow sound. The sixties furnishings were low-key, and limited for lounging. Johnny's curtain was solid blue; the Neapolitan curtain was introduced later, in Burbank.

Broadcaster Tom Snyder told *TV Guide* about his first impression of meeting Carson face-to-face on the air: "You are sitting in this awful chair," he said. "I mean a chair that has got to be the most uncomfortable chair in the history of television. At the break, I say, 'Johnny, is this chair uncomfortable on purpose?' He says, "Yep. That's right. I need all the weapons I can get to keep people off their guard.'"

Carl Reiner argues that it was not like a home at all, but rather an employment atmosphere: "You feel like you're in an office being interviewed," he says. "But if you know you have the qualifications for the job, you don't feel so bad."

Johnny was proud of the house he built. One night, guest host Dick Shawn turned the desk and chairs over on their side in a fit of comedy when his material failed. This infuriated Carson, and Shawn was not invited to repeat his guest-hosting chores.

On occasion, the desk became part of the show's comedy and the prop department brought in perfectly replicated balsa-wood "breakaway" desks for gags. Carnac stumbled right on top of one, demolishing it. For a bit celebrating NBC's hit mini-series *Shogun,* a samurai warrior chopped it into bits one night. Steve Martin blew the desk up with dynamite. At Christmastime one year, Johnny had a forklift haul in a holiday fruitcake and place it atop his desk only to have it crash clear through.

Johnny's set was, for the most part, sacred—with the exception of Bob Hope, who

# Moonlighting

Everyone knows Johnny Carson from *The Tonight Show* and maybe even a few stints as host of the Academy Awards, but few remember that he was on the sitcom *Get Smart* twice, or that he played a talk-show host with Connie Francis in the long forgotten 1964 flick *Looking for Love.* The following is a catalog of Johnny's guest appearances over the years. (This list excludes Johnny's own programs as host and his *Tonight Show* anniversary specials. And keep in mind, it would be nearly impossible to list the many films and episodic television programs that have included clips of *The Tonight Show* over the years, visible in the background or used in a pivotal fashion—such as the memorable episode of NBC's *Columbo* in which the mystery was solved using Johnny's program as a key in the investigation.)

## Specials

Oh Johnny!
Johnny Carson Discovers Cypress Gardens
Joys
Life Goes to War
A Love Letter to Jack Benny
Johnny Goes Home
Johnny Carson's Greatest Practical Jokes
James Stewart: A Wonderful Life
NBC's 60th Anniversary Celebration
Laurel & Hardy: A Tribute to the Boys
The Arthur Murray Party for Bob Hope
The Sun City Scandals
Kraft Music Hall: Friars Club Roasts Jack
    Benny
Kraft Music Hall: Friars Club Roasts Johnny
    Carson
CBS Salutes Lucy: The First 25 Years
Jerry Lewis Labor Day Telethon (1978)
Lucy Moves to NBC
Breakfast in Beverly Hills
Life's Most Embarrassing Moments
The Academy Awards (host; five times:
    '79–'82; '84)
Sheena Easton Act One
It's Howdy Doody Time
American Teacher Awards
Bob Hope: The First 90 Years
The Kennedy Center Honors: A Celebration
    of the Performing Arts (1993)

## Episodic

Playhouse 90
U.S. Steel Hour
The Jack Benny Program
New Comedy Showcase (pilot)
Get Smart
NBC Children's Theatre ("Stuart Little")
Bob Hope Chrysler Theatre
Here's Lucy
The Mary Tyler Moore Show (voice-over)
Night Court
Newhart
Cheers
The Simpsons (voice-over)

## Talk/Variety Programs

The Ed Sullivan Show
Timex All-Star Comedy Show
The Sammy Davis Jr. Show
Jack Benny's Carnival Nights
The Red Skelton Show
Colgate Comedy Hour
The Polly Bergen Show
The Jack Benny Show
The Jack Paar Show
The Steve Allen Show
Arthur Murray Party
The Garry Moore Show
Steve Allen Plymouth Show
Dinah Shore Chevy Show
Dick Clark's World of Talent
Perry Como's Kraft Music Hall
Celebrity Talent Scouts
Here's Hollywood
The Don Rickles Show
The Smothers Brothers Comedy Hour
Rowan & Martin's Laugh-In

Slinging the insults on the NBC special *The Friars Club Roasts Jack Benny* are roastmaster Johnny Carson, Alan King, Ed Sullivan, Dennis Day, Phil Harris, Jack Benny, George Burns, and Milton Berle. (January 1970)

*Above,* Don Adams as Maxwell Smart, with Johnny Carson in a cameo appearance on the hit sitcom *Get Smart* in 1966. *Below,* Johnny whispers his secret to host Garry Moore during an appearance on the CBS game show *I've Got a Secret* in 1959.

The Phil Donahue Show
The Dinah Shore Show
The David Frost Show
The Dick Cavett Show
Tomorrow
Dean Martin's Man of the Week Celebrity Roast
The Merv Griffin Show
Star Search
Late Night with David Letterman
TV's Bloopers and Practical Jokes

## Game Shows

Who's in the Picture?
What's My Line?
Pantomime Quiz
I've Got a Secret
To Tell the Truth
Password

## Films

Looking for Love (1964)
Cancel My Reservation (1972)

Las Vegas makes me
feel so young!
Johnny Carson

Advertising his live Las Vegas show at the Sahara, this publicity postcard featured an early snapshot of Johnny as a little tyke.

cleared the studio to tape specials in Studio One on occasion. Untouched for years were his set pieces, like the microphone, cigarette lighter, two-headed pencils, and cigarette box. One night, Johnny discovered the cigarette box broken. His cherished memento, which he had brought from New York, had been tampered with during the previous night's show by a guest host. It had been beaten. The lid was in pieces. And he found out his pal Don Rickles was the culprit.

"He was having one of his fits," Doc tattled.

"How could you tell?" Johnny joked, still visibly irked.

Johnny suddenly looked over to his director, got a nod to go ahead, and shot up from his seat, grabbing a hand mike. The director knew instinctively what he was going to do. Johnny waved the cameraman to follow him right across the hallway in to the next studio where Johnny knew Rickles was in the middle of taping his sitcom *CPO Sharkey* in front of a live audience. Johnny burst into the studio, halted the taping and lashed a verbal beating to the man who delivers them best. Rickles was stunned and apologetic, attempting to cover his embarrassment with humor. Johnny joked about it, of course, and the bit was outrageously funny and out of character for Johnny as well as the show itself.

■ ■ ■

For quite a stretch, Johnny Carson might have been the most recognizable man in America, a fact that pushed him further into a private existence at home. Even today, it's not easy for him to emerge form his residence for a quiet moment in public. For years, people who approached him either wanted an autograph or to audition their spoon-playing act right there at his restaurant table for him, fame glittering in their eye. He'd been asked for autographs while standing at a urinal and people even followed him home from work as he drove the course from NBC to Malibu. Over the years, Carson learned to deal with the compromise, this sometimes painful fate of fame.

HERE'S JOHNNY!

John William Carson was born in Corning, Iowa, on October 23, 1925, to Homer Lloyd (nicknamed "Kit") and Ruth Hook Carson. He grew up in Norfolk, Nebraska, the territory he really regards as his roots.

It might be hard to believe that young John was a shy kid, uncomfortable in crowds. His childhood was secure; his family, which included an older sister, Catherine, and a younger brother, Richard, spent family vacations on a lake in Minnesota. His father was a utility company lineman who became a manager for the Nebraska Light and Power Company. The family's faith was Methodist, and school did not seem to be a problem for young John. In fact, he learned early on that his quirky Popeye impression and talent for telling jokes called attention to him, releasing a little of the shyness.

Prolific screenwriter Nora Ephron might have been the first to write a biography of Carson in the late 1960s. She described his childhood in great detail:

> The Carsons settled in a large white frame house at 306 South Thirteenth Street, on a tree-lined block in a fairly nice neighborhood. (In 1966, the Norfolk Centennial Committee put a twelve-foot-high billboard in front of the house, with an enormous picture of Carson on it and, in monstrous letters, "Johnny Carson lived here!") The Carson boys went through their early years doing what most Norfolk boys did: they went skinny dipping and fishing in the nearby Elkhorn River; they learned to hunt the pheasant that thrive in the vicinity and shoot at a rifle range their father built in the basement; they sold *Saturday Evening Post* subscriptions door-to-door; they kept fast-multiplying white rats; they went exploring in the woods with satchels full of peanut butter and jelly sandwiches. "I could have paved a highway with all the peanut butter and jelly sandwiches that I made for them," Mrs. Carson recalled. And though Johnny can't remember it, Dick Carson well recalls the early mischief the two boys got into. One Christmas, he recalled, the two of them shot all the balls off the Christmas tree with beebee guns. Another Christmas, the two of them were playfully throwing a grapefruit in the living room when Johnny threw it extra hard at Dick, who ducked. The grapefruit splattered all over the brand new wallpaper.

The young Nebraskan becomes "The Great Carsoni" in 1949.

Johnny has said he prefers not to dwell on the old days, reluctant to relive it all, especially his childhood. "Looking back is kind of a silly thing to do," he said years ago.

"Houses are always larger. You see them through a child's eye." But Johnny adjusted and mellowed and eventually he did go back—several times, in fact, right in front of the camera's eye. In the 1960s he and his brother Dick returned to Norfolk on a strange mission, and again in 1982 Johnny went back to the midwest as part of a nostalgic televised special, which was filmed (not videotaped), called simply *Johnny Goes Home.*

In 1966, Johnny and his brother Dick returned to their old frame house in Norfolk for a day to unearth a time capsule Johnny had buried there when he was young. Dick Carson, who at that time was the director on *The Tonight Show,* told Nora Ephron about the odd excursion. "We didn't tell anyone we were coming," he said. "We wanted to get some color shots for the show of Johnny digging up this old can . . . he insisted he knew exactly where the can was, just two feet from the garage. I forget the name of the woman who's living there now, but can you imagine the look on her face when I rang the bell and said, 'Excuse me ma'am, but Johnny Carson is here . . . do you mind if we tear up your backyard a little?'"

By the time they were through, the brothers had dug a trench half the length of the garage and come up empty. Neighbors curiously converged and others helped look, including a reporter for the local paper, but still no coffee can. Johnny left very disappointed. Ultimately, the neighbors kept searching and found the can with the help of a metal detector. They shipped it, unopened, to Johnny in New York, where the host unsealed the can on network television.

Ensign John Carson served in the navy during World War II.

Early on, maybe at age twelve or so, John stumbled across *Hoffman's Book of Magic* and quickly became engrossed in the art of illusion and sleight-of-hand, enthralled with the whole history and process of prestidigitation. He sent away for mail-order magic kits and practiced card tricks, pestering his family with "pick a card . . . c'mon, take a card" until they were sick of it. He was noticeably becoming better at the tricks, applying his own technique.

At age fourteen, young John appeared "live" at the Norfolk Rotary Club, which earned him three dollars. His mother had sewn him a big black cape he swung on his shoulders, and he became the first Mighty Carson Art Player in his first routine—as "The Great Carsoni." He was encouraged by his parents to pursue his magical hobby, and he entertained at parties for his family.

HERE'S JOHNNY!

At Norfolk High School, John appeared in student productions and wrote a humor column for the school newspaper. To earn funds to pay for his magic tricks, he ushered at the Granada Theater and sold magazine subscriptions. He graduated in 1943 at the height of World War II and entered the navy, where he attended midshipmen's school at Columbia University. He served the rest of the war aboard the USS *Pennsylvania* in the Pacific Ocean. Reportedly, he was "the only officer to entertain enlisted men in the ship's shows."

He earned a B.A. degree at the University of Nebraska, where he was a member of Phi Gamma Delta fraternity. His senior thesis, entitled "Comedy Writing," was a study in the art via analysis of radio comedians like Jack Benny, Bob Hope, and Fred Allen—all of whom he worked with later in his career. Just prior to his graduation in 1949, he obtained his first professional radio job at KRAB in Lincoln, Nebraska. Later, he found work at WOW radio in Omaha before moving to California, where he became an "all-purpose" announcer at KNXT-TV (a CBS affiliate) in Los Angeles and was given his own half-hour comedy show on Sunday afternoons, *Carson's Cellar*. The young dark-haired comic hosted the show until mid-1953, and it caught the attention of Groucho Marx, Fred Allen, and Red Skelton, who all graced the little show with an appearance. Carson's first notable television appearance in prime time

Carson never disappointed worldwide audiences, proving to be a classy and appealing host for the Oscars, having led five Academy Award telecasts (1979–1982, 1984). Here, he is shown with a frail John Wayne during the 1979 broadcast; it would be the Duke's last television appearance.

on an established program was with his idol, Jack Benny, in 1952. He mimicked Benny's stance and stare, and comically offered suggestions to the master as to "how to do Benny." He suggested to Benny that he spoke too slowly and that he shouldn't put his hands up to his face so often. Benny quizzed, "How long have *you* been in show business?"

The Benny show went better than Johnny had ever hoped for and the two comedians—mentor and protégé—became close friends. Carson also got to know Red Skelton and wrote for him on his CBS television show. In August 1954, fate turned Johnny's way when a breakaway door malfunctioned during rehearsal just two hours before airtime and Skelton was knocked unconscious. The producer hastily asked Johnny to go on in lieu of Skelton, and with a nearly improvised monologue he'd constructed while driving to the studio, he impressed audiences. He also impressed CBS executives, who handed him his own program, *The Johnny Carson Show,* which lasted thirty-nine weeks. It was a rocky start, and the show went through seven writers and even more directors before it was canned. Johnny felt he needed a change.

On borrowed money, he shifted coasts and landed in New York in 1956. During the next few years he joined the Friars Club and made guest appearances on television, and even found himself on Broadway, in a play opposite Marsha Hunt called *The Tunnel of Love.* By this time, his self-confidence was restored. Johnny was offered the job as host of the network show *Earn Your Vacation* when he was twenty-nine. He also appeared as a substitute host for Jack Paar on CBS-TV's *The Morning Show.* In 1957, he was hired as host of the ABC-TV quiz show *Who Do You Trust?* which lasted five years with Carson as the master of ceremonies. It was on this show that he met announcer Ed McMahon.

While hosting the game show, Johnny was offered the job as host of the new *Tonight Show* on NBC in 1958, prior to Jack Paar, but Johnny declined, based on his security with his current employment. Then, in 1962, NBC secretly boosted its offer and lured Carson into the night. His appointment as Paar's successor was supposed to be a secret, but word got out, and for a few months prior to actually taking the wheel, the

Carson pitched to Mickey Mantle at Yankee Stadium as part of a bit on *The Tonight Show* during his first year as host.

HERE'S JOHNNY!

Johnny and his first wife, Jody, landed on the cover of *TV Guide* in September 1955. It was the first of twenty-five *TV Guide* covers for Johnny. (Cover photo by Gabi Rona; reprinted with permission from *TV Guide,* News America Publications)

anticipation mounted not only with audiences, but inside Carson himself. How could he have known that it would be a perpetual gig that took him almost to the new millennium?

During his years on *The Tonight Show* Johnny became itchy and wanted to do more than guest spots, so he headlined in Las Vegas regularly as well as completing some highly successful runs in Atlantic City. This was all while hosting the show and being a husband and a dad to three sons.

## ■ MARRIED LIFE

> *She says, "Johnny, I want a divorce from you." And I said, "But we're not even married." She says, "Yeah, but I want to skip right to the goodies."*
>
> JOHNNY CARSON [REFERRING
> TO A LADY WHO STOPPED
> HIM ON THE STREET]

To say his married life has been tumultuous is to let the man off easy. Johnny Carson has admitted that his devotion to his career caused his marriages to suffer. Although he's been down the aisle fewer times than Elizabeth Taylor or Mickey Rooney, his personal life has been just as much tabloid fodder as anyone's, to Johnny's dismay and disgust.

His first marriage, to college sweetheart Jody Wolcott, took place in Nebraska, in 1949. The couple had three boys, Chris, Ricky, and Cory. In 1963, they obtained a "quickie" divorce in Mexico.

Airline stewardess JoAnne Copeland was his second wife. They were married in 1963, not long after he began his duties on *The Tonight Show.* Johnny's career unfortunately put pressure on the marriage because in taking over the nightly show he became a workaholic. He won the hearts and ratings of his fans, but he did not pick up points in the marital department. JoAnne left after seven years. Their divorce was

*Above,* Johnny and JoAnne (née Copeland) share a glass of champagne at a small reception in the Carson apartment after their marriage on August 17, 1963, at New York's Marble Collegiate Church on Fifth Avenue. Johnny was thirty-seven and JoAnne was thirty-one. *Above right,* Johnny and his third wife, Joanna, posed for the cover of *Look* in 1979. *Right,* In 1981, Carson—known for maintaining privacy in his personal life—sternly read from a copy of the *National Enquirer* and denounced an article about his marriage as "scurrilous," saying the publication "stinks." He concluded, "I'm going to call the *National Enquirer,* and the people who wrote this, liars. Now that's slander. You know where I am, gentlemen. . . . I'll be happy to defend that charge against you."

splashed across the news and made final in 1972, just as he was making a fresh start in sunny California. Following a protracted divorce, JoAnne received a million dollars in cash and art and $100,000 a year in alimony for life.

At a party celebrating the tenth anniversary of Johnny's *Tonight Show* in 1972, Johnny announced that he and former model Joanna Holland had been secretly married that afternoon, shocking all of his friends and associates at the party. Johnny was forty-six, Joanna was thirty-three, and the two moved into a luxurious five-million-dollar Bel Air mansion that once belonged to movie producer Mervyn LeRoy. During a televised Dean Martin roast for Johnny, his pal Bob Newhart noted, "Johnny's first wife was named Jody. His second was JoAnne, and now he's married to Joanna . . . the man just won't go for new towels."

On March 8, 1983, Joanna filed for divorce in Los Angeles. Over the next two years, a battle ensued that would set many ignominious records. One writer observed at the time, "Joanna didn't just want to take Johnny to the cleaners, she wanted to leave him hanging on the clothesline out back." Johnny could do nothing but joke about it on the show: "My producer, Freddy de Cordova, really gave me something I needed for Christmas. He gave me a gift certificate to the legal office of Jacoby & Meyers."

Joanna's application asked the judge to order Johnny to pay her an astounding $220,000 a month in temporary alimony in order to maintain a standard of living which she enjoyed during the years of marriage.

Johnny joked in the monologue again: "Passed by my house yesterday—in a tour bus."

Joanna Carson sought $500,000 in attorney's fees and other outlandish amounts such as $270 a month to care for her cat. How could he pass up that detail in the monologue? Well, he couldn't. "I heard from my cat's lawyer," he said one night. "My cat wants twelve thousand dollars a week for Tender Vittles."

Author James Albert, who profiled this famous divorce in his book, *Pay Dirt*, wrote: "As Judge Olson and the attorneys argued over the details, Johnny braced himself. He knew full well that under California's community property laws, Joanna was entitled to 50 percent of all the assets accumulated during the marriage even though he was the one who worked and earned virtually 100 percent of the couple's income during that time. . . . What emerged on August 30, 1985, was an eighty-page divorce settlement to which Johnny and Joanna agreed." Albert pointed out that the whopping, meticulously drawn document was more detailed and lengthier than the World War I armistice with Germany, the World War II Japanese and Germany Instruments of Surrender, the 1782 treaty between England and the American colonies ending the Revolutionary War, the Louisiana Purchase, the Treaty of Ghent ending the War of 1812 and the United Nations Charter—combined.

After three divorces took a chunk of his sizable earnings and angered him with their public displays but still left him a wealthy man (albeit skeptical about marrying again), Johnny once again headed for the altar and married Alex Mass on June 20, 1987. He was sixty-one and she was thirty-five, and it looks like Johnny finally got it right on the fourth try. He and Alex reside in Malibu, near the beach where Johnny first saw Alex walking . . . and was intrigued by the beautiful woman he saw.

## ■ "THROUGH THICK AND THICK"

Possibly the only constant element in the adult life of Johnny Carson has been his pal, Ed McMahon. He was there for him when he did perhaps the hardest thing he could do on the show one night, discuss the death of his son, Rick.

Aside from certain jokes through the years, Johnny always strived to keep his personal life out of the public eye, but this time, he poignantly discussed one of his family members. With members of the audience wiping away tears and Johnny fighting them back himself, his voice quivered and choked with emotion as he delivered a brief tribute to his son, who had died in a freak automobile accident.

Johnny and his fourth wife, the former Alex Maas.

When Johnny returned from a hiatus on July 17, 1991, audiences wondered if he might mention the death of his son Rick, a thirty-nine-year-old professional photographer. Johnny was, of course, greeted with wild applause and support in the studio. He joked as usual, which attests to his performing abilities, and then, maybe for the first time, he let the audience in on his pain. The tragedy was visible; in a mere month the sixty-five-year-old Carson seemed to have aged a decade. In the show's final minutes, Johnny broke the years of silence about his family and presented a touching tribute to his son. Carson described Rick as "an exuberant young man, fun to be around. . . . He tried so darn hard to please," he said. Carson closed the show with a nice picture of his son, since the newspapers were running a

On December 29, 1993, Johnny Carson was honored along with Georg Solti, Arthur Mitchell, Stephen Sondheim, and Marion Williams on *The Kennedy Center Honors: A Celebration of the Performing Arts.* Johnny has not returned to television since.

driver's license photo. Then Johnny introduced a series of beautiful landscape photographs captured by Rick.

## ■ WHERE'S JOHNNY?

When Johnny left, he just walked out the door at NBC, got in a helicopter, and flew home. That evening, he threw a wingding on his Malibu estate the likes of which the *Tonight Show* staff had never seen, and he went around and greeted everyone, making sure it was an evening to remember. Later that night, he got into bed and shut off the alarm clock for good.

Outside of contributing a few humor pieces to *The New Yorker* and a foreword for the political humor book *Bob Hope's Dear Prez, I Wanna Tell Ya!* (published in 1993), Johnny has retired and hung a sign outside his door that reads "Gone Fishing." He exited his post at *The Tonight Show* in May 1992 and promised us all to be back, but as of yet, has not found the right avenue. He spoke briefly to writer Bill Zehme for an

*Esquire* article commemorating the tenth year since he left NBC, and outside of that, he has remained a private retiree, content with his life. "I think I left at the right time," says the tanned seventy-six-year-old Malibu resident, who underwent heart bypass surgery three years ago. "You've got to know when to get the hell off the stage and the timing was right for me. The reason I really don't go back or do interviews is because I just let the work speak for itself."

## Ed McMahon: Hi-Yoooooo!

*I'll probably be rolling Johnny out in a wheelchair. . . . The Tonight Show*
*is good for at least another five years, maybe longer. Who knows?*

—Ed McMahon, 1973

Laurel & Hardy weren't teamed for this many years. Neither were Abbott & Costello. Don't even think about Martin & Lewis. Have you considered that Ed McMahon and Johnny Carson celebrated nearly thirty-five years together as host and sidekick when they retired from *The Tonight Show* in 1992?

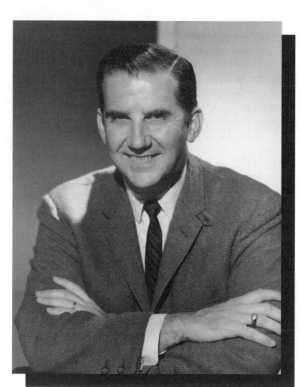

"Big Ed" McMahon, America's most famous second banana, had already briefly teamed with Carson prior to *The Tonight Show* in 1962.

Their professional relationship began in 1957 when McMahon, living in Philadelphia next door to Dick Clark, was called for an interview in New York about announcing a new show with Johnny Carson. "I met Johnny for about five minutes," McMahon recalls clearly. "We were both looking out the window at the changing of a theater marquee across the street: *Bells Are Ringing* at the Schubert. We hardly even looked at each other." McMahon did not believe he had the job, but he got called back to the city soon after and found that he had won the prize: announcing ABC-TV's new show, *Who Do You Trust?* with host Johnny Carson. The producers liked the "size difference" between the two, and they felt they'd work well together, complementing each other's styles. When *The Tonight Show* came around, Carson insisted that McMahon come along as his second banana, a title that McMahon has never found fault or guilt in.

"I'm also companion, assistant, consultant, and devil's advocate," he said not quite ten years into the show. He could've added straight man, resident huckster, and one of the most visible men on television during those days. His role on *The Tonight Show* was a "tough"

*Right,* Stirred, not shaken: Johnny is either checking if Ed's giant cocktail is well-chilled, or he's reducing the head of a beer with his finger. Hard to tell. *Below,* ALF imitates Carnac in an episode of the furry alien's '80s sitcom.

# The Old-Fashioned Way

It's no secret that Ed McMahon's all-time favorite comedian is the irascible William Claude Dunkenfield, aka W. C. Fields. The opening lines of McMahon's own book, *Here's Ed,* quote the legendary comedian who was known for his quick wit, a habitude toward the juice, and an aversion to kids. McMahon opened his memoirs, "Those who knew my idol, W. C. Fields, have told me that when a young writer asked for permission to write the story of his life, the great one replied, 'Please do. Capital idea. Do it right away. I can't wait to see how it turns out.'"

McMahon, an imposing figure like the heavyset Fields, began his career in Philadelphia as Fields himself did, and both men developed a 98-proof reputation for a taste or two. During McMahon's nightclub routine in the 1970s, he devoted an entire routine to the art of imbibing. It was called his "Salute to Great Drinkers," and in it he worked out some of his best Fields impressions. "I was in love with a beautiful blonde once. She drove me to drink; it's the one thing I'm indebted to her for." He'd also slip in lines like, "I've been asked if I ever get the DT's. I don't know. It's hard to tell where Hollywood ends and the DT's begin."

At NBC, as well as at his home office, McMahon decorated his surroundings with statues of W. C. Fields, trinkets, and even a ventriloquist dummy of the comedian sitting atop shelves that also featured Fields in framed portraits or scenes from select films. One classic shot in McMahon's office shows Fields displaying his extraordinary talents with the pool cue. In the early 1970s, McMahon was happy to help welcome Ronald J. Fields, grandson of the famed comedian, to plug his book on *The Tonight Show.* It's obvious that the incomparable W. C. Fields was quite an influence on McMahon. For years, McMahon favored eating at the posh L.A. restaurant Chasens in the very seat once kept in reserve for Fields. The Hollywood Chamber of Commerce awarded McMahon his star on the Hollywood Walk of Fame, right in front of the old Roosevelt Hotel on Hollywood Boulevard—next to W. C. Fields' star. Why, Ed even had a cat named W. C.

But even that's not all. McMahon named his firstborn child, a daughter, Claudia in honor of his idol. Yes, it's true.

Ed McMahon's nightclub act served up pure 100-proof homage to his favorite film comedian, W. C. Fields: "It was a woman who drove me to drink. And you know, I never even wrote to thank her."

one, he told Bob Costas on NBC's *Later*: "It really is difficult. You have to be in when needed and out of the way when not. I can't get in [Johnny's] way but I have to help him. I've got to support him. Sort of the pusher who helps him get through the hour. But I can't look like I'm doing anything."

That was McMahon's success, to gauge quickly and assess with lightning speed what would happen on the show and what he could do next to make it funny. McMahon's rarely been given credit for his own comic abilities and timing, but he possessed both. During one show, Johnny was at center stage in front of the main curtain, poking his head very near a cage that housed a cougar. When the animal hissed and lunged at Johnny, he ran across the stage to towering Ed and jumped off the floor into his arms. The two had a Laurel and Hardy kind of symmetry at times that was defined early on in their teaming.

When they were paired on *Who Do You Trust?* Johnny would routinely set fire to Ed's script and sometimes his cue cards with his cigarette lighter. "The first time it happened, I kept reading the lines, but it was black type on charcoal and my fingers were burning," he

In the summer of 1968, Ed McMahon did double duty when he also served as guest host of the NBC musical variety series *The Kraft Music Hall.*

says. "It got a big laugh from the audience, so Johnny never stopped doing it—every show for four years." Years later, on *The Tonight Show,* Ed reversed the gag while Johnny struggled through a comedy bit at the desk. "He was reading a piece of material that clearly wasn't going anywhere. I picked up the cigarette lighter from his desk and set fire to the paper. Johnny looked at me and said, 'You're absolutely right.' then dropped the blazing paper in the wastebasket while Doc played taps. It was a great moment."

McMahon once referred to himself as a "thirty-year overnight success," because he'd been in the business so long. From the time he was old enough to appreciate radio, he began to envision himself—and then train himself—as an announcer. He knew he was destined for broadcasting. "When I was twelve, I was talking into a flashlight and reading *Time* magazine aloud in front of mirrors," he said.

He was born on March 6, 1923, in Detroit, Michigan, but grew up in Lowell,

Not wishing to grossly outshine the competing talent, flamboyant entertainer Liberace dressed conservatively when he appeared as a guest celebrity on TV's *Star Search* with Ed McMahon in the 1980s.

Massachusetts. He attended Boston College and began his broadcasting career at a Lowell radio station, WLLH. During World War II, McMahon became a pilot and flight instructor in the Marine Corps, and "emceed every show on the base," he said. "Wherever there was a microphone, I was."

He later attended the Catholic University of America and received a degree in speech and drama. Soon after, he took his first job at a television station in Philadelphia. The Korean War curtailed any plans he may have had, and he served as a fighter pilot until 1954.

Always a big fellow, the six-foot-four Irishman struggled to keep his weight down, but he says his stature is the result of his Irish grandmother's cooking habits. He played football for Boston College in his late teens and tried to exercise as much as possible. Looks have always been important to him, he has said—so much so that in 1973 he revealed that he traveled to the Bahamas "to get myself injected with those sheep cells," he told writer William Wolf. "You've heard about the treatment. It has really helped me to keep looking youthful. It's good for your skin, hair, and in general revitalizes your body organs."

Did you know Ed even wrote a diet book for those who were "born overweight" as he says? His 1970s book *Slimming Down* provided advice about how to shed unwanted pounds. His average weight over the years was around 240 pounds, but in the past ten years he has gotten it down to a healthier 200 pounds on average.

During his *Tonight Show* tenure, McMahon developed the acting bug and wanted to break into films. He had roles in films such as *The Incident, Slaughter's Big Rip-Off, Fun With Dick and Jane,* and *Butterfly.* His television roles included everything from a clown on the early children's show *Big Top* to cameos on *ChiPs* and *ALF.* While still on *The Tonight Show,* he hosted nine seasons of the syndicated talent show *Star Search,* and he is currently launching a newer version. "I wonder how many pages I have to turn before finding one of my discoveries from *Star Search,*" he told the *National Enquirer.* "Usually in the first five pages there's somebody doing something who started on my show." *Star Search* aired from 1983 to 1995 and introduced a bevy of talented kids who went on to the big time, including Britney Spears, Rosie O'Donnell,

Brad Garrett, Drew Carey, Sinbad, Jenny Jones, LeAnn Rimes, Justin Timberlake, and Christina Aguilera.

McMahon's visibility during his thirty-plus years with Johnny never waned. He was a TV huckster for the sponsor's commercials (Budweiser, Alpo dog food, as well as an array of insurance firms). Perhaps his most recognized catchphrase outside of "Here's Johnny!" and "Hi-yooooo!" would be "You may have already won ten million dollars," from his long-running Publisher's Clearinghouse Sweepstakes campaign. Ed was a popular spokesman for Budweiser beer, but he was never allowed to actually sip the foamy beverage on camera. He could merely hold it up and wet his lips with anticipation.

When you think of Ed McMahon, you also think of his loud booming laugh, heard over and above the audience most nights, mostly because he was near a mike. And his reputation for taking a drink now and then became an ongoing joke over the years. Unfortunately, the joke became the public's perception of reality and, Ed admitted, that bothered him at times. Johnny's cracks over the years ("Ed's baby learned to crawl by watching Ed come home at night") became more frequent, despite the fact that it was actually Carson who suffered with a drinking problem for a while.

Over the years, McMahon took the inflated drunk jokes with the humor with which they were intended, but he admitted to Bob Costas that he was sensitive about it, ". . . only because it affected my kids. That bothered me when one of my children will say to me that someone had said to them, 'Does your father really drink like they say he drinks?'

"Hey, I'm a big Irishman. Irish are supposed to have a reputation for being heavy drinkers and my defense is you couldn't run my schedule and be a heavy drinker. I figure the people believe that it's just a joke, part of our relationship. It started on *Who Do You Trust?* Of course, what would happen is we'd go out after the show and we'd have a won-

Ed McMahon became the consummate co-host with a rhythm for appropriate interjections.

derful time. Johnny would have a much more wonderful time than I had. We hung out a lot. We did drink. The next day, he would put me in his shoes and say, 'Boy, did you drink a lot last night.' That's how it started."

Ed toured Las Vegas and traveled the nightclub circuit for a while, itching for

Musician and orchestra leader Milton DeLugg jokes with Ed on *The Tonight Show* in 1966. DeLugg briefly became the show's bandleader following Skitch Henderson and preceding Doc Severinsen. Years later, DeLugg's orchestra played to a whole new TV generation when they whipped up the music on *The Gong Show* (1976–1980).

something to augment his announcing chores. He even appeared briefly on Broadway in *The Impossible Years,* substituting for Alan King. For several decades, he has co-hosted the *Jerry Lewis Muscular Dystrophy Telethon* as well as being as a goodwill ambassador in holiday parades such as Macy's Thanksgiving Day Parade and the Hollywood Christmas Parade.

Ed McMahon's married life has been almost as choppy as Johnny's. McMahon was separated in 1973 from his wife of twenty-seven years, the former Alyce Ferrell. They had four children. When he decided to move with *The Tonight Show* out west, news reports indicated that he was abandoning his wife, but he told the press his marriage was already in trouble at that time. Amid a heavily publicized separation, McMahon finally divorced in 1976. He remarried in 1976 to Victoria Valentine, and the McMahons adopted a little girl. The couple were divorced in 1989. Ed eventually married again and he and his wife, Pamela, live in Beverly Hills.

Like a towering beacon still standing in Hollywood, Ed was there to represent *The Tonight Show* gang on NBC's seventy-fifth anniversary special in 2002. Discussing *The Tonight Show* on CNN on the occasion of the tenth anniversary of the final show, he said that he knew the end was approaching as the show neared three decades. "I'd talk with [Johnny] during commercials and he'd say to me, 'Well, Ed, should we do another year?' and I'd say 'Yeah, we might as well.' The last several years he was renewing on a yearly basis."

Ed and Johnny are still great friends after all these years, through "thick and thick" as Johnny used to say. The two got together for a little reminiscing when their retirement hit ten years, and Ed confirms that these days Johnny is content "and has no regrets or attitude about it at all . . . his appraisal of the whole thing is 'Ed . . . I did it.'

"It surprises me, because for a while, I think he wanted to do something," McMahon says. "When I'd talk to him during the early years after his departure he'd say, 'I haven't found anything yet, Ed, I haven't found it.' I thought for sure he'd do the Oscars. It would have been perfect—work one day a year. That's where he was headed."

# "DOC"

*Johnny: Interesting item today in the paper . . . Jimmy Carter, the president, is backing the decriminalization of marijuana. A lot of controversy there, but he declared support for the removal of all federal criminal penalties for possession of "an ounce or less" of marijuana—which is bad news for our band, because they don't know what "an ounce or less" means.*

*Doc: It means you're about out.*

Doc Severinsen, now in his early seventies, says he misses the days and nights of *The Tonight Show,* one of the best gigs a musician could have, but he still tours with members of his old band and loves the gypsy life on the road. "It's the life of a musician," he recently told writer Phil Potempa. "And when you perform with a sixteen-piece big band, you're never alone. We perform a little bit of everything, from big band music to pop."

Little Doc Severinsen grew up in Arlington, Oregon. His father, Carl Severinsen, was a dentist. He named his son Carl, so his nickname became "Little Doc." The name eventually wore off. "I couldn't wait to drop the 'Little' part of that nickname," he admits.

Born on July 7, 1927, in the cattle country of Arlington, which had a population of all of six hundred at that time, Little Doc Severinsen was small when his father would sit at the edge of his bed at night and play a violin. "He was a very good player, so it's a nice recollection

Doc Severinsen was on a collision course with the loud, wacky styles of the seventies.

Tonight Show bandleader Skitch Henderson (center) was priming trumpeter Doc Severinsen for the top spot in the mid-1960s.

to have," Doc told *Down Beat* magazine. "I started on trumpet quite by accident. My father wanted me to be a violinist like him, but I didn't take to it at all. In desperation he asked me what I would like to play and I picked the trombone because I liked the way it looked with the slide as played in the town band. There wasn't an extra one in town and I was too small for trombone anyway. But Herb Clarke, who worked at the Shell service station, had a cornet lying in his attic that I started with."

His father was a great source of creative energy for him, he says. "He was a real taskmaster, a true perfectionist. I nearly went batty trying to please him, but he was my first inspiration," he says.

Doc's biggest musical influences, like Harry James, Ziggy Elman, and Louis Armstrong, came by way of the radio when he was young. At the tender age of thirteen, he auditioned for Tommy Dorsey's band "as a fluke," he says, which left him with a growing ambition to one day play with Dorsey. By seventeen, he left home to tour with the Ted Fio Rito Orchestra, a short-lived gig. The army intervened during World War II, and after his discharge, Severinsen caught the tail end of the big-band era, joining Charlie Barnet a few times between1947 and 1949.

While stationed at Fort Lewis, Washington, Doc heard his first Dizzy Gillespie records, which "spun my head around," he said in a 1970s interview, with the vernacular of a beatnik. "Dizzy explored new territory. I tried to imitate Dizzy, to find out what this cat was layin' down. The guys in the band figured I was ready to join the Japanese army, the wild stuff I tried to play on my horn. I was really groovin' high."

Eventually, Doc sat in with Dorsey—a dream come true—and also Benny Goodman, Barnet, and others. "With Charlie Barnet, we never played one commercial tune," he explained. "It was what you'd call a musician's band. Also it was my first mixed band, meaning I could sit next to some soul brothers and really swing."

In 1949, Severinsen landed in New York and worked as a studio musician at NBC. He played in the house band when Steve Allen was hosting *Tonight!* and on through Jack Paar, and he caught the eye of music director Skitch Henderson. "Skitch was always great to promote the fellows in the band," Severinsen said in 1981. "He kept raising my level of visibility to the point that it was understood that when he took off, I would take over." In 1967, he ended his term as the anonymous studio musician and took over as the bandleader on *The Tonight Show*. Eventually, he became one of Johnny's stooges on the show, occasionally delivering some ad-libbed zingers which had Johnny convulsing in laughter. In *Down Beat* magazine, Doc recalled a few high

Still at it, Doc Severinsen headlined on the PBS special *The Cincinnati Pops Big Band Hit Parade* in 1998. (Photo by Mark Lyons; courtesy of PBS Television)

points from his thousands of *Tonight Show* tapings:

> I think the *Tonight Show* is the perfect home for any musician; it's certainly been a great place for me. I loved having Louis Armstrong, Dizzy Gillespie, Harry James and all the other musicians on. To have Joe Williams decide to fake something with the entire band faking a chart that you would swear they spent hours writing, was exciting. I'll never forget Miles Davis at the time his record *Bitches Brew* was out. Needless to say, his music was much too advanced for most people on the show. Miles came out, turned his back on the camera, and just wailed. I thought it was wonderful.

Severinsen will name a host of trumpeters he prefers and admires, like when the topic of his prime idol, Louis Armstrong, arises. "Satchmo Armstrong was the granddaddy of anybody who picks up the horn," he says. "I never felt I was of age until I heard Louis and could absorb his personality. The way he would feel the music . . . when Louis played his horn or when he sang, he said it all." Doc also enjoys Freddie Hubbard, Wynton Marsalis, and Chris Botti.

With threads as loud as his trumpet, Doc dressed to be noticed. The flashy wardrobe became part of his personality, on the show and off. Everyone asks him about his clothes, and he tires of it. The trademark loud outerwear stuck with him after Johnny cracked a few jokes and eventually, Doc liked dressing that way, shopping for new additions to his closet while on the road frequently.

Over the years, Doc recorded several albums with the *Tonight Show* band, which garnered him some Grammy awards. He also toured for a few years with his fusion group called Xebron, a name which came from "a little place I created in my mind to get away from the world." He's led the *Tonight Show* orchestra in the Playboy Jazz Festival at the Hollywood Bowl, recorded more than thirty albums, and toured with a jazz group called Facets in the late 1980s.

His style varies incredibly. Although perhaps best known for his superb trumpet playing, he's one of today's premier instrumentalists with a range of recordings from big-band sounds to Dixieland, traditional jazz to country music. He continues to

HERE'S JOHNNY!

By the early 1970s, Doc Severinsen developed the "Liberace syndrome," whereby an entertainer dresses to be noticed. It's a matter of showmanship. For Severinsen, it all began with some brightly colored ties that elicited comments from Johnny. But Severinsen was more than just Carson's sidekick in a loud jacket; he was a serious musician who led the last of TV's great swing bands.

accompany a battery of symphony orchestras around the country as guest conductor and performer, most notably associated with the Phoenix Symphony Orchestra.

Doc has five children and has been married three times. His third wife, television writer Emily Marshall, was working as a secretary to *Tonight Show* producer Fred de Cordova when they met. When he's not trekking around the globe playing, he enjoys horses, cooking Italian dishes, and collecting art.

## TOMMY NEWSOM

*Things never go right with Tommy . . . his inflatable woman has PMS.*

—JOHNNY CARSON

In a *Tonight Show* parody of *This Is Your Life*, Johnny played the moderator who stopped the show, sat Tommy Newsom down, and began a tribute that put it all in perspective. The opening went like this:

> Born Thomas "Tapioca" Newsom in the sleepy southern seaport town of Portsmouth, Virginia, on February 25, 1929, appropriately enough, the year of the Great Depression.
>
> You were born to a proud, but dull, Virginia family. Tommy, you are a direct descendant of a boring Revolutionary war hero, Nathan Hale

Newsom, who when captured by the British, said, "I regret that I have no life to give for my country."

. . . And at the age of two, you were abandoned by your parents at Pismo Beach, California, and raised by a herd of wild clams. The year was 1941. War broke out and you answered your nation's call. You volunteered for an elite commando unit, the Polyester Berets. . . .

The character that is Tommy Newsom was one that was cultivated over the years and molded into a glob of, well, nothingness. The *This Is Your Life* parody correctly reported his age and birthplace, but disregard the clams, he says.

Lack of personality aside, the real Tommy Newsom is a kind, gentle, mostly serious man with a pleasant Virginia coastal accent and a round face that resembles everybody's favorite uncle. Cautious in nature, he rarely offered tales about the band's unofficial watering hole across the street from NBC, Chadney's. "The band had been known to raise a glass on the break occasionally," he admitted years ago. Many a ticket-holder waiting in line outside the studio had witnessed a sweating band member or two, hustling across the busy street in their dark blue blazer, out of breath as they made a mad dash back to the studio.

Johnny never bantered long with Tommy on the show. Usually, Newsom was out front subbing for Doc Severinsen, and Carson would ask him a simple question, which somehow hit home runs almost every time. They were innocuous things, but coming from the blank-faced Newsom, they just came out funny.

"One night somebody from the audience asked Johnny why there weren't any girls in the band," recalls Newsom. "He looked over at me and said, 'Yeah, Tommy, why are there no girls in the band?' I said, 'Well, we had one but we ate her.'

"It just popped out."

Those brief ad-libbed exchanges were often hilarious. "Sometimes I'd say something off the wall and it tickled him."

Johnny's informal chats with band member Tommy Newsom were breezy and funny.

HERE'S JOHNNY!

Newsom, who became assistant musical director on *The Tonight Show* in 1968, is not the simpleton Johnny joked about, but he does admit that some of the humor was valid. "I never took Johnny's comments personally," he says. "It's like they're talking about a third person. Of course there is a kernel of truth in all of those things. I don't lead a very exciting existence. Not anything the press would love. I hope I'm a little more animated than they portrayed me. It was good ammunition for the writers."

Tommy began his career playing saxophone with *The Tonight Show* the summer before Johnny's entrance as host in 1962. On the strength of his touring with Benny Goodman in Russia, he was hired as a "reed man" for one week's work and ended up staying thirty years. "It was heaven for me because I'd been freelancing around New York, you know. Scuffling," he says. "*The Tonight Show* was a steady job and a wonderful band to join."

Oddly enough, during all those years, Newsom, along with the other mainstays in the band, were on the payroll as "temporary employees" with NBC. "We were employed by NBC, but that was a way around giving us a pension. We were 'temporary employees' for thirty years. Can you believe that?

"I get no pension from NBC," he admits. "Mine comes from the musicians union, and years ago my medical was covered through AFTRA. As I was in front of the camera a little bit more, some people got me to join the television union and they did me a big favor. They got me raises and a health plan and a pension."

Newsom plays the clarinet, the flute, the saxophone, and the piano. He attended the College of William and Mary but was graduated form the Peabody Conservatory of Music in Baltimore, where he studied piano and sax. Following three years as a member of the Air Force Band from 1953 to 1956, he received an M.A. in music education from Columbia University. He and his wife, Pat, lived in Tarzana, California, until 1994 when an earthquake changed their minds. "We decided to look for a place that didn't shake so much," he says, and after almost twenty-five years in Southern California, Tommy and his wife moved back to his hometown of Portsmouth, Virginia.

Tommy continues to play on occasion at jazz festivals and arranges music for his old boss, Doc Severinsen. He recently sat in with former *Tonight Show* music director Skitch Henderson and the Virginia Symphony Orchestra. "I have to practice more often these days because there's more distance between engagements and you get rusty if you don't," he says. "I love it. I'll play till I drop."

# INDEX

## A

Abbott & Costello, 195–96, 226
Abrahamson, Tillie, 126
Academy Awards, 219
Adams, Don, 15, 32, 48, 215
Agnew, Spiro, 190
Agoglia, John, 23
Aguilera, Christina, 231
Albert, James, 223
Allen, Fred, 15, 219
Allen, Steve, 11, 13, 31–34, 36, 38, 39, 108, 162, 170, 235
Allen, Tim, 149
Allen, Woody, 149
Ames, Ed, 82
Amsterdam, Morey, 26–30, 35
Anderson, Louie, x, 140, 142–56
Andreoli, Rick, 202, 204
Andrews, Bart, 33
Anka, Paul, 192–93
Ann-Margret, 89
Arquette, Alexis, 39
Arquette, Cliff, 39
Arquette, David, 39
Arquette, Lewis, 39
Arquette, Patricia, 39
Arquette, Rosanna, 39
Ashe, Arthur, 108
Aunt Blabby, 187
Austin, John, 112–13
Averback, Hy, 32
Aykroyd, Dan, 12, 82

## B

Bacharach, Burt, 155
Bald, Wambly, 29
Barathy, Rick, 125
Bayouth, Michael, 201
Beardsley, Helen and Frank, 139
Beatles, 39
Benjamin, Richard, 162
Bennett, Tony, 43, 207
*Benny Goodman Story, The*, 32
Benny, Jack, 13, 15, 48–49, 86–87, 145, 215, 220

Bergen, Edgar, 49
Berle, Milton, 49, 215
Berman, Shelly, 33
Besser, Joe, 7
Bishop, Joey, 41, 86–87, 153, 155
Black, Bill, 133, 137
Black, Minnie, 131
Black, Shirley Temple, 178
Blake, Robert, 11, 93–95, 142, 152, 155, 212
Blanc, Mel, 49
Bob & Ray, 49
*Bob Hope's Dear Prez, I Wanna Tell Ya!*, 225
Bolger, Ray, 4
Boyd, William "Hopalong Cassidy," 3, 81
Brando, Marlon, 167
Brenner, David, 121, 149, 155
*Broadway Open House*, 25–30, 35
Brooks, Mel, 43, 207
Bruce, Lenny, 33
Buckley, William F. Jr., x
Budinger, Victoria May "Miss Vicki," 68, 72–73
Burbank Mug Shop, 160
Burnett, Carol, 39
Burns, George, ix, 49, 86–87, 90–91, 193, 215
Byner, John, 89–90, 144, 146

## C

Cagney, Jimmy, 18, 144
*Candid Camera*, 101
Canon, Maureen, 27
Capote, Truman, 94–95
Carey, Drew, 148–49, 231
Carlin, George, 155, 196, 207
Carnac the Magnificent, 70–71
Carne, Judy, 201
Carrey, Jim, 149
Carson, Chris, 213, 221
Carson, Cory, 213, 221
Carson, Dick, 11, 62, 217
Carson, Homer Lloyd, 217
Carson, Rick, 12, 208, 213, 221, 224–25

Carson, Ruth Hook, 217
*Carson's Cellar*, 116, 219
Carter, Jack, 41, 145
Carvey, Dana, 144–46
Caselotti, Adriana, 132
Cass, Peggy, 38, 40
Cavett, Dick, 100, 148–49, 155
Charles, Ray, 147
Chase, Chevy, 155
*Chicago Sun-Times*, 119
Coates, Paul, 36
Connery, Sean, 167
Conreid, Hans, 38
Considine, Bob, 36
Convy, Bert, 162
Conway, Tim, 32
Copeland, JoAnne, 221–23
Corzine, CF, 132–33
Cosby, Bill, 39, 121, 149, 155, 159
Cosford, Bill, 51
Costas, Bob, 48, 83, 229
*CPO Sharkey*, 216
Crane, Les, 100
Crawford, Joan, 43–44
Cronkite, Walter, 185
Crosby, Ken, 158–59, 162–63
Crystal, Billy, 155
Csonka, Larry, 183
Cummings, Bob, 41
Curtis, Billy, 18
Cuscuna, Susan, 202

## D

Dagmar, 27, 29–31
Dana, Bill, 32
Danza, Tony, 155
Davidson, John, 11, 119, 155
Davis, Sammy Jr., 92, 94, 128, 161
Dawson, Richard, 155
Day, Dennis, 215
de Cordova, Fred, 6–7, 48, 49, 50, 57, 102, 118, 124, 145, 155, 158, 162, 182
Dean, Jimmy, 41, 153
Dell & Abbott, 27
DeLouise, Dom, 155

DeLugg, Milton, 27–30, 31, 232
DeNiro, Robert, 81
Denver, John, 155
Diamond, Selma, 38, 152
*Dick Van Dyke Show, The,* 29, 30, 108–109
Dickinson, Angie, 77
Dill, Dean, 11
Diller, Phyllis, viii, 39, 68–69, 72, 73, 103, 107–108, 120, 149
Donahue, Phil, 103
Douglas, Mike, 100, 119
Dow, Tony, 93
*Down Beat* magazine, 235–36
Downs, Hugh, 38, 41
Dunn, Elaine, 27
Durgin, Don, 86–87
Durston, Edward, 112–13

**E**

*Earn Your Vacation,* 220
Eastwood, Clint, 18, 207
Edelman, Murray, 183, 185
Edelstein, Andrew, 69
El Moldo, 59
Elliot, Chris, 162
Embery, Joan, 11, 170–75, 176
Engor, Virginia Ruth. *See* Dagmar.
Ephron, Nora, 217
*Esquire* magazine, 206, 226
Essex, California, 125
Esterly, Glenn, 119

**F**

Feinstein, Barry, 113
Fern, Art, 64, 111
Fields, Greg, 60–65
Fields, W. C., 228
Flynn, Harry, 78
Fonda, Jane, 77
Fowler, Jim, 175
Fowler, Tamara Ann, 158, 167
Francis, Arlene, 41
Francis, Connie, 214
*Fred Allen Show, The,* 28
Friedman, Hal, 30
Funt, Allen, 101

**G**

Gabor, Zsa Zsa, 38, 77, 89
Gaddis, Louise, 126
Galioto, Charles, 137
Gallop, Frank, 27
Garagiola, Joe, 155
Gardner, Hy, 36
Garland, Judy, 10, 38
Garrett, Brad, 231
Garver, Jack, 58
*Get Smart,* 214–15
Gielgud, John, 81
Gingold, Hermione, 38
Gleason, Jackie, 3, 15, 48, 83–85, 144, 193
Glenesk, Rev. William, 72–73
Goldberg, Whoopi, 149
Goodman, Dody, 38
Goodwin, Danny, 122
Gorme, Eydie, 32
Gorshin, Frank, 145
Goulet, Robert, 155
Graham, Virginia, 170
Grant, Cary, 3, 81
Grant, Jack, 58, 160
Greco, Buddy, 27
Griffin, Merv, 41, 100, 119, 144
Grodin, Charles, 207

**H**

Hackett, Buddy, x, 12, 19, 99, 104–106, 207
Hagler, Marvelous Marvin, 84
Hall, Arsenio, 100, 159
Hansen, Allison, Brooke, Claire, and Darcy, 137
Harris, Phil, 215
Hart, Mary, 113
Hartman, Phil, 145–46
Harvey, Jane, 27
Haskell, Jack, 41
Hawn, Goldie, 201
Hayes, Peter Lind, 41
Healy, Mary, 41
Henderson, Florence, 68
Henderson, Skitch, 31, 32, 33, 43, 45, 192, 232, 234, 235, 239
Herlihy, Ed, 41
Herman, Pee-wee, 63, 103
Heston, Charlton, 85, 88
Hill, Benny, 3, 81

Hill, Frank, 126
Holland, Joanna, 223
*Hollywood Reporter,* 19
Holt, Mildred, 126–27
Hope, Bob, 15, 19, 48, 79, 193, 213
Hoyos, Andrew, 201
Hull, Rod, 53
Hunt, Marsha, 220

**I**

Iglesias, Julio, 79, 128
Ingels, Marty, 88
Irving, Amy, 127
*It's a Wonderful Life,* 114
Ives, Burl, 38

**J**

Jackson, Kate, 162
Jarvis, Jeff, 8–9
*Jet* magazine, 189
*Johnny Carson Discovers Cypress Gardens,* 58
*Johnny Carson Show, The,* 220
"Johnny's Theme," 192–93
Johnson, Lyndon B., 185, 199
Jones, Jenny, 231
Jones, Shirley, 89

**K**

Kann, Stan, 120–21
Kaplan, Gabe, 149
Kaufman, Bel, 54
Kelley, Douglas Ward, 194
Kelly, Betty and Bob, 128–29
*Kennedy Center Honors, The,* 225
Kennedy, John F., 37, 48
Kennedy, Robert F., 38
Kermit the Frog, 155
Kersik, Vlosta, 131–32
Kiick, Jim, 183
Kilgallen, Dorothy, 39
King, Alan, ix, 149, 215
Klein, Robert, 149
Knotts, Don, 32
Kovacs, Ernie, 33, 34
Kupcinet, Irv, 36

## L

*L.A. Times*, 51, 102, 159, 162
Lamas, Fernando, 154
Landon, Michael, 12, 75–82, 128, 155
Lassally, Peter, 156, 162
*Late Shift, The*, 24, 144
*Laugh-In*, 69, 75, 201
Laurel & Hardy, 15, 226
Lavin, Cheryl, 38
Lawrence, Steve, 32, 41
Leachman, Cloris, 115
Lemmon, Jack, viii
Leno, Jay, 11, 22, 23–24, 35, 137, 144, 149, 155, 161, 170, 192, 199
Leonard, Jack E., 27, 39, 41
Lerner, Max, 191
Lester, Jerry, 25, 35
Letterman, David, 22, 23–25, 117, 144, 149, 155, 199, 207, 212
Levant, Oscar, 38
Lewis, Jenny. *See* Dagmar.
Lewis, Jerry, ix, 41, 86–87, 153, 155
Lewis, Richard, 149
Liberace, 230
Lindsey, George "Goober," 89–90
Linkletter, Art, 41, 113, 124, 170
Linkletter, Diane, 113
Little, Rich, 24, 144–46, 155
Littlefield, Warren, 23
Locke, Don, 17, 202, 204
Lofflin, John, 179–200
Lombardo, Carmen, 99
Lucas, Nick, 68, 72
Lynde, Paul, 115

## M

*Mad* magazine, 100
Maher, Bill, 149, 151–52
Mailer, Norman, 194
Malone, Ray, 27
Mandrell, Barbara, 155
Manilow, Barry, 128
Mantle, Mickey, 220
March, Hal, 41
Marsh, Jean, 154
Martin, Dean, 86–87, 153, 167

Martin, Dick, 86–87
Martin, Steve, 51, 149, 207, 213
Marx, Groucho, 15, 41, 43–44, 196–98, 219
Mason, Jackie, 32
Mass, Alex, 223
Mathers, Jerry, 93
Maxwell, Elsa, 38
McBride, Mary Margaret, 38
McCawley, Jim, 143, 152
McCormick, Pat, 52, 54–55, 60–61
McKay, Bertie, 132
McMahon, Ed, 40, 42–43, 45, 52, 57, 83, 88, 90, 161, 176, 206, 209, 220, 224, 226–32
Meadows, Audrey, 32
Meadows, Jayne, 32
Melis, José, 38
Meriwether, Lee, 150
Midler, Bette, 207–208
Mighty Carson Art Players, 64, 111, 116
Miller, Jack, 72
Mills, Wilbur, 185
Minnelli, Liza, 106
Mitchell, Arthur, 225
Moore, Gary, 215
Moore, Roger, 155
*Morning Show, The*, 220
Mr. T, 147
Mulholland, Robert, 22
Murphy, Eddie, 149, 196
Murphy, Mary, 101
Murray, Jan, 41

## N

Nabors, Jim, 32, 119
*National Enquirer*, 78, 222
NBC pages, 158–67
Nelson, Willie, 79
*New York Times, The*, 49
*New Yorker, The*, 225
Newhart, Bob, 11, 39, 149, 155
Newsom, Tommy, 163–64, 237–39
*Newsweek*, 38
Newton, Wayne, 50, 155
Nichols, Barbara, 27
Nicholson, Jack, 81
Nixon, Richard, 38, 56
Nye, Louis, 32

## O

O'Brien, Conan, 199
O'Connor, Donald, 41
O'Donnell, Rosie, 230
Olney, Alma and Robert, 160
"One for My Baby (And One More for the Road)," 207

## P

Paar, Jack, ix, 10, 34, 36–40, 108, 220, 235
Pacino, Al, 81
pages. *See* NBC pages.
Palmer, Arnold, 77
Parton, Dolly, 84, 160
Peppard, George, 212
Peterson, Cassandra, 103
Philbin, Regis, 153, 162
Pine, Joe, 194
Postman, Neil, 180, 199
Poston, Tom, viii, 32, 48
Potempa, Phil, 233
Presley, Elvis, 81
Price, Vincent, 155
Prinze, Freddie, 151, 155
Pryor, Richard, 111, 149
*Purple Rain*, 150

## Q

Quinn, Bobby, 58

## R

Randall, Tony, 33–34, 96, 98–99, 170
Rayburn, Gene, 32
Reagan, Nancy, 181
Reagan, Ronald, 86–87, 144–45, 181, 195–96
Reed, Oliver, 92
Reese, Della, 154
Reilly, Charles Nelson, 118–19
Reiner, Carl, x, 36, 89–90, 108–109, 213
Reiner, Rob, 155
Reynolds, Burt, 93, 155, 190
Reynolds, Debbie, 89
Reynolds, William, 81
Rhodes, Joe, 141–56
Rich, Buddy, 88

HERE'S JOHNNY!